A Baptist's Theology

R. Wayne Stacy, editor

SMYTH&HELWYS
PUBLISHING, INCORPORATED · MACON, GEORGIA

Smyth & Helwys Publishing, Inc.
6316 Peake Road
Macon, Georgia 31210-3960
1-800-747-3016
©1999 by Smyth & Helwys Publishing

R. Wayne Stacy

The paper used in this publication meets the minimum requirements of
American National Standard for Information Sciences—Permanence of
Paper for Printed Library Materials.
ANSI Z39.48–1984. (alk. paper)

Library of Congress Cataloging-in-Publication Data

R. Wayne Stacy, editor.
    A Baptist's theology.
    (alk. paper)
    1. Baptists—Doctrines.
    I. Stacy, R. Wayne.
    BX6331.2.B2945   1999
    230.—dc21   99-39704
                                     CIP
ISBN 1-573132-265-3

Contents

Introduction

R. Wayne Stacy

The past twenty years have seen intense theological foment among Baptists in general and Baptists in the South in particular. However, while theologically generated rancor has been high, there has been precious little theological discourse, and this scholarly discussion has tended to be conducted in a climate that for the most part has been reactionary, divisive, and counterproductive. For too long we Baptists have defined our theology by delineating what we're *against* rather than what we're *for*, what we don't believe rather than what we do. It is time for a constructive theology, especially for us Baptists who have been referred to by that anemic adjective "moderate." (Personally, I reject the label "moderate." While in theological discourse I always try to begin with the question rather than the answer, I am nonetheless "passionate," not "moderate," about the things I believe.) At this time in our history, Baptists need some fresh, creative thinking about what we're *for* rather than remaining fixated on and defined by what we're *against*. This book was borne out of the desire to meet that need.

The idea for the book was originally conceived in response to a question put to me some time ago from a most unlikely source. Since the early 1980s Baptists and Roman Catholics in North Carolina have met annually for a "Baptist-Catholic Dialogue" jointly sponsored by the Diocese of Raleigh and the Evangelism Division of the Baptist State Convention of North Carolina. It is a splendid event in which Baptists, Roman Catholics, and Protestants of all stripes come together to hear papers read by Baptist and Roman Catholic scholars on subjects that have tended to divide us, such as church authority versus scriptural authority, ministry as pastor versus priest, the Lord's Supper as symbol versus sacrament, and infant baptism versus believer's baptism.

I first became aware of the conference when I moved to North Carolina in 1991 to become pastor of the First Baptist Church of Raleigh. I was invited to deliver the Baptist paper that year titled "Conflicts Resulting from Biblical Interpretation in the Baptist Tradition." Father Roland Murphy of the Washington Theological Union delivered the Roman Catholic paper. Given the recent foment in Baptist life over the nature and authority of the

Scriptures, I felt it important in my presentation to speak to the whole issue of biblical inerrancy and the degree to which it is an appropriate model for understanding the Scripture's authority in the life of the believer. The news media carried a story on the conference, including some of my remarks in which I was critical of the term inerrancy.

(I do hold a high view of Scripture in which I believe, contrary to the views of some, that the Bible doesn't just *contain* the word of God, but *is* the word of God. This means, among other things, that Christians are obliged to regard the Bible as having authority over their lives *both* when they like what it says and when they don't. Rather, my reservations with the term "inerrancy" grow out of the fact that I do not believe that this nonbiblical term is the best model for describing the nature of the Bible's authority.)

It did not come as a surprise to me when I received an angry letter in the mail from someone who had read the news reports of the conference. What did surprise me, however, was that the letter did not come from a Baptist; it was from a Catholic woman in Florida. She said that she watched a well-known Baptist preacher on television every Sunday and, being Catholic and assuming that Baptist ministers like Catholic priests all shared the same views about things theological, was shocked that a Baptist minister in North Carolina could actually be permitted publicly to express views that were at odds with the views of this one who was obviously Southern Baptist's authoritative spokesperson in such matters. I didn't have the heart to tell her that her own confession was not the monolithic theological citadel she presumed, but I did try to disabuse her of the notion that any one Baptist could speak authoritatively for another, even one who speaks each week *ex televisia.* Such freedom, I assured her, grows out of the Baptist principle known as "the priesthood of the believer" or "soul competency." We exchanged correspondences for a while, but I am not sanguine that I ever really explained to her satisfaction this rather curious Baptist idiosyncrasy.

Then, in the spring of 1998, it happened again. I was invited to deliver the Baptist paper at the Baptist-Catholic Conference, this time on the subject of baptism. The conference theme was, "Do You Know What Baptism Does to You?" Father William Ruhl, formerly of Catholic University of America and now pastor of the host church, read the Catholic paper. In the course of the day's activities a surprising degree of theological agreement emerged between the two of us, which startled many in attendance. The theology of baptism they heard being articulated from a Baptist scholar was not at all what many had assumed to be an "orthodox" Baptist theology of baptism. Again, I worked as hard as I could to explain that Baptist polity, unlike our more "episcopal" brothers and sisters, does not permit one Baptist to speak authoritatively for another. But many in the audience, including many Baptists, could not grasp the implications of the "priesthood of the believer" that could allow a Baptist to articulate a theology that differed at significant points from what they had always assumed to be Baptist "orthodoxy."

(Incidentally, part of the confusion lay in the fact that most in attendance assumed that Baptist "orthodoxy" regarding baptism coalesced around the idea of "dunking" or immersion. However, historically the issue for Baptists has been believer's baptism.)

Finally, one exasperated Roman Catholic priest asked me this question: "Is there a Baptist theology anywhere in which individual Baptist scholars like yourself articulate their views, not speaking for Baptists in general but for themselves as individual Baptists, in such a way that we might get a handle on this?" It was a disarming question. In essence he was saying: "We're accustomed to working within ecclesiologically determined parameters, guidelines, and guardrails within which theological diversity is either deemed orthodox or heretical. But this Baptist way of doing theology in which each Baptist may (and must) articulate his/her own individual *Baptist's* theology, no more and no less, is new to us. Can you point us to a place where we can see what such a theology would look like?"

I had to say, "Well, no, I can't. Individual Baptists have articulated theologies of one sort or another—Mullins, Moody, McClendon, Hendricks, Humphreys, and Stagg, to name a few—but there really isn't a book like the one you've described in which individual Baptists present an individual *Baptist's* theology of God, humanity, sin, Scripture, church, salvation, sacraments, and eschatology." Then I added: "But there ought to be."

There is something uniquely Baptist about a theology in which individual Baptists, rather than just one Baptist, express their own diverse views, not attempting to speak for all Baptists in these matters—which no Baptist can. Rather, such a theology would truly be a Baptist's theology in which a group of us individual Baptist thinkers offers to our brothers and sisters the benefit of the best thinking we can do on things theological in the hope that our theologizing might encourage theirs. You can't get more "baptistic" than that! After some encouragement from conferees and others, I approached Smyth & Helwys about the project. It seemed to me that the timing was right for such a theology.

Coincidentally, there looms now on the Baptist landscape a new network of theological schools in which Baptist scholars are engaged in just this kind of creative theologizing. These schools, which recently formed the Consortium of Theological Schools Partnering with the Cooperative Baptist Fellowship (CBF), include:

- Baptist House of Studies at the Divinity School, Duke University
- Baptist Studies at Brite Divinity School, Texas Christian University
- Baptist Studies Program, Candler School of Theology, Emory University
- Campbell University Divinity School
- M. Christopher White School of Divinity, Gardner-Webb University
- Logsdon School of Theology, Hardin-Simmons University
- McAfee School of Theology, Mercer University
- Wake Forest University Divinity School
- Baptist Theological Seminary at Richmond
- Central Baptist Theological Seminary
- Truett Theological Seminary, Baylor University

At least in part, all eleven schools are in some measure a response to the foment in Baptist life over the past twenty years precipitated by the fact that Baptists have forgotten one of their most cherished core values: that no one Baptist can speak with authority for another in matters of faith. It occurred to me: Why not ask the deans of these new schools (or their designees) to write a chapter in such a Baptist's theology? These are the people who will shape to a large degree the next generation of Baptist ministers and, consequently, much of Baptist life and theology for the new millennium. What better group of theologians is there with which to compose a new theology for individual Baptists? Furthermore, such a volume would have the added benefit of introducing these new theological schools to a wider audience, highlighting the fact that it really is a new day for Baptists, both theologically and denominationally.

Moreover, I wanted such a book to be a book of practical, or popular, theology rather than a critical theology written only for the guild of scholars. I often quip that in the minds of many laypersons a theologian is one who says more and more about less and less to fewer and fewer. I envisioned this book being a practical theology, one that could help to answer the Roman Catholic priest's question and that might be useful to Baptist pastors, laypersons, and students.

With the encouragement of Smyth & Helwys, the book I envisioned has become a reality. Nearly all of the contributors represent schools belonging to the Consortium of Theological Schools Partnering with CBF. All but two of them are the deans of their respective schools. The only contributor who is not directly related to one of the Consortium schools is Gary Parker, Coordinator for Baptist Principles for the CBF. Given his close working relationship with the Consortium, it seemed only natural that he should be one of the book's contributors.

The book is designed and organized as a systematic theology. A systematic theology treats doctrines, or aspects, of the Christian faith from the standpoint of an assumed theological "system," or overarching perspective often confessional in nature—in this case, "Baptist"—and then moves into and out of the biblical text to the degree deemed necessary by the particular theologian in order to substantiate or document from the biblical text the perspectives being espoused. Typical theological themes/doctrines explored in such an approach include the doctrines of God, revelation, humanity, sin, Scripture, salvation, church, the ordinances (or sacraments), and eschatology. A brief perusal of the table of contents reveals that this is the approach taken in this volume.

Moreover, a systematic theology, as opposed to some other organizing scheme, is better suited for a book of this kind in that each chapter stands on its own merits. Not only are individual chapters structured and organized differently, but differing conventions are employed by the various writers. For example, while all writers utilize gender-inclusive language for persons, some prefer to use masculine pronouns for God (He, His, Him), while others do not. Furthermore, the individual personalities of the writers will be clearly discernible even to the casual reader. The reader will quickly note that the writers, though sharing much in common, do not always agree at every point. Again, this is as it should be in a true Baptist's theology. This approach makes the volume more user-friendly and serviceable to the reader. Readers can simply "dip in" at whatever point interests them without having to follow a central thesis developed throughout the entire volume, which is typically the case with a systematic theology written by a single author. As a resource for the reader, a list of contributors along with a brief biographical sketch appears at the conclusion of the book.

Often, writers will comment in the introduction of a volume that a book is never merely the work of just one person. No false modesty is being exercised by this writer when he says that this book, from start to finish, was a collaborative effort. I gratefully acknowledge the excellent and timely work of my colleagues at the various divinity schools/seminaries in contributing to this collection of essays. They represent the finest in Baptist scholarship, and the best in Baptist statesmanship and churchmanship.

Also, I gratefully acknowledge the staff of Smyth & Helwys for their willingness to take a risk on a venture such as this. They could not have been more helpful, supportive, and gracious. I must also say "thank you" to my administrative assistant, Laura Back. In the throes of a busy, hectic divinity school schedule that included, among other things, a self-study for the Association of Theological Schools, Laura made the time to help me push this project to conclusion. Finally, I express gratitude to Cheryl, who for the past twenty-nine years has been both my wife and best friend. In the words of the apostle Paul, I can say to her: "I thank my God every time I think about you."

Revelation
William L. Hendricks

How does God break through to God's creation? The answer, in one word, is *revelation*. Behind and beyond this one word there are many assumptions, related matters, and definitions that are necessary to answer the question.

Assumptions

We all have assumptions in every area of life. In the mechanical realm we assume the brakes of our car will work. In the area of cooking we assume that we will use the correct ingredients without first reading the package. In relationships we assume a trust and confidence in those we love. Any of these assumptions can break down, and when they do there are drastic results, and we have to check our assumptions and rearrange our priorities.

The life of faith, also, has its basic assumptions. As Christians, we need to be clear about our basic assumptions or presuppositions. There are five basic assumptions on which the Christian faith—Baptist beliefs and all others—rest.

The first assumption begins where scripture begins: *God is.* The Bible never argues the case. The majestic words "in the beginning God" contain a basic assumption, namely, that God is. This assumption is called "theism," or a belief in God. All Christians start with the basic affirmation, "I believe in God . . .," but not all people begin with that assumption. Persons who intentionally and consciously do not believe in God are atheists, literally, no-God people. It is important for Baptists to give reasons for and to make rational arguments about their God-belief. The formal discipline for arguing a case for God is called "apologetics," or speaking a word on behalf of someone or something. It is good to argue God's case. It is not necessary to convince all opponents of belief in God. Faith may be strengthened by argument, but unbelief cannot be overcome by argument alone.

The second basic assumption is that *God speaks.* The point of this presupposition is evident. It would do humanity no good to worship a God who does not speak, who does not break through into our world. There has been much discussion about how God speaks and by what means God has revealed God's self to the human community. In the following pages we will take up the vital question as to how God breaks through. It is our basic assumption that God does speak. Please note that when we say God speaks, we are using a metaphor. God's actions are also part of God's speech.

The other side of the assumption that God speaks is that *humanity receives and understands* what God is saying. There are people who grant God's existence but do not believe that humans can know or understand a message from God. This view is called "agnosticism." Agnosticism, unlike atheism, does not explicitly deny that God exists; it says that we cannot know if God exists. The practical results of atheism and agnosticism are the same. Atheism often feels the necessity of trying to prove that God does not exist. Agnosticism does not enter the argument at all. Atheism shakes its head "no" to God questions. Agnosticism merely shrugs its shoulders.

The fourth assumption of the Christian faith is controversial: *God does not reveal all of God's self to humanity.* This view, which I share, is based on the supposition that finite persons in their earthly existence cannot know, interpret, or assimilate all that God knows, does, and is. The Latin phrase for this view is *finiti non capax infiniti*—finite persons are not fully capable of knowing the infinite God. This position uses scriptural references such as Isaiah 55:8-9.

> For my thoughts are not your thoughts, nor are your ways my ways, says the Lord. For as the heavens are higher than the earth, so are my ways higher than your ways and my thoughts than your thoughts.

There is in this view, also, an understanding about the distinctive difference between God and humankind. The alternative fourth presupposition is that humans can know and assimilate all that God is and does. This view uses biblical verses such as Amos 3:7. "Surely the Lord God does nothing, without revealing his secret to his servants the prophets."

Many Baptist ministers today assume that humans can fully and completely know the infinite God. The Latin phrase for this view is *finiti capax infiniti*—finite humans are capable of fully knowing an Infinite God. It is important which version of this assumption one accepts. The issue cannot be settled by prooftexts from the Bible. The assumption has to do with one's views of God and of the limitedness or lack of limits of humans.

The final assumption of the Christian faith is *what God has revealed of God's self is true to who God really is.* We cannot know all of God, but we can confidently say that what is revealed is correct and is an accurate account of who God actually is. The basic nature of God is revealed in scripture and supremely in Jesus Christ. God is love, not hate. God is involved in, not unconcerned with, creation.

Without these basic assumptions, the Christian faith and Baptist expressions of faith would not make sense. Having made clear what we take for granted, we can now move on to some basic definitions.

Terminology

It has been said that seventy percent of learning a new subject is understanding the vocabulary. Like every discipline, theology uses its own vocabulary. It is, therefore, important to have clear and well-defined meanings for a Baptist theology. The term "theology" is based on two Greek words: *theos* (God) and *logos* (a word or study about something). We may define theology as a study of God and all things pertaining to God. Theology is not just a formal study about God, but a way of understanding all of life and relating everything to God. Theology is a basic outlook, a climate of thought that involves God, our understanding of God, in every arena of our existence.

Biblical theology is an attempt to understand and spell out the various insights the Bible expresses about God. *Historical theology* is a recounting of what thoughtful people in every age have said about God. *Systematic theology* is an organization of Christian thinking around certain topics, specifically, a system that describes coherent and comprehensive insights about God and all things pertaining to God. *Practical theology,* which includes ethics and pastoral theology, seeks to apply the insights of the other theologies to the world in which we live. These definitions will help one to sort out the various types of God-talk.

When we know the theories about God and all things pertaining to God, we need to put theory into practice in everyday life. The truth of the matter is that actual Christian living leads us to ask about Christian theology. Worship, praise, and service come before theory, study, and system-making.

Revelatory Triad

The first topic in systematic theology is usually revelation, not to be confused with the last book of the Bible. The word "revelation" means to pull back the curtain so that what is behind the scenes may be viewed. The theological concept of revelation describes how God comes into our world. The book of Revelation draws back the curtain on the struggle of good and evil and the outcome of that battle. Good news! God wins! Granted the theological idea of revelation means drawing back a curtain so that God reveals God's self, but the deeper question is how this process of unveiling happens. How does God make the divine reality known, understood, and operable in every age? These questions lead us to further definitions. Theology is a wonderfully intricate, interwoven way of looking at reality and letting ourselves be grasped by God.

Revelation includes three other theological topics: manifestation, inspiration, and illumination. Together these form what I call the "revelatory triad." You will recognize that the metaphor is taken from music. Musical triads are three notes sounded together to make a chord. The three notes of the revelatory triad need to be held together in order to answer fully the question how God speaks. But we will build the chord by defining these three processes individually.

Manifestation

Manifestation means that God enters our time and space in special arenas to speak God's will and to perform God's special acts. God uses many things and people to provide an awareness of the divine way. In the Old Testament, Moses' burning bush, Baalam's frightened donkey, and the minds and messages of the prophets were means of divine communication. In the New Testament, God used miracles, the apostles' preaching, and the predictions of Old Testament prophets to bless and guide those chosen to be recipients of the divine message. The manifestation of God comes in our history and in ways the recipients can understand God's will and message.

The insights of manifestation come in a given context, such as Corinth, and are received and framed in a particular language or thought pattern, such as Greek. Even when the message of God is symbolic or coded, as in the symbols of the book of Revelation, the major meaning of the symbols is clear—God will win. The primary act of manifestation in the Hebrew Scriptures is the deliverance of the Hebrew slaves from Egypt. The mighty works surrounding Israel's deliverance from bondage is the major focus of the Old Testament. This marvel is followed by wilderness wanderings, the establishment of the monarchy, and the prophetic promises of God and warnings of judgment. The whole history of God's dealings with Israel, both in action and in interpretation, is the manifestation of God to a specific people for a certain purpose. The people were the Israelites; the purpose was to be a light of God to all the other nations.

All of this saga is an interpretation of what God was doing in God's creation with a small group of people whom God would use to bless all people. These acts and their understanding were at God's initiative. This epochal story and its historical and poetic sidelights (for example, Psalms and Proverbs) become definitive for all the people of that time, and by extension, the people of all times, including our own, to see and understand God.

The definitive manifestation of God in the Old Testament, that by which we interpret God in all ages as a covenantal, redemptive God, is the Exodus. The definitive manifestation of God in the New Testament is the Christ event. The birth, life, teachings, miracles, death, and resurrection of Jesus Christ are the defining acts of God. As the Exodus formed the redemptive community of Israel, so the Christ event formed the church, the redeemed community of God. Apostolic preaching and epistles to churches instructive in matters of faith and practice are analogous to prophetic messages of the Old Testament.

The Exodus and the Resurrection are the accounts of God's actions that give meaning and definition to what God is like. God is the one who leads people to deliverance. God is one who, through God's Son, will redeem all who believe and deliver them, at last, into God's own presence. This is the way God manifested God's self as the delivering, redeeming God who overcomes whatever threatens creation. This is good news indeed. Yet it seems so much in the past. Did God just live and act long ago and far away? How do we know all of this? Is our God only the God of the past? These questions drive us on to the second note of the revelatory triad, namely, to the concept of inspiration.

Inspiration

The word inspiration means "breathed into." The Greek term *theopneustia* means "God-breathed." The modern use of the term inspiration implies that anything that pleases or incites us in a positive way is "inspiring." We need an exact and theological definition. I would propose the following: "Inspiration is God guiding certain persons rightly to perceive, record, interpret, and transmit the record of God's definitive manifestations." That is quite a mouthful, but you can see how this definition fits on top of the idea of manifestation. There is a not-so-funny story called Wholly Moses in which a person other than Moses sees the bush burn and hears the divine voice and goes off on an entirely different tangent. The idea of inspiration presupposes that the right people receive, understand, and correctly report God's actions and message.

There is nothing mechanical about the process of inspiration. The *dictation theory* that said God placed the biblical writers in a trance and dictated to them word for word has long been discredited. This view would not account for the hundreds of variant readings we have in the thousands of early manuscripts. It is remarkable and also an evidence of inspiration that, despite many variations, the Bible contains a powerfully coherent message that can redeem and motivate people in every age. Since the time of the Reformation, different scholars, in order to bolster biblical authority, have given various theories as to how the Bible is inspired.

The *verbal theory* says that the words of scripture are inspired. Obviously, if we see the Bible as an inspired book, the words would be the vehicles of inspiration. To tighten the verbal theory, some speak of a plenary verbal theory of inspiration, which means that each word used is the exact word the Spirit intended. Again, the minor differences in the numerous ancient manuscripts would make it impossible to nail down which word was the original. In order to meet this objection, some modern scholars—including some Baptists—have suggested an original autograph theory, which states that every word of the original autographs (written by the historical authors) was divinely inspired. The dilemma of this theory, acknowledged by all, is that we do not have any original autographs. It seems self-defeating to have a theory for which there is no demonstrable evidence.

Theories of inspiration seem to answer the wrong question. The Bible gives no answer as to *how* the Bible is inspired. The biblical materials assume that the accounts are words that tell the story of God's dealings with creation, Israel, and the Church. Inspiration is to be judged by its results, not its method. There are numerous references that indicate "God spoke," or "the word of the Lord came unto. . . ." The idea of inspiration is used twice in the New Testament: "All scripture is inspired by God and is useful for teaching, for reproof, for correction, and for training in righteousness" (2 Tim 3:16). "No prophecy ever came by human will, but men and women moved by the Holy Spirit spoke from God" (2 Pet 1:21). These passages obviously refer to the Old Testament, but by extension the early churches and later Baptists used them to apply to the New Testament.

Our definition of inspiration includes more than biblical allusions. Inspiration, to be consistent, must extend beyond the original writers to those who draw the accounts together and who helped to preserve them. The Bible, as we know it, was not put in definitive form (a canon or rule of accepted scriptures) until about AD 400. Human insight and effort were instrumental in that whole process. Baptists would confess that the Spirit of God was also active through the entire process. The story of the preservation of scripture is a thrilling saga. This story is a far greater evidence of inspiration, God's involvement in the process, than hypothetical ideas as to how the Bible was inspired.

Inspiration with its results—the Bible, the word of God in written form—gives trustworthy accounts of God's definitive manifestations. Baptists have been known as a "people of the Book." This label is a compliment. Fidelity to our understanding of scripture reinforces the chord of continuity of God's definitive acts and the account of them in scripture. But other questions must be answered: How did we get the Bible in our language? What accounts for the various interpretations of the Bible? To what arenas of life does the inspiration of scripture apply?

The question of translation of the ancient manuscripts is important. The Bible was originally written in Hebrew (in the Old Testament) and Greek (in the New Testament). A small portion of the Old Testament was written in Aramaic. The history of biblical translation is a complex and lengthy subject. Suffice it to say, we owe a debt of gratitude to those scholars, ancient and modern, who have given their lives to translating the Bible into more than a thousand languages. Since the 1940s Christians have had a great number of translations from which to choose. The large number of translations available to us today can pose a problem or a pleasure. The problem arises when we begin to teach memory verses to children, youth, and even ourselves. In my opinion, every congregation should choose a translation for memory work and for use in pew Bibles. The pleasure of having many translations is that we may see a variety of texts that should challenge us to engage in a more serious Bible study and bring forth the richness of different ways of stating the biblical messages.

Granted the inspired text of scripture, there is no guarantee of one definitive interpretation. The various understandings and interpretations of the Bible stand behind and are the cause of numerous denominations and many theological disputes. We must live with various biblical interpretations, but there are some basic rules for good biblical interpretation.

There is, in fact, a whole area of study about interpretation. It is called "hermeneutics." Some basic principles of interpretation are: (1) Take a passage in context. (2) Consider what kind of literature a given passage is, for example, poetry, history, or epistle. (3) Use commentaries that will enhance understanding of the history, background, and ancient customs of biblical times.

We have sounded two notes of a three-note chord. Revelation involves manifestation, inspiration, and illumination. If we had only God's ancient definitive acts (manifestation) and if we had only a book recording those accounts (inspiration), we would have only echoes and accounts of what happened in the past. One of the hallmarks of Baptists is their insistence on a personal, vital relationship with God, here and now, in our time. This leads us to the third key in the chord of revelation: illumination.

Illumination

Illumination literally means to turn on a light enabling persons to see. This can be a physical light or a mental or spiritual understanding. A useful theological definition of illumination is the divine act of giving persons in every age an understanding of God through the inspired record of God's definitive manifestation (the Bible) in matters sufficient to salvation.

God who entered creation and showed God's self to be a delivering redeemer continues the divine work. Just as God worked by the Spirit to create, so God moved to deliver Israel and to act redemptively through Jesus Christ. That same Spirit of God makes scripture come alive and enters our experience, incorporating us into God's kingdom. Revelation is historical. God enters our time and space to grasp us and include us in the redemptive plan intended for all the world. You may well ask, "Does God not continue to reveal who God is to people today?" The answer is yes. But what God does today always fits the patterns and promises of what has been done before. God is a specialist in doing new things, yet the new things God does are consistent with what God did before.

When it comes to biblical interpretation, I claim that all people, in reading scripture, can discern God's love and realize the salvation given in Jesus Christ. All can understand things sufficient to salvation. No person or group can claim *the* infallible interpretation of all scripture. This is so because the Bible is like a diamond rather than a book of mathematics. No one can catch all of the flashes of light that occur when the sun's rays hit a diamond. These flashes depend on the viewer, on the way the jewel is held. Therefore circumstances, context, and individual and group needs will find from time to time a special awareness and guidance in scripture. From the days of Anabaptists forward we have tended to trust group interpretation more than one individual's opinion. From the days of technical biblical studies forward we have used these guidelines to reinforce our biblical interpretations.

The idea of illumination places the inspired account of God's manifestation (the Bible) within the reach of all. Illumination does not guarantee to any group or person *the* final infallible interpretation of scripture. The text of scripture is the Christian fact. It is a possession of all denominations and Christians. The various interpretations of scripture form the heritage of each Christian community. What all Christian communities, including Baptists, need to do is find the best interpretations of their heritage and reinforce or reconfigure them in the light of scripture and the realities of their own context.

So we have heard the full chord of revelation. Its three notes, manifestation, inspiration, and illumination need to be sounded together. By discussing them separately we can see how God has held together and extended God's self to the world. If we dwell exclusively on one note we fall into problems. For example, we may emphasize only God's action in the days of old and in the days of Christ's incarnation and the accounts of the early church. This approach, purely a historical and archaeological view, is *arid historicism*. Arid historicism means that we leave all of God's work in the past. Questions then arise. So what? How do we know about it? Does it have any meaning today?

Scripture describes God's acts in the past. There is a record of God's acts and their meaning. The guidance of God's Spirit in causing the various biblical accounts to come into being, to be collected, and to be preserved is the remarkable process of inspiration.

Because of inspiration we have *the* Christian book. But we cannot be content to keep God in a book, not even the "Good Book." We cannot use the Bible without acknowledging God's acts behind the biblical accounts. Nor can we ignore the movements of God in history, including our own history. To use the Bible without an awareness as to what lies behind it or what God has done since is bibliolatry, the worship of scripture. The Bible is part of revelation. We do not worship scripture; we worship the God who lies beyond the Bible and who is expressed and made known in scripture. The Bible is authoritative because it is God's word. Scripture points to the God who gives this book its redemptive significance.

Manifestation and inspiration lead us on to illumination. Illumination is active in our heritage and our group and individual experience. Illumination is where we come in as congregations and believers. But if we stress only our experience or descend to a defensive, "God told me" level, we run the risk of "cut-loose mysticism." Cut-loose mysticism is the error of putting our own corporate or individual experience above scripture as the norm for Christian belief and action. A student once told me, "I don't care what the Bible says. God told me . . . ." That is cut-loose mysticism. It is more prevalent in Baptist life today than it should be. When one's claims run counter to evident and clear teachings of the Scripture, we have an authority problem. Manifestation, inspiration, and illumination are all required to build the chord of revelation. When this understanding is one-sided or incomplete, we have a need to ask what is the authority of our faith. On what do we build our case and stake our claim?

Authority

We face authority issues every day. Who put that sign there? Which of the television commercials should I believe? Among the claims of various religions, which is most nearly correct? Finally, the skeptic in all of us asks, "Says who?"

Jesus faced the authority question in his many confrontations with the religious leaders of his day, the sharpest of which is expressed in John 8. When the religious leaders asked Jesus about his authority, he pointed even beyond himself to God. That is where we must start. *The authority of the Christian faith is the triune God as revealed in scripture, conveyed in a heritage, and made real in experience.*

All authority ultimately comes from God. God is the source, the ground of being, the one who lets be, the maker of heaven and earth. To be more specific, it is the triune God—Father, Son, and Holy Spirit—the fullness of God, who creates and redeems the world. I mention God's triunity because that is a distinctively Christian understanding of God drawn from biblical implications by the early churches.

The two distinctive doctrines of the Christian faith are the incarnation of Jesus Christ and the trinity. Who is our ultimate authority? God. Which God? The maker of heaven and earth, the God and Father of our Lord and Savior, Jesus Christ? So say the scriptures and the earliest expressions of the believing community. But how do we know God? How has God revealed God's self?

God has revealed God's self definitively in the Bible, but how shall we interpret the Bible? "No man is an island." We all have a Christian heritage. Mine is a Baptist heritage that is indebted to and enriched by other Christian traditions. Many times Baptists want to jump straight from God or even straight from the Bible to one's own experience. That won't work. All of us inevitably are shaped by the time and circumstances of our lives. We have a heritage or a context, even if we know nothing of the Baptist story but what happened in our home church or our own home. We need to learn about Baptist traditions, for they have shaped who Baptists are in the modern world.

The last part of our authority statement extends to the experience of our church life and our private lives. I would encourage Baptists to listen to the church, the redeemed community to which one is attached, with great respect and much care. The corporate life of the church is more likely to be attuned to what God is saying in the life of the community than is the individual. This is not always the case, but those who find themselves in a perpetual series of disagreements with a series of churches may want to evaluate themselves carefully.

If we put these elements of authority—triune God, scripture, heritage, and experience—out of order, we risk theological confusion. Some years ago I spoke to a large group of pastors. I suggested that we were in danger of putting the Bible in the place of God and of placing our experience above everything. Soon after that speaking engagement I received a letter from a prominent pastor who said he did not understand what I said. He continued, "The Bible is God, and God is the Bible." That was a classic case of bibliolatry. In all things God must have the preeminence. Some in Baptist life today would want to place their individual experience as the highest authority. Although our experience is the point at which we connect with God, our own experience is too fragile and varies too much to make it our final authority. Let us leave the first and final place with God.[1] Our authority is not to be perceived in a strong-armed fashion. The well-known hymn, "My Faith Has Found a Resting Place" expresses the testimony that accepts God's redemptive love and actions as a final expression of authority. Two other questions must be raised. Are there other sources of revelation? Are the claims of other religions legitimate?

Other Sources of Revelation

Is God confined in the pages of a book, even a Holy Book? No, not at all. Reread the paragraphs that affirm God is God and Lord of all. Where else may we see traces of God? Look around. The world God has made, and which we seem bent on destroying, bears the marks of its maker. The knowledge we can draw of the sublimity and grandeur of God is sometimes called "general revelation." General revelation is sometimes contrasted with special revelation. Biblical corroboration for general revelation is found in Romans 1, which says that everyone should be able to see the evidences of God, the Creator, in the world God has made. But this is only a general idea that there is a God. It does not say what that God is like. The idea of general revelation is often coupled with the notion of an innate conscience that is present in all people, which gives them a sense of what is right or wrong. General revelation and conscience were supposed to make all persons guilty before God.

The older view of general revelation has come under much criticism in recent years. Modern urban people have little firsthand exposure to nature. Children and youth in our world commit heinous crimes, demonstrating no sense of right or wrong. It has been suggested that ours is an amoral generation. I prefer to classify the grandeur of God's world and the common morality (which comes from a residual Christian culture in our society) as preparation for revelation. All that humans know and can determine, I label "discovery." I prefer to give the term revelation to those special acts by which God unveils God's self as the loving Redeemer, culminating in the life, death, burial, and resurrection of Jesus Christ.

Older church traditions and modern optimistic views of human nature suggest that human reason can find and demonstrate logically proofs for God's existence. This line of thought held by Thomas Aquinas (1224–1274) and Immanuel Kant (1724–1804) is called "natural theology." Natural theology suggests that by our innate, natural rational powers we can establish the necessary existence of a higher power. Natural theology can assist believers in providing underpinning for faith. The persuasive arguments of powerful modern philosophers have weakened older philosophical "proofs" for God's existence. Natural theology is a highly sophisticated system that is of little practical help to the average Christian. Natural theology is not to be confused with a theology of nature, which is a Christian discourse about God's world. A theology of nature involves appreciation and wonder for God's creation and a determination to care for God's world. Christians should be concerned about ecology in all of its dimensions. This is "our Father's world," and God has asked us to take care of it.

For me, revelation is always special. We all draw intimations about a creator from the world around us. We are shaped in our morality and outlook by our world. There are logical arguments that reinforce views about a Supreme Being. All of these are discoveries that lead to the threshold of revelation. The question remains: Are other religions recipients of revelation also?

Religious Pluralism

In twentieth-century America many Baptists have met people who do not make our assumptions and who do not share our views of revelation. This is a twofold challenge to modern believers. We need to understand and be able to interpret our faith. We also need to understand and dialogue with the faith of others. Most of us know a Buddhist or a Moslem who is a good, moral person and an earnest believer in his or her religion. What does Christian theology say to religious pluralism?

A Proper Attitude

There are four basic attitudes for thinking about other religions. The first is a defensive attitude called "they-are-all-of-the-devil." This attitude reasons that my faith is correct because it is from God. Since other faiths are different from my faith, they must be of the devil. This is not an informed position. It is certainly not a view that will permit one to dialogue with people of other religions. In earlier days some Baptists even took the "they're-of-the-devil" view about different Christian denominations. Much hostility, argument, and ill will resulted. There is little to be gained by this first view except bitter fruit.

A second attitude for looking at world religions is what I call the "stair-step" approach. This approach ranks world religions according to the criteria of the one building the staircase. The poor, so-called primitive religions, who often are too ill-prepared to respond to these comparative arguments, usually wind up on the bottom of the stairs. The person who lands on the top stair is the one who builds the staircase, the one who makes the rules for the comparison. This comparative attitude usually appears arrogant and does not help in open-faced interfaith dialogue.

A third attitude for looking at other faiths is to pick and choose parts of each world religion and to try to put them together so that the chooser ends up with a super faith including parts of many faiths. I call this third approach the "stew-pot" method. An older generation used to clean out the ice box and put all the remnants of several leftovers together. These stews were often hard on the digestive system. The problems with the "stew-pot" approach toward varied religions are many. All religions do not say the same thing. Each religion has its distinctives. All religions grow in their own soil. The religions of the East (Hinduism, Buddhism, Shinto, and so on) have a different worldview from the religions of the West (Judaism, Christianity, and Islam). The results of an eclectic (pick and choose selectively) religion usually pleases noone. It is as someone said of an elephant: "It looks like it was put together by a committee."

The fourth attitude, which I strongly recommend, is called "listening love." The attitude of listening love does just what the name implies. It hears the other religions. It is not defensive, but tries to understand the other's viewpoint. This means one must know one's faith and know about the other's faith. Listening love requires a courteous dialogue between both views. Then, by confidence, the Christian must leave the discussion with God. I have heard all of the objections to the listening attitude. They run something like this: "But I must win the intellectual argument, or God will look bad"; "I am threatened by religious discussions when I'm not on my turf"; "I don't know anything about that other faith." To name these arguments is to answer them. God's honor is not bound up with our argumentation. If your own faith and beliefs are secure, there is not any turf that should threaten you. Learn from others and about others so that you can give a positive witness of your faith.

Resolving Pluralism

In a shrinking world drawn together by the media and public transportation, pluralism is an "in-your-face" fact. Pluralism is the reality of multiple perspectives that do not reduce to one satisfying simple answer (unity). I predict that in the twenty-first century pluralism will pose the largest problem for interactive religious communities. Mosques, Ashrams, Buddhist temples and Bahai churches are springing up all over the United States. It is a trend that will only multiply, so far as anyone can predict. How can pluralism be resolved and brought into one simple solution? I do not believe that it can be resolved. Moreover, intellectual solutions seldom resolve problems of the heart.

I do not have any fool-proof resolution to this challenge, nor do I know anyone who does. There are some helpful hints. All religions have three parts: *doctrine, worship practices,* and *ethics.* The strongest bridge we can build with other religions is in the area of ethics. Most religions want to respect life and preserve the world. We should start with our points of agreement. We should cooperate to eradicate the senseless waste of human life in wars and the greedy use of natural resources. This friendly cooperation and ecological cooperation will not bring a full Christian salvation to all who cooperate. But these united actions will certainly help humanity and help save the planet. God would certainly be glorified in these attitudes and actions. The best proof of any religion is found not in intellectual arguments, but in ethical actions. Christians believe that God is a God of justice and love. The best way to reinforce this belief is for Christians to be loving and just. We must indeed be known by our fruits. There is no more convincing way to demonstrate and give evidence of our faith. But the question persists. What happens to people who are not Christians, those who do not know Christ either because of non-acquaintance or non-acceptance?

The old twofold answer is still standard fare. All people are judged by the light they have, and it is God who judges nations and people. This provisional answer has given impetus to our responsibility for evangelism and missions. I am fond of the answer that says wherever there is truth, goodness, and beauty they must have come directly or indirectly from God. The Christian looks through the focused telescope of Christ. Christ is the one through whom God is most clearly seen. That is a Christian predisposition, and I share it. In the beginning, God. In the end, God. God has pulled back the curtain to reveal who God is and who we are. It is an interesting show, this drama of revelation.

Postscript

Older Baptist confessions of faith[2] began with statements about God. Then they spoke about how God revealed God's self. That is probably a wise thing to do. Yet, when you set up a systematic theology, it seems appropriate to start with how God comes to us. I have taught Baptist ministers for forty-two years. This chapter has been influenced by many streams of theology, from both the Christian perspective and that of other faith groups. In keeping with the purpose of this book I have forborne from technical footnotes and quoting extensively from scholarly works. I have appended a select bibliography of theological works by Baptists. The many sources I have used have been put through my Baptist sieve. The reader is welcome to this distillation. It is accompanied by my fervent wishes that it will help readers understand their faith and rejoice in their Baptist roots.

Notes

[1]See *Sacred Mandates of Conscience,* ed. Jeff Pool (Macon GA: Smyth & Helwys Publishing, Inc., 1997) 102-21.

[2]William Lumpkin, *Baptist Confessions of Faith* (Valley Forge PA: Judson Press, 1969). See also William Hendricks, "God, The Bible, and Authority," in *Sacred Mandates of Conscience,* 102-21.

Selected Bibliography

Basden, Paul, and David S. Dockery, eds. *The People of God: Essays on the Believers' Church.* Nashville: Broadman Press, 1991.

Bush, L. Russ, and Tom J. Nettles. *Baptists and the Bible.* Chicago: Moody Press, 1980.

Bunyan, John. *Grace Abounding to the Chief of Sinners* and *The Pilgrim's Progress.* London: Oxford University Press, 1966.

Conner, W. T. *Christian Doctrine.* Nashville: Broadman Press, 1937.

Conyers, A. J. *A Basic Christian Theology.* Nashville: Broadman & Holman Publishers, 1995.

Cunningham, Richard B. *The Christian Faith and Its Contemporary Rivals.* Nashville: Broadman Press, 1988.

Deweese, Charles W. *Baptist Church Covenants.* Nashville: Broadman Press, 1990.

Erickson, Millard J. *Christian Theology.* Grand Rapids: Baker Book House, 1983.

Garrett, James Leo. *Systematic Theology: Biblical, Historical, & Evangelical.* Volume 1. Grand Rapids: Wm. B. Eerdmans Publishing, Co., 1990.

Gilkey, Langdon. *Maker of Heaven and Earth: A Study of the Christian Doctrine of Creation.* Garden City NY: Doubleday & Co., 1959.

_____. *Reaping the Whirlwind: A Christian Interpretation of History.* New York: Seabury Press, 1976.

Grenz, Stanley J. *Theology for the Community of God.* Nashville: Broadman & Holman Publishers, 1994.

Hendricks, William L. *A Theology for Aging.* Nashville: Broadman Press, 1986.

_____. *A Theology for Children.* Nashville: Broadman Press, 1980.

_____. *Who Is Jesus Christ? Layman's Library of Christian Doctrine.* Volume 2. Nashville: Broadman Press, 1985.

Henry, Carl F. H., ed. *Revelation and the Bible: Contemporary Evangelical Thought.* Grand Rapids: Baker Book House, 1958.

Hunt, Boyd. *Reedemed! Eschatological Redemption and the Kingdom of God.* Nashville: Broadman & Holman Publishers, 1993.

Humphreys, Fisher. *Thinking about God: An Introduction to Christian Theology.* New Orleans: Insight Press, 1974.

Lumpkin, William L. *Baptist Confessions of Faith.* Valley Forge PA: Judson Press, 1959.

Marshall, Molly T. *What It Means To Be Human.* Macon GA: Smyth & Helwys Publishing, Inc., 1995.

McClendon, James Wm., Jr. *Doctrine: Systematic Theology.* Volume 2. Nashville: Abingdon Press, 1994.

Moody, Dale. *The Word of Truth: A Summary of Christian Doctrine Based on Biblical Revelation.* Grand Rapids: Wm. B. Eerdmans Publishing Co., 1981.

Mullins, E. Y. *The Christian Religion in Its Doctrinal Expression.* Nashville: Broadman Press, 1917.

_____. *Why Is Christianity True?* Philadelphia: Judson Press, 1905.

Patterson, Robert E., ed. *Science, Faith, and Revelation: An Approach to Christian Philosophy.* Nashville: Broadman Press, 1979.

Pinnock, Clark H. *The Scripture Principle.* San Francisco: Harper and Row, 1984.

Rauschenbusch, Walter. *A Theology for the Social Gospel.* Nashville: Abingdon Press, 1945.

Roark, Dallas M. *The Christian Faith: An Introduction to Christian Thought.* Nashville: Broadman Press, 1969.

Robinson, H. Wheeler. *The Life and Faith of the Baptists.* London: Kingsgate Press, 1946.

Strong, A. H. *Systematic Theology.* Philadelphia: Judson Press, 1907.

Wade, Charles R., Carol Bowman, and N. Lee Bowman. *The Jesus Principle: Building Churches in the Likeness of Christ.* Arlington TX: Clear Stream Publishing, 1998.

Ward, Wayne E., and Joseph F. Green, eds. *Is the Bible a Human Book? Fifteen Baptist Leaders Speak Out.* Nashville: Broadman Press, 1970.

God

Gary L. Parker

One Sunday morning in April in a white steepled, red-bricked church in Georgia, a young pastor gathered the children at the front of the sanctuary to lead them in the children's sermon. As usual, he asked the children a question: "What has a bushy tail, eats nuts, and lives in trees?" For a second, none of the kids answered. The parents, watching quietly in the pews, instantly thought of the answer: "bushy tail, eats nuts, lives in trees—a squirrel!" But before any of the kids could offer that obvious response, a boy with ears big enough to pick up satellite transmissions threw up his hand and shouted, "God!" The whole congregation erupted with laughter. The big-eared boy turned red with embarrassment. The preacher, feeling bad for the child, decided the best thing to do was to give the youngster a chance to explain his reasoning. So he asked the boy: "Why do you think that something that has a bushy tail, eats nuts, and lives in trees is God?" The boy shook his big ears side to side and said, "Preacher, I know the answer you're looking for is 'squirrel.' But . . . it seems to me, here in church and all, we ought to be talking about God." Out of the mouths of babes! We ought to be talking about God, and in this chapter we will.

Clarifications

In any book of theology, whether written by a Baptist or a person of any other religious tradition, the "oughtness" of talking about God immediately raises its head and demands attention. The word "theology" means exactly that—the study of God. To have a theology of any kind means to engage in the process of doing "God-talk."[1] It means gaining some understanding of what we mean when we say "God." It means pondering the nature of God, the work of God, how God relates to humans, and how that relationship affects our personal lives.

Yet, even as we do this, we find it absolutely necessary to establish some parameters for our discussion. In a limited chapter such as this I can in no way touch every base that a systematic theologian would touch in a book-length manuscript. It would be easier to drink all the water of the Mississippi River through a straw than to deal sufficiently with "God" in twenty pages! To narrow my focus, then, I want to state six qualifications to this discussion.

(1) I assume the existence of God. I am a believer in the reality of a divine being, a holy force, a "personal deity" and will not in any way try to "prove" God to the reader.[2]

(2) Speaking of God means I have to choose what aspects of God I want to discuss. In traditional Baptist theologies, the writer typically follows a pattern of considering the "nature" of God and the "attributes" of God. Though I'll touch on each of these, I won't follow this deductive pattern nearly so stringently as many do.[3] As a result, what I choose to say about God might not match what you would choose given the same opportunity.

(3) As a Baptist, I begin my effort to speak of God by asking what the Bible says about God. Though the Bible isn't the only source of knowledge about God, a Baptist typically starts digging through the pages of holy writ to get answers to questions related to holy matters.[4] Certainly, we have had our debates over how God uses the Bible to communicate the history of the interaction between the divine and the human.[5] Yet, in spite of our disagreements, Baptists have believed that God transmitted through human beings the history, poetry, parables, narratives, prayers, and discourses that came together over the centuries to become our Holy Book. And we have believed that this Holy Book reveals to us all we need to know of God to live as people of faith.

(4) Speaking of a Baptist's theology of God implies that perhaps a "Baptist's theology" will somehow differ from that of other Christian traditions. Though I'm certain this is true to some extent in the case of each individual believer, it may not be as true in terms of "orthodox" Christian faith. In other words, for example, though a Baptist's theology of the Lord's Supper will differ significantly from that of many other Christian expressions, I'm not sure that is equally true of a Baptist's theology of God. In many ways the bigger the issue, the more unanimity of our common belief.

(5) Though I will speak in ways that I hope are theologically respectable to the professor, I am primarily directing my words to the layperson. By the nature of this assignment, I cannot define every term, examine every implication, and consider every nuance of the statements I'll make. I'm sure the professional academic can

find scores of "bones to pick" with me, but I have to paint with a broad brush in this circumstance.

(6) No one can really describe God in the frail clothing of human language. Though philosophers have tried in erudite words, poets have tried in rhythmic verse, preachers have tried in fiery sermons, musicians have tried in soaring hymns, and theologians have tried in complicated prose, no one ever completely succeeds. The best we can do is use the shorthand of analogy and metaphor. Yet the language used, no matter how grand, will never do justice to the totality of God. God is always more than any figure of speech that I, or anyone else, might suggest.

Let me give a short example. First John tells us, "God is love." We hear this as an admirable description of God. But what a human understands as love is never adequate to describe the manner in which God loves. God's love, therefore, is not exactly what we understand as love. So, God is love, but God's love is far purer than even the best of our loves.[6] God is love, but God is more than the analogy of love can embrace.

Ultimately, it seems that we always find this the case. Though we have to describe God in human categories, our descriptions will always falter in doing God justice. Yet, even with the poverty of our language, the believer still feels compelled to think of and to speak of God. The question therefore is not, "Will we speak of God?" but "What shall we say of God when we speak?" To that question, let us now turn our attention.

God as Mystery

Several years ago I attended an interdenominational writer's conference where a number of well-known authors were scheduled to speak. At about seven on the first evening of the conference one of these speakers, a mid-fiftyish male with thinning hair and a popular television program, stood and walked to the pulpit. A hush fell over the audience in the man's celebrity-like presence. He took a deep breath and then said. "If you want to know what God is like, then listen to me tonight. I'm going to tell you who God is and what God wants you to do with your life."

Hearing his opening line, I began to squirm. Although I suspect the man didn't mean to come across as confident as he sounded, his assurance that he knew "what God is like" and "who God is" made me uncomfortable. To my way of thinking, he was claiming too much. He was going too far. He was offering something I didn't think he could deliver as easily and glibly as he seemed to think.

Striving to know God as completely as possible is a commendable act. But the plain truth is that God never allows us to know everything we might desire to know. To some extent, God always remains a question mark to us, an abyss too deep and dark to see to the bottom, a mountain too tall to climb, a "mystery wrapped in a riddle inside an enigma."[7] To claim anything else, it seems to me, is to sin. The finite can never completely grasp the infinite; the sinful can never fully understand the holy. The Scriptures make this plain. In Exodus 33, Moses cried out to God: "Show me your glory." And God answered: "I will make all my goodness pass before you . . . but you cannot see my face, for no one shall see me and live."

Before we can say anything else, I think it is necessary to hear this reminder: No matter how much we know of God, there still exists even more of God that is unknowable. If we could somehow paint a picture that contains the sum of our knowledge about God, much of the canvas would remain blank—no paint, a black sheet of mystery. Knowing God fully would overwhelm us in the same manner that an Atlantic hurricane overwhelms a beach house. Karl Barth referred to this incomplete knowledge as the "hiddenness of God," saying,

> God's revelation is precisely his revelation as the hidden God. And therefore, faith in God's revelation can only give a very humble answer to the question, "Who is God?" and it is faith which will confess God as the God of majesty, and therefore, as the God unknown to us.[8]

Isaiah 55:8-9 echoes this sentiment: "For my thoughts are not your thoughts, nor are my ways your ways, says the Lord. For as the heavens are higher than the earth, so are my ways higher than your ways and my thoughts than your thoughts."

Like an ant trying to understand an atom, a human being cannot fully understand God. So, to speak of God, we must first accept the divine "unknowability" of the One of whom we speak.

God by Gallup

Though we admit that we can't know everything about God, we still have to acknowledge that Americans are more than a bit intrigued with the notion of deity. By any stretch of the imagination, God is popular these days. When pollsters ask Americans if they believe in God, 95 to 98 percent reply positively. Wherever we turn, we can find evidence of this belief—television and radio talk shows, Internet web sites, bookstores and library shelves, church parking lots on Sunday mornings, billboards on highways. God is everywhere!

A couple of years ago I sat at a major college football game and watched an airplane pull a banner that read, "God loves you." No matter where we look, we see that belief in God is a popular pastime. And that's good. Yet we can't help but ask a series of questions: Who is this God in whom the masses believe? What is the nature of this God? Does this God interact with human beings? If so, in what way? If not, why not? It is one thing to say, "I believe in God." It is still another to define what we mean by that statement.

In a December 1998 article in *Life* magazine titled, "When You Think of God, What Do You See?" Frank McCourt said, "America's God is vaguely defined." Speaking of America's multiple images of God, he continued, "Within these are many different views of God (sometimes Gods, plural); sometimes 'exalted beings' (possessing a divine essence)."[9]

To paraphrase McCourt's article into common slang, we might say that America is "lousy" with gods. That condition, however, can leave us with no true sense of the nature of the God in whom we believe. Unless we're careful, our God will end up meaningless to us—indefinite, nondefinable, and not specific. For most of us, that condition will leave us as empty as believing in no God at all.

God in Full

Those of us with roots in the soil of Baptist life typically want more definition of God than that offered by McCourt's article in *Life*. We want some substance to the term, some specificity to the subject. We want God to become more than the "oblong ooze" of which church historian Martin Marty spoke while discussing modern America's concept of God.[10] Thankfully for us, in spite of the mystery of which

I spoke at the beginning of this discussion, the Scriptures offer us all the specificity we need. The Scriptures, in fact, tell us of a God who wants us to know the character and the nature of the One who created us and loves us.

God as Revealer

Though a veil of mystery always separates us to some extent from God, that doesn't mean we can't know anything at all. In fact, just the opposite is true. Out of mystery, God chooses to reveal. Though we can't know God as a result of our own power or intellect, we can know God because of the choice God makes to show us the divine person.[11] For purposes we can't fully fathom and out of motivations we can't completely grasp, God made a decision to show human beings something of the nature and character of holiness.

We call this act "revelation," and it's really the beginning point to understanding the nature of God. After all, to reveal anything at all says something about the one doing the revealing. It is only when we open ourselves to other persons that we come into relationship with them. Thus, God's decision to reveal even a bit of the divine character shows us God's desire to relate to us. And that, I believe, is the first thing we can definitively say about God: God wants to relate to human beings and shows us this desire by the choice to unwrap some of the mystery so we might see and know the holy.

God in Creation

Typically, theologians describe the method of God's revelation as twofold: God reveals in natural revelation and then in special or historical revelation. In natural revelation God reveals through two methods, first through the wondrous world in which we live. In traditional theologies the writers often begin by describing God as the "Creator." After all, the Bible begins this way: "In the beginning when God created the heavens and the earth." Our earliest view of God shows us a deity making something from nothing (*creatio ex nihilio*), making light and darkness from a void, making life from the vast emptiness of that which wasn't.

Certainly, God's creativity is different from any human ability to build and establish. Whereas a human can make something out of inanimate material, only God can create something out of nothing and then breathe life into it. A human can carve the image of a bird from a piece of wood, but God created the tree from which the wood is taken and the bird who sits and chirps in it while it still lives.[12] Therefore, God is both involved with the created order and yet still "beyond it." In theological terms, God is both transcendent and yet immanent in the process of the created world.

If we accept God as the Creator, then we inevitably ask this question: What does the creation tell us about God? I think it tells us at least two things.

One, God has a purpose for the world. Though we may not know that purpose just by looking at the rhythm of the seasons or the consistency of day and night, the very precision of what we see tells us of a God of design, a God of direction, a God with a plan.[13]

Two, I believe the created order shows us a God of artistry, a God of beauty and goodness. Surely, I acknowledge the destructiveness of certain aspects of nature.[14] But, even with that, I see God as a generous artist, draping the world with scattered bits of holiness for us to enjoy and consider. Skilled with a brush and paints, God dabs the world with sunsets and azaleas and Texas bluebonnets. As a sculptor, God pushes up mountains, digs out oceans, and fills up waterfalls with white cascades. As a musician, God writes the song of a whippoorwill at dusk, the laughter of a two-year-old at the sight of a clown, and the crunch of snow underfoot in January.

I could carry this analogy further, but I hope these examples make the point. Nature reveals something crucial to us. God is a God of design, and a part of that design is to shower the world with beauty so we might see it and grasp something of the grandeur of the Almighty. As the writer of James said, "Every generous act of giving, with every perfect gift, is from above, coming down from the Father of lights, with whom there is no variation or shadow due to change" (1:17).

God and Human Conscience

Not only do we know something of God through the revelation of the natural world, but also through the revelation given in the inner self of each person as we deal with the sense of right and wrong apparently wired into our DNA. Though arguments often arise as to whether or not this "conscience" is innate in each person or implanted through cultural and social norms, the fact of a sense of "oughtness" within each person is indisputable.[15] Speaking of this conscience, Paul said,

> When Gentiles, who do not possess the law, do instinctively what the law requires, these, though not having the law, are a law to themselves. They show that what the law requires is written on their hearts, to which their own conscience also bears witness. (Rom 2:14-15a)

Like a computer that comes loaded with the most up-to-date software, a human being comes crying into the world loaded with a sense of right and wrong. This innate sense, though inevitably warped by sin, gives at least some evidence of a divine and holy power lurking in the recesses of each human spirit. After all, if this sense of morality comes with birth and if we believe that this sense comes from a God who created us, then it shows that God must care about right and wrong, morality and immorality, good and evil. Why program this sense into us if it's not important to the Divine Programmer? Just as creation reveals to us a God of purpose and beauty, so the conscience shows us a God of virtue and morality.

We find one of the traditional ways of describing God at this point. God is known as holy, not only because God is completely "unique" and "wholly other" from all that God created, but God is holy also in the sense of existing as pure Good, pure Virtue. In God we find nothing impure, nothing evil, nothing of fault.[16]

Certainly, neither the created order nor the inner conscience can tell us everything we want to know of God. Though they might lead us to some vague sense of belief in a divine being, they reveal little about God's interaction with the world. If all we knew of God was what we saw in creation and felt in conscience, then a deistic God (who set the world in motion but then stepped back and out of involvement with it) would serve us quite well. But we want more than that. We want to know not only that God "is," but also more of what God is like. To know that, however, requires a deeper, fuller revelation. To know God intimately means we have to see God act in specific, historical ways.

God as "Actor"

Though I have chosen the word "actor" to describe God's historical "acts" of revelation, I don't mean by the term what we think of when we see a Broadway play performed. We know from experience that actors and actresses are people who only pretend to be the characters they portray. When I speak here of God as "actor," I want to convey in the word the truth that God gets involved in the context of our world. God moves, communicates, and acts in the historical setting of human life. Through this divine action, we see more and more of the nature of God.

Typically, theologians have called this divine action "special" or "historical" revelation. By it, they refer to God's repeated works within human history. From the beginning of Jewish history—the call of Abraham, the deliverance from Egypt, the formation of the nation of Israel, the captivity years, the return to the land of promise and beyond—God has performed mighty deeds that demonstrate the character of the Almighty.

As the culmination of this Jewish history, Christians believe that God enacted the unique event we see in the life of Jesus Christ. For the Christian, Jesus embodies and brings to fruition all that God has done. As Hebrews 1:1-3 reminds us,

> Long ago God spoke to our ancestors in many and varied ways by the prophets, but in these last days he has spoken to us by a Son, whom he appointed heir of all things, through whom he also created the worlds. He is the reflection of God's glory and the exact imprint of God's very being . . .

If you want to see what God is like, look into the face of Jesus. In the life, death, resurrection, and continuing presence of Jesus we most completely discover the nature of God. And, quite amazingly, what we discover in Jesus is that God is a personal God.

God as Personal

As I declare that God is personal, I need to remind you of what I said in my sixth qualification. Any analogy of God will always fall short of saying all we want it to say about God. Suggesting that God is a "person" or a "personality" automatically throws up a number of red flags to those who want to make sure we keep God properly enthroned as the "holy other," completely unique and distinct from the frailties and limitations of human beings.[17] I understand that caution. Speaking of God as a person is not to suggest that God is a person as we are persons. God is not flesh and bones. I agree with Jesus who told the Samaritan woman at the well that "God is spirit, and those who worship him must worship in spirit and truth" (John 4:24).

At the same time, however, the word "person" does describe God in the sense that God has existence as a "being"—even if a "being" beyond anything we can imagine, that God has an intentional will, that God has consciousness (God "thinks" and even "feels"), and that God communicates.

To those who want to dismiss the idea of God as "person," I ask about the alternative. Is it better to call God "impersonal?" Shall we see God as some kind of cosmic machine or as a static energy without purpose? Shall we define God as an impersonal force, a nebulous "holy fog," existent but unaware of that existence or of human beings? Is it better to speak of God as the "ground of being," as Paul Tillich suggested, or as "a being"—with the understanding that by the phrase we don't suggest a "being" like a human but something totally different, unique and distinct?[18]

Saying that God is "personal" is a much higher concept than the alternative. If we are to believe that God interacts with us in any way at all, we have to use the term, even as poverty-stricken as it is. Certainly, to believe that God came in Jesus is to understand God as a personal being.

The Bible constantly describes God in this way. Time and time again in Scripture we see language that describes God in specifically human terms. The Bible describes God as demonstrating traits similar to those of human personalities. God loves; God grieves; God gets angry; God is jealous; God has purpose; God speaks; and God sees. To stay faithful to a biblical portrait of the divine is to accept the paradox that God is both transcendent and personal. As C. C. J. Webb said it:

> Controversy about the "personality" of God will be found to turn upon the difficulty involved in reconciling the finitude which seems essential to human personality with the absoluteness and infinity, or at least omnipresence and omnipotence, which we are accustomed to ascribe to God.[19]

In spite of the difficulties, then, we accept that God has "personal" characteristics. In fact, the Bible gives names to God to demonstrate the divine persona. Those names are familiar to us— God the Father, God the Son, and God the Holy Spirit. To these personal images of God we now turn.

God as Father

I realize that the use of the term "father" to describe God creates a number of difficulties for some readers. Those who grew up with abusive, neglectful, or distant fathers feel negative emotional baggage when they hear God described this way. And those who reject any use of masculine language in relationship to God erect immediate barriers when the word falls on their ears.

Certainly, the use of the word "father" should not be taken to mean that God is any more "masculine" than "feminine." Though, for the most part, scripture describes God in masculine terms, certain passages do picture God in more feminine images. For example, Isaiah 66:13 puts these words in the mouth of God: "As a mother comforts her child, so I will comfort you." And Deuteronomy 32:18, speaking against those who had forsaken God, reads, "You forgot the God who gave you birth." Finally, from the mouth of Jesus, we hear these words in Matthew 23:37 as he laments over Jerusalem: "How often have I desired to gather your children together as a hen gathers her brood under her wings."

The point I want to make is this: if God is indeed spirit instead of flesh and bone, as Jesus said God was, then neither term for gender fully satisfies our needs at this point. No gender designation fully captures the character of God. Yet, even with these qualifications, to stay true to biblical language we have to acknowledge the use of the term "father" to designate something of the sustaining, protecting, encouraging, teaching, and guiding characteristics of the Almighty. In the New Testament alone, God is described as "Father" about 120 times. Most significantly to the believer, Jesus referred to God this way repeatedly. In perhaps the most complete text regarding what Jesus believed about God, John 13–17, he spoke of the mansions in the "Father's house"; he equated himself as "one" with the Father and suggested that he was going "to the Father." He prayed to the Father to send "the Counselor" to the disciples; he

promised the "love" of the Father to those who loved him; he gave
the believers the right to pray to the Father and receive what they
asked. He said the Spirit "proceeds" from the Father and that the
Father was with him in all he did. Finally, Jesus prayed to the Father
for the disciples, saying, "Holy Father, protect them in your name
. . . that they may be one, even as we are one" (17:11b).

If we could separate the word "father" from all its negative con-
notations, I think we could see again that, in its purest sense, the
designation pictures God as a personal being who cares for, sacrifices for, and provides for the children created by the holy will.

Permit me a short, personal illustration. I am the father of two
daughters. And I, like all parents, looked forward to the day when
each of them would begin to talk. Most especially, I looked forward
to the day they would say, "Daddy." To be honest, I can't recall precisely when that day happened, and I can't recall if either of my girls
said "Daddy" before they said "Mommy." But I do recall the feeling
that welled up in me then and that wells up in me now when either
of my girls calls me "Father" or "Daddy."

That feeling comes to me not because I'm masculine—no
doubt, my wife experiences an equal intensity of feeling when our
daughters call her "Mother"—but because of the relationship I have
with my girls. The word "Father" as a name for God refers to
relationship—to mutual love, care and provision for—far more
than it does to gender. As a symbol of that relationship, we find
value in the term.

God as Son

When Baptists speak of God, we don't speak of a distant God, separated from us like the stages of a rocket jettisoned from the master
ship. We don't speak of a deistic God, one who wound up the
universe, then left it to run on its own devices.

Instead, the Christian God comes to us in a particular, personal
form. In fact, the God of the believer comes to us in the one manner
we can most readily understand. God comes to us in an historical
being—in the person of Jesus Christ. In Jesus, God made divinity
available to humanity. In Jesus, God stepped into human shoes,
breathed dusty air, and ate crusty bread. In Jesus, God got stom-
achaches and sweated under the arms. In Jesus, God's face turned

red with anger at hard-heartedness, God's voice thundered at intolerance, and God's eyes wept at sin. In Jesus, God's hands ripped as nails penetrated them, and God's heart exploded as death had its way. In Jesus, God identified with the human condition and became our divine fellow-struggler.

When we speak of God, then, we speak ultimately and always of the One who came to embrace us in the person of Jesus. Theologians call this act of identification with the human race "the incarnation." By this, we mean the profound act of God pouring divinity into human flesh.[20] John's Gospel said it in the most sublime way. "In the beginning was the Word, and the Word was with God, and the Word was God. . . . And the Word became flesh and lived among us, . . . full of grace and truth" (1:1, 14).

When I speak of God, I find myself coming back to this key truth: God is most personal in the life, death, and resurrection of Jesus Christ. We dare not forget this. It lies at the base of all we want to say about God. Without this as our foundation stone, our voices instantly slam shut. Either God came to us in Jesus or we have no need to talk about God.

To accept this proposition, however, is to make a profound decision of faith. I don't want to minimize what this signifies. Saying that God came to us in Jesus means we have to accept the reality of a world open to divine involvement. To say it negatively, it means we have to reject the notion of a closed universe, one in which cause and effect closes off all possibility of the supernatural. Accepting the incarnation—the miraculous life, atoning death, and bodily resurrection of Jesus—leads us right into the heart of the darkest mystery. No human mind can grasp the "method" or understand the "how" of God's work in these acts in history. Yet the Christian faith rises or falls with these assertions.

In Jesus, the transcendent God became visible. In Jesus, the abstract God became concrete. In Jesus, the fearsome God became approachable. In Jesus, the mysterious God became understandable. In Jesus, the divinity received a heart, two kidneys, ten toes, hair on his chest, and a voice with which to tell us that God loves us. Not a bad life's work, it seems to me.

God as Holy Spirit

Did you ever close your eyes and try to get a mental image of the Holy Spirit? What did you see? A gray fog? The leaves of a tree rustling in a soft breeze? A picture of Casper the Friendly Ghost? Of the three "persons" of the Trinity, I suspect we have the most trouble envisioning the Holy Spirit. After all, how can a person see a "spirit"? In all honesty, we can't. The Spirit exists, according to scripture, but not in visible form. The Spirit works as God works, but not in ways we can fully grasp. Yet, in spite of our inability to "see" the Spirit, the Scriptures indicate the reality of the Spirit as strongly as they indicate the reality of Jesus.

In the Old Testament the Holy Spirit is *ruach*, the power that moves and creates and empowers both individuals and the nation of Israel. In the New Testament the Spirit is *pneuma*, the mysterious power of God that comes and goes as it wills to carry out the work of the Father and the Son. In John 14–16 Jesus speaks of the Holy Spirit as the *paracletos*, the one "laid alongside" the believer to help through all the passages of life.

Significantly, we see the Holy Spirit at work in the life of Jesus from the beginning. The Holy Spirit "conceived" the child in the womb of Mary. The Holy Spirit blessed Jesus at his baptism. The Holy Spirit led Jesus into the wilderness temptation and filled him as he initiated his public ministry in Galilee. When Jesus preached to the synagogue in Nazareth, he pointed to the Spirit as having "anointed" him to preach "good news to the poor."[21] Over and over again in the life of Jesus, the Holy Spirit, referred to as "He" on numerous occasions, led Jesus and empowered him to do his holy work.

Not only did the Spirit create and empower Jesus, but the Spirit also leads the believer to faith and creates and empowers the church as believers become part of a spiritual community. The Spirit sets us free from our sin. The Spirit assures us that we are "children of God." The Spirit gives spiritual gifts to the believers for the "common good" of the church.[22]

From Pentecost forward to the present day, the Holy Spirit has heated the seeds of faith and brought them to flower in individuals and in community. As the physical presence of Jesus ended, the spiritual presence of God continued. We find that presence in the power of the Holy Spirit in our lives today.

Taken together, the images of God as Father, Son, and Holy Spirit comprise, in traditional terms, what we call the Holy Trinity. To best grasp what we mean when we think of God, we need to consider these in total now that we have considered them as distinct manifestations of God.

God as Trinity

When we begin to consider the Trinity, we don't get into much complicated language, and we don't delve into ancient church history. Instead, more than likely, we turn to the world around us to see if it offers any images that help us grasp the mystery of how one God can exist in three different "persons." Fortunately for us, it does. Three common analogies come to mind. First, just as the compound H_2O exists as steam, ice, and water—one substance, three expressions—so God exists as one being in three forms. Second, just as a human can exist in multiple relationships and yet be one—a woman as wife, mother, sister, and daughter, for example—so God can exist in similar manner as one God demonstrating different characteristics based on different needs. Using the human analogy in a slightly different way, the church father Augustine suggested that just as a person exists as memory, mind, and will, so God can exist in three.[23]

Obviously, such analogies don't satisfy the arguments of those who choose to see God as other than Trinitarian. Yet the doctrine is a universal Christian belief, not just a Baptist one, in spite of these arguments and in spite of the fact that the word "trinity" doesn't appear in the Bible. Let me suggest four reasons for the historical acceptance of this way of understanding God.

(1) The Bible supports the concept of the Trinity even if it does not specifically mention it. In the New Testament alone, more than 120 passages refer to Father, Son, and Holy Spirit together.[24]

(2) The church has always preached it. Peter said in his Pentecost message, "This Jesus God raised up, and of that we are all witnesses. Being therefore exalted at the right hand of God, and having received from the Father the promise of the Holy Spirit, he has poured out this that you both see and hear" (Acts 2:32-33).

(3) New believers were baptized into the Trinity. The Great Commission (Matt 28:19) commands the disciples to baptize the

converts in the "name of the Father and of the Son and of the Holy Spirit."

(4) The early church defended, clarified, and communicated it. Against those who suggested that Jesus and the Spirit were "demigods" or that God had taken on three roles at consecutive moments in history (modalism) or that the three represented a "trias" (three different gods), the church threw up a formidable defense. Defenders insisted that each "person" of the Trinity was equal and of the same essence within the Godhead. In the early third century a writer named Tertullian coined the Latin words *trinitas* and *personae* as a way of describing the "three persons" of Father, Son, and Holy Spirit. Though distinct, the three persons of the Trinity shared what the Greeks called one *ousia* ("essence"), or what the Latins referred to as one *substantia* ("one substance") of God. By the end of the fourth century the notion had taken firm hold in Christian belief. A synod at Constantinople wrote a letter to the church at Rome, saying, "The Father, Son, and Holy Spirit have the same Divinity, the same substance, and the same power; and the three perfect hypostases or three perfect persons, are co-equal and co-eternal."[25]

Of all the arguments for the Trinity, I think this simple one makes the most sense: The Trinity puts three "faces" on God, three faces we recognize, three persons we experience in our personal faith, three images we see in the Bible. Therefore, we accept the doctrine as essential to Christian truth and as vital for our lives.

A Personal Theology of God

I have spoken of God in many ways. I have described God as the Revealer who shows design and purpose in creation and virtue and morality in the conscience. I have described God as personal, with the revelation of this personal nature seen in the Father, the Son, and the Holy Spirit. Finally, I have described God as Trinitarian, one person unique and uncreated in essence and yet three in "person" or "manifestation."

To conclude this chapter, I want to outline in a short form what I see as the yet unstated, but nevertheless key, implications of my descriptions of God. Obviously, any such outline runs the risk of omitting something that someone else would see as critical. Yet, writers have always accepted that risk, and so must I.

First, I say what all others also inevitably say—God is Love. Though this has been stated over and over again, I don't see how I can leave out the statement most often used to sum up the nature of God. As the Bible often describes it, God's love compelled the gift of Jesus to our world.

By saying God is love, I don't mean to oversentimentalize God to the extent of leaving out God's concern about our sin. Like a parent with a child, love sometimes demands toughness along with compassion. Loving someone doesn't mean accepting everything they do as "okay." Though I tell my children every night that I love them, that doesn't mean I applaud everything they do. Neither does it mean they don't have to deal with the consequences of their actions when those actions transgress some family norm or morality.

God is love in the sense that God comes to us in persuasion rather than in coercion. God comes to us in mercy rather than in rigidity. God comes to us with open hands rather than with clenched fists. God comes to us in spite of our sins and offers us a divine embrace when we have turned from our failures and asked for reconciliation.

Second, God is interactive with the created world. From creation to exodus to incarnation to resurrection to salvation, I see the holy hands of God doing mighty acts in the midst of human history. I accept the mystery of the miraculous through which God intervenes in the stream of our lives to do the unexplainable and the unrepeatable. To reject the possibility of God's intervention in my world is to reject the possibility of God in any form that a believer would recognize. I know this belief leaves me open to charges of irrationality to those who demand empirical proof of everything, but to suggest that God cannot or does not work in our history is to suggest a God either too weak to matter or too distant to care.

How can any of us who claim Christian faith accept anything less? If our faith centers in the resurrection, then we have to conclude that God can and does intervene in human history. As Paul said, "If Christ has not been raised, then our proclamation has been in vain and your faith has been in vain" (1 Cor 15:14).

I understand that the idea of God as interactive raises the question of why God doesn't end all the suffering that exists in the world. After all, goes the question: If God can get involved and if

God does get involved, then why not just eradicate all evil and pain and establish a world without any of the troubles so readily at hand?

Though this is not the place to answer fully that question, I point to two characteristics of the world I experience. First, I refer to the freedom I believe God allows within the created order. As a result of freedom, humans choose to do evil, and that evil results in the suffering and tragedy we experience.

Second, I point to the mystery I experience in the world. Though God can and does interact with us, we cannot determine or even identify when and how that interaction might occur. In certain moments God intervenes. At others times God does not intervene. I acknowledge the reality of mystery at this point. Though the "miraculous" occurs, I cannot presume upon it. Though I have seen that which I call miraculous, I know that others can see the same event and interpret it in entirely different ways.

At this point, of course, faith enters the picture. I and the skeptic both live by faith—the skeptic in "faith" that life exists only as the product of chance circumstance, I in faith that life exists as the product of a God of love and purpose. I like my odds better than those of the skeptic. As one unknown man said it, "The chances of the world existing as it does as a result of mere circumstance is about the same as the chances of a monkey sitting down at a keyboard and typing out the dictionary."

Third, I believe God is gracious. By this I mean that God has extended an unearned and undeserved mercy toward the created. Though Israel faltered and sinned numerous times, God continued to demonstrate a willingness to forgive. Though we don't deserve it, God provides the same grace toward each of us. Like a parent who gives the children a room full of Christmas presents in spite of the fact that the child has been "naughty and not nice," so God extends to us the gift of grace in spite of our transgressions.

This grace, "greater than all our sin," comes to us most visibly in Jesus Christ and his atoning death upon the cross. Since we don't have nearly enough space here to describe all the theories of the atonement, let me offer this simple statement: the crucifixion of Jesus served as the final staging ground for God's ultimate act of grace. In the event of the cross, both of the thieves beside Jesus received the opportunity of forgiveness and new life. So do we. As we read in Ephesians 2:8-9, "For by grace you have been saved through faith . . . it is the gift of God—not the result of works, so that no one may boast."

I believe God is infinite and, therefore, triumphant. When I look at our contemporary world, I cannot help but wonder about the future. Will we manage to corral the evil that threatens us on so many fronts? Will we keep the nuclear genie in the bottle? Will we protect the environment so we can continue to exist with enough food and water for all the earth's inhabitants? Will we find a way of peace between races, nations, and religions? Will we maintain control over the chemicals and biological weapons that can now destroy us? Who knows? Questions such as these defy any of us to answer them.

Yet, in spite of all that pulls us toward despair, the Bible tell us of a God who ultimately exists beyond it all and who triumphs over it all. The Scriptures show us a God who emerges victorious over anything and everything that would threaten the divine will.

Several years ago I preached a series of seven messages from the book of Revelation. I began the last of those sermons with these words: "Today I'm going to tell you in five words everything you ever need to know about the book of Revelation. If you can remember these five words, you don't need to know anything else about this book. Are you ready? Here they are—the five words you need to remember about Revelation. 'In the end God wins!' That's it. All you need to know about Revelation. In the end God wins."

I'm not saying here that this is all we need to know about God, but it's certainly a good point to conclude this chapter. In the end God wins—eternally, infinitely. God is triumphant over sin, death, and the struggles of life. This knowledge may not satisfy all our questions, but it can certainly calm all our fears.

Notes

[1]Some philosophers suggest that we can't even speak of "God." To do so, according to this view, is to immediately objectify the deity and, thus, make "God" less than what God is. Christian faith, however, suggests that we can and should speak of God for the simple reason that God has chosen to interact with human beings. In other words, God began the dialogue with us and so gives us our permission to speak. For a discussion of the problem of language in relationship to God, see John McQuarrie, *Principles of Christian Theology* (New York: Charles Scribner's Sons, 1977) 123-48.

[2]For a short overview of the basic arguments for the existence of God, see *The Range of Philosophy,* edited by Harold Titus, Maylon Hepp, and Marilyn Smith (New York: Van Nostrand Co., 1975) 276-85. In these pages, the cosmological, ontological, and teleological arguments are offered and explained.

[3]Baptist theologians such as John Dagg, *A Manual of Theology* (Harrisonburg VA: Gano Books, 1982, first published in 1857), and A. H. Strong, *Systematic Theology* (Nashville: Fleming H. Revell, 1954, first published in 1907), referred to God's existence and attributes and God's nature and attributes.

[4]I know that speaking of a "typical" Baptist is dangerous, but it seems to me a safe statement to say that Baptists, at least in theory, begin with the Bible when they want to deal with religious issues.

[5]This is not the time for a discussion of the varying theories concerning biblical inspiration. For one treatment of this issue, see Clark Pinnock, *The Scripture Principle* (San Francisco: Harper & Row, 1984).

[6]Theologians have terms to describe this process of using an analogy, then negating it, then moving beyond it to describe God. They call this process *via analogia, via negativa,* and *via eminentia,* the way of analogy, the way of negation, and the way of eminence. God is like this. Then God is not like this. Then God is like this but more than this.

[7]This was Winston Churchill's assessment of Russia as he spoke to the British people in October 1939.

[8]Karl Barth, *The Knowledge of God and the Service of God* (New York: Hodder, 1938) 28.

[9]Frank McCourt, "God in America: When You Think of God, What Do You See?" *Life* (1 December 1998) 60.

[10]Though I cannot find the reference for this quote, I recall Martin Marty, distinguished church historian from the University of Chicago, saying this of God.

[11]I use the word "person" to speak of God, even though I haven't yet defined it. I will speak more precisely of this word in a subsequent section of this chapter.

[12]To say God is creator of the world also implies that God can intervene in the world God created. Though God created the world to respond to cause and effect, this should not lead to the notion that God cannot intervene in the world if God so chooses.

[13]It is instructive to remember here that one of the arguments for the existence of God comes from the argument of design. The sheer fact of the order of the universe leads some to say that such order has to have a designer behind it.

[14]This is not the forum for a discussion of evil, but most evil—that is, death and suffering—that comes to the world comes not from the natural order but from what humans have done to distort, destroy, or misuse the natural order. Certainly if we believe that the natural world suffered from the "fall" that occurred as a result of human sin, then we have to conclude that in its original purity the world, as God created it, experienced none of the tragedy we now witness.

[15]Studies show that even psychotic killers and pathological liars have a sense of right and wrong. Though the sense is warped to the point of being unrecognizable to most of us, even the most evil persons of society seem to have a moral code

of some kind, even though their notion of morality is certainly different from that of "normal" people.

[16]In the notion of "moral oughtness" Immanuel Kant found what he saw as the only reasonable "proof of God." In Kant's thought, "oughtness" is *a priori* (a part of the natural self) and, therefore, superior to scientific proofs. And, since if there is any "good" there has to be a "Supreme Good," he moved to the idea of the *summum bonum*, that is, a "Supreme Being." As Kant said it, "It is morally necessary to assume the existence of God." Quoted in James C. Livingston, *Modern Christian Thought: From the Enlightenment to Vatican II* (New York: Macmillan, 1971) 70.

[17]Paul Tillich, Rudolf Bultmann, and others suggest that to call God a "being" of any kind, much less a "personal being," is inappropriate. Thinkers such as these refer often to God as the "ground of being," but not a "being" as we think of that term. Certainly God is not a being as humans are beings (in terms of our frailties and limitations), but God is a being in the sense that God has existence and purpose in the universe.

[18]Paul Tillich and others used this term in their efforts to maintain the uniqueness of God.

[19]C. C. J. Webb, *Problems in the Relations of God and Man* (London: Nisbet and Co., Ltd., 1924) 216.

[20]The word for this act is *kenosis*, the emptying of God into the human. In this act, God took on the limitations of the flesh, including the limitations that led to suffering and death.

[21]See Matt 1:20; 3:16; 4:1; Luke 4:14, 16-21 for specific references to the accounts.

[22]See Rom 8 and 1 Cor 12:1-7 for these references.

[23]This was Augustine's suggestion in his work *The Trinity,* translated by Edmund Hill (New York: New City Press, 1991). This is called a "psychological analogy."

[24]Fisher Humphreys, in *Thinking About God* (New Orleans: Insight Press, 1974) 120, quotes this figure.

[25]See Theodoret, *A History of the Church,* vol. 5 (London: Bohn, 1854) 9, for the complete quote.

Persons
Molly T. Marshall

The longer I study and teach constructive theology to seminarians, the more impressed I become with the remarkable intellectual heritage of the Christian tradition. Although my students ruefully contend that I assign too much of it to be digested each semester, they also are encouraged to know that their questions have usually already been considered by gifted forebears. And indeed, many of those forebears' hard-wrought conclusions continue to illuminate the glory of the gospel of Jesus Christ. The scriptures, the creeds, the confessions, the hymns, and the scholarly treatises all bear witness to a faith that seeks understanding. We know that faith without works is dead; but, can faith live without questions? Probably not very well.

Theologians, preachers, and common Christians have given their best efforts, indeed their very lives, to pursuing knowledge of their Maker and what has been made. Proper humility admits that apprehension of the truth of God was all they could labor toward. Comprehension, that is, a complete understanding, remains beyond human capacity. And yet we strive to gain insight into the meaning of our lives before God.

Centuries of reflection on the divine movement in human history have taught us that God could not be studied unaided, that is without the doctrine of revelation. Even the great Aquinas conceded this. Yet we have presumed that we could by observation and analysis gain a clear perception of what it means to be human.[1] But we are mysterious, too. Perhaps along with the acknowledgment that the divine is beyond our knowing without self-revelation, we should also humbly confess that we cannot understand humans without knowledge from beyond ourselves. Hence, Calvin's dictum with which he begins the *Institutes* remains true: "Nearly all the wisdom we possess, that is to say, true and sound wisdom, consists of two parts: the knowledge of God and of ourselves."[2] He was persuaded, and I believe rightly so, that knowledge about humans was illusive apart from the contemplation of God, and conversely, that we could not have accurate knowledge of God if we failed to scrutinize ourselves. Thus, theologically we never study divine being except through the lens of human being, and we can only begin to understand the human being after the likeness of God.

Traditionally the study of creaturely being follows the threefold structure of creation—fall—redemption. Obviously these are not separable doctrines; each is ingredient to understanding the others. I will employ this structure in a somewhat modified form in this chapter as a means for constructing a contemporary theology of persons from a Baptist perspective. In the first section I will explore the meaning of creation in the image of God; in the second I will consider the christological image of God as determinative for true humanity; and in the third section I will probe the transformation of humans into the fullness of their calling, being conformed to the image of Christ.

After Our Likeness

Then God said, "Let us make humankind in our image, according to our likeness" (Gen 1:26). In the history of theological inquiry there is perhaps no more fascinating and perplexing a phrase than this. Questions abound and press for answers: What is God's image, and how can humans bear it? What does it mean to be like God? Why does God say, "Let *us* . . . ?" (To whom does "us" refer?) Why were the humans the only ones to receive this ascription?

Following the practice of so many theological textbooks, it would be tempting to trace the history of exegesis and theological construction surrounding this biblical passage.[3] The history of interpretation of the meaning of *imago Dei* is marked both by percipient insight and wayward missteps. I will refrain from retracing this well-worn historical trajectory, believing that it will be more profitable to engage newer analyses.

Created for God and for Community

There is a wonderful, personal connection between God and the human creation implied in the biblical narrative. The deliberate decision of the divine to create creatures who would correspond to the divine community suggests largesse of generous love and fecundity. In Dante's lyrical words, "From the Creator's love came forth in glory the world."[4] James Weldon Johnson's epic poem "God's Trombones" boldly declares that God created out of loneliness and that somehow the human was to fill this void in the divine life. Winsome though this idea is, orthodox Christianity has always claimed that

God's creation issued out of an orientation to share life in expansive, nonconstricting ways. Indeed, drawing upon the ancient cabalistic understanding of *zinsum* (God's own self-limitation), Jürgen Moltmann contends that the only constriction is God's own withdrawing so as to allow space for creation to flourish.[5] God's voluntary self-limitation means that divine power will not be exercised in a dominative, unilateral manner. Humanity was created for God, and yet created for our own sake. Indeed, it would be out of character for God not to bequeath the enrichment that shared life offers. In an ebullient declaration, Augustine said it was sheerly out of God's goodness that creation came to be by saying, "And by the words, 'God saw that it was good,' it is sufficiently intimated that God made what was made not from any necessity, nor for the sake of supplying any want, but solely from its own goodness, i.e., because it was Good."[6]

God created humans as creatures who could be addressed and respond; the "answering character" of our lives enables us to hear the voice of God and offer our voices in response. We are the *homo loquens*, the creature that speaks and prays and laughs. Hendrikus Berkhof describes the human as a "respondable being"[7] that allows both a freedom and a destiny. That we were not created "according to our kind" but after the divine likeness is suggestive of a particular dignity accorded human beings. The etiological narratives of Genesis proclaim that human existence is a gift from God, that we have responsibility toward God and toward the world, and that we must live within limits.

God's creation of humanity "after our likeness" denotes a plural subject, a linguistic nuance that has vexed interpreters for generations. Traditional exegetes have attempted to read the Trinity back into the Genesis text; however, this has proved difficult since an understanding of the Trinity is properly a postbiblical doctrinal development.[8] For one such as Karl Barth, seeing the Trinity in this text is a dogmatic judgment, which he acknowledges is not the original meaning.[9] Others have suggested that the plural is God together with the heavenly court or a grammatical construction that denotes a plural of deliberation.[10] Although I do not believe the Priestly writer has a full trinitarian understanding in mind when writing about the creation of humanity, it is fair to argue that the author's perception of divine being construes a richness of relationship that requires plural description. And certainly Christians would confess that the triune expression of God was active in bringing forth all of creation. God's creating work is expressed through the brooding Spirit and the active Word. The dynamic movement of divine creativity evokes a symphony of life, which God deigns to allow enriching God's own unfolding life. God's own trinitarian history with creation is an expression of self-giving and gathering in, of creative novelty and honoring faith's promise.

Although we might not share Barth's treatment of the Genesis text, especially as it relates to the ordering of male and female, his intuition is correct, however, when he argues that humanity was created for community, just as God dwells eternally in community.[11] The human creature derives personal identity from relating to others. Just as a child knows its worth and has its personhood validated by the attentive touch of caregivers, so we throughout our lives are drawn toward wholeness through the level of communion we experience. "It is not good for the earth creature to be alone," as Phyllis Trible translates Genesis 2:18. Her insight is provocative: human sexuality is understood through "otherness" in the human community.[12] It is only in the presence of this other that the lonely being discovers the potentiality of becoming human together. God makes this truth clearly known: we cannot be human alone.

Issues related to human sexuality provide a veritable minefield for a theology of persons. Most ecclesial bodies in our day seek to understand how contemporary human experience interfaces with the biblical witness crafted in a distant social context. Because of the emotionally charged nature of the topics, careful biblical hermeneutical procedures are often abandoned to less nuanced approaches, replete with proof texts and adamant denunciations. Our understanding of sexual orientation, male/female equality, marriage, contraception, childlessness, and celibacy have moved far beyond the biological and philosophical perceptions of early Christianity.[13] Rather than seeing sexual desire as the chief expression of human perversity (Augustine's dark legacy), we should affirm human sexuality as good. Ethicist James Nelson calls us to this essential approbation:

> Even though much of the church throughout much of its history has been remiss on this score, the foundations for sexual affirmation are central to Christianity's theological tenets. Christianity is

a religion of incarnation, and an incarnationalist faith affirms the body as good. We can be both fully spiritual and fully sexual; indeed, that is our destiny.[14]

Baptists have allowed the Puritan impress to linger in this area. Whereas Hester Prynne of Hawthorne's *Scarlet Letter* "feared no one but God," we too often fear what others might think to forge clearer, more informed understanding in the realm of human sexuality.

Humanity as *Imago Trinitatis*

Recently writers have begun to speak of humans as *imago trinitatis* rather than *imago Dei* in order to stress the communal nature of personal identity.[15] This is a helpful development in constructive theology, as most of the West historically followed Augustine's notion that the individual could image God alone.[16] Augustine reduces the *imago Dei* to the human soul, which he primarily identifies as the human mind; there God's image resides. In *De Trinitate* he wrote, "And there is a certain image of the Trinity: the mind itself and its knowledge."[17] Moltmann offers a sustained critique of Augustine's approach (as well as that of Aquinas) because it isolates and turns the individual in upon self; it does not allow for the social communion to be the bearer of God's own image. Moltmann rather argues for an open, relational view of the image:

> It is the *relations* in the Trinity that are the levels represented on earth through the *imago Trinitatis*, not the levels of the trinitarian *constitution. Just as* the three Persons of the Trinity are "one" in a wholly unique way, so, *similarly,* human beings are *imago Trinitatis* in their personal fellowship with one another.[18]

This understanding greatly changes our understanding of the *imago.* No longer is it a personal endowment, a possession; rather it is a practice, a way of being together as humans that reflects the divine communion. As Catherine Mowry LaCugna wrote, "Living trinitarian faith means living God's life: Living from and for God, from and for others."[19]

The ancient writers, John of Damascus and later the Cappadocians,[20] described the relations within the triune being of God using the term *perichoresis.* Literally the Greek term describes a circulatory movement within the being of God as love and energy flow from one person to another, thereby establishing identity through relationship. Jürgen Moltmann describes this triune movement:

> In the *perichoresis,* the very thing that divides them becomes that which binds them together. The "circulation" of the eternal divine life becomes perfect through the fellowship and unity of the three different persons in eternal love . . .
>
> The doctrine of the *perichoresis* links together in a brilliant way the threeness and the unity, without reducing the threeness to the unity, or dissolving the unity in the threeness.[21]

While we can never live in the purity of self-giving that characterizes the inner life of God, we can, nevertheless, learn to live with embrace rather than exclusion.[22] The interdependence, freedom, mutuality, and dynamism of the relations within the triune God become the model for all human relations and the very space in which these can occur.

Humans were not only created for communion with God and community among the human family, but we were also instructed to care for the world in which we were placed. The granting of dominion by God delineates an enduring job description, a vocation that we exercise on behalf of all creation. For most of Christian history, theology has studied the human by way of connection and contrast with God and has basically ignored the worldly context in which we live. Hall contends that the key question put to all human beings in this day is: "What is your attitude toward *this world?*"[23] Scripture and the healthy part of Christian tradition compel us to profess the goodness of God's creation. Of course, given the weight of the tragic[24] and of human sin, it requires faith for us to confess the continuing goodness of a radically distorted creation.

Often when describing the contours of creaturely being, the human has been abstracted from the natural world as if it was not foundational to self-understanding. This kind of dualism has marked far too much of Christian anthropology.[25] Feminist theology has been teaching us over the past three decades that negative attitudes toward embodiedness, women, and the earth are all bound up together.[26] The legacy of Greek philosophy and patriarchal theology conspires to legitimate a hierarchy of spirit/flesh, male/female, rationality/emotionality, and human/nonhuman.

Currently, a promising trajectory is the new ecological sensitivity in theology.[27] Not only does this address the human hegemony over against nature, but it also offers the proper interface between creation and redemption. Just as we cannot be human without others, so we cannot live the fullness of embodied existence apart from all of nature and our fellow creatures in the world. As we well know, the largest threat to the continuation of life on our planet is no longer nuclear warfare. As Michael Welker reminds us, the "worst way in which human beings are endangering themselves [and all other living creatures] is the erosion . . . of their biological-natural environments."[28] We are suffocating in our ever-higher pile of garbage; living creatures are forced from plains and wetlands so that we might "develop" the area; we use resources with profligacy; species are becoming extinct—not through the grinding process of cosmic evolution, but through human violence. All creation is groaning; its subjection is far beyond what God intended when it was "subjected in hope" as Romans 8:20 puts it.

Effacing the Image

We have already anticipated this section on human sinfulness in the description of the effects of human violence toward nature. In classical theology, Augustine blamed all the ills of the world on the sin of the primeval pair. While that is too simplistic a view, we cannot gainsay the reality that human selfishness and negligence have wreaked devastation upon the creation God gave us for our home, which we were designated to tend, populate, and cherish.

Interestingly, there is no stated orthodox doctrine of sin comparable to the doctrines of Christology or Trinity. Yet speak of it we must, for self-inflicted, sinful wounds mark our lives. A Christian theology of persons, however, never properly begins with fallenness; it always sees sin as "not the way it's supposed to be," in the words of Cornelius Plantinga, Jr.[29]

Created for community with God, one another, and the world in which they were placed, humans quickly displayed a propensity to be *incurvatum in se*, curved in upon themselves, breaking communion with their Maker and Friend. Their self-assertion against their finitude led them to challenge the limit set by God and to try to secure their own identity, hopefully establishing themselves "as wise as God."

Theologians have pressed this brief biblical story of humanity's ruptured relationship with God for precise delineations of the origin and nature of sin, usually embellishing the straightforward narrative. If one follows the Augustinian construction, which places perfect humans in a perfect garden, it is very hard to discern the origin of sin. The precipitous nature of their "fall" presupposes an elevated state, which is then lost. The logical problem of evil arising out of perfection can never be satisfactorily addressed in this proto-logical scheme. Further, original perfection lost, then restored in Christ, basically makes Christ dispensable; if humans were as God intended them prior to sin, the incarnation becomes an afterthought only capable of repristinating the original creation.[30]

More satisfactory is the Irenaean intuition, which does not posit perfection in the past, but in the future.[31] It is an eschatological vision, which allows for consummation to be forged through the groaning process of creation and human history. The immaturity and weakness of our human forebears produce the occasion for the "fall upwards," to use Irenaeus' felicitous phrase. And Jesus Christ recapitulates all the stages of life as our pioneer and pattern, showing us how God intended that we live.[32] Thus our future is greater than Genesis' depiction of our idyllic past; God does not let the human "no" be the end to the conversation.

How does the original and continuing "opposition to grace," as Daniel Migliore describes sin,[33] affect the image of God? Since it was more a practice than a possession, a calling rather than a faculty, we cannot speak of the image as lost. Yet we must speak about it being effaced, obscured, and distorted by sin.[34] We need forgiveness for things done and left undone, as the *Book of Common Prayer* inscribes it. Only in Christ is our likeness to God restored; only in his Body do we live out the community for which we were created.

In Our Likeness

Now the focus of the "our" shifts. Whereas in the first section we examined what it means to be created after the likeness of God, we must now consider something equally profound, laden with irrevocable meaning: God has become one of us, "being born in human likeness" as the great hymn of Philippians sings forth. One of *us* is Jesus the Christ, "born of a woman, born under the law" (Gal 4:4).

What does the Word become flesh mean about human identity? In what way is the human being lifted to a new potentiality by becoming a vehicle to bear the divine? What is the significance of this new event in the divine life? Since Christology is not the focus of this chapter, this section will necessarily be briefer than the first.

During my doctoral study I became acquainted with the writings of Karl Rahner, one of the most significant Roman Catholic theologians of the second half of the twentieth century. Much of his intricate Thomistic argument about nature and grace was foreign to me, but I found his incarnational theology to have breathtaking implications. In brief, he set forth the idea that because God had made a home in our midst as one of us, the whole horizon of humanity had been transformed. "That the Word became flesh is the ultimate expression of God's self-giving, thereby endowing the creature with the possibility of being assumed, of 'becoming the material of a possible history of God.' "[35] Because humanity could bear the divine as word made flesh, all flesh is now oriented towards God. Rahner calls this the "supernatural existential." God has accepted humanity in the Christ, and we are beckoned freely to receive this grace.

Rahner claims that Jesus Christ is true humanity, who demonstrates how God intended all humans to live before God. In this affirmation Rahner is joined by many other contemporary theologians who, though committed fully to Chalcedonian Christology with its dual affirmation of humanity and divinity, feel that too much has been made of Jesus' otherness, his difference from the rest of us. My Cambridge teacher John A. T. Robinson loved to speak of Jesus as the only "normal" person ever to live. Likewise, my other beloved teacher, Dale Moody, articulated a Spirit Christology, which assumed that we could also live fully from God and fully for others.[36] If human identity is bound up with this one who, though sent from God, is fully contextualized in the human story, our theology of persons must necessarily be shaped by the Christ who is "the image of the invisible God" and in whom "the fullness of God was pleased to dwell" (Col 1:15, 19). Our self-understanding is dependent upon finding the connections with him that can allow *imitatio Christi.*

At this point in the essay we could examine many areas of the life, death, and resurrection of Jesus to inform our understanding of normative humanity. Given the space limitations, however, we can only examine three briefly to see how the truly human life of Jesus calls us to the dignity of being fully human.

Commitment to Vocation

One of the most striking aspects of Jesus' life was his unwavering sense of vocation. Too often we telescope the life of Jesus, interpreting him as knowing all the outcomes ahead of time, for example, seeing him as a twelve-year-old prodigy in the Temple who already had figured out his messianic identity and unique relationship to God, or fully comprehending from the outset the forerunner role that John the Baptist was to play.[37] Over against these views that tend to ignore personal, spiritual, and theological growth, we should consider the life of Jesus as one who sought God with all his heart and soul and mind and strength. Ben Witherington perceives that "Jesus manifested a normal progressive historical consciousness."[38] Rather than trying to ascertain exactly when Jesus first knew that God was calling him to be the Savior of the world, it would be more profitable to grant him an awakening sense of vocation throughout his life.

N. T. Wright proposes the following hypothesis about Jesus' sense of vocation:

> He believed that it was his own task not only to announce, but also to enact and embody, the three major kingdom-themes, namely, the return from exile, the defeat of evil, and the return of YAHWEH to Zion. This motivated him to pursue certain identifiable aims and objectives.[39]

The importance of this statement for our purposes is Jesus' own searing sense of vocation in relation to God and humanity. Certainly Jesus was persuaded that the work he did was not simply his own; it was the work of the One who sent him. His sense of dependence upon God to be able to do his vocation is palpable throughout the Gospels.[40] Further, Christ's sense of being empowered for his ministry by the presence of God is echoed in Paul, who wrote: "It is no longer I who lives, but it is Christ who lives in me" (Gal 2:20). This acknowledgment by the Apostle is paradigmatic for followers of Jesus Christ.

Commitment to vocation is perhaps the most defining aspect of a person's life. Whether this be professional ministry, the arts, parenting, civil service, common labor, or the myriad of occupations by which we earn our living, each has an opportunity to see this as a calling from God and a means to exercise her or his discipleship to Christ. In our day we are witnessing a plethora of "second-career" persons entering new vocations. They are learning the importance of work as service and as self-expression[41]; they are learning that a deep sense of well-being is related to giving themselves to something they enjoy, something they believe will make a contribution to living in the reign of God.

Celebration of Friendship

A second and often neglected aspect of Jesus' normative humanity is his valuing and delight in human friendship. The key text for this perception is found in the fourth Gospel:

> This is my commandment, that you love one another as I have loved you. No one has greater love than this, to lay down one's life for one's friends. You are my friends if you do what I command you. I do not call you servants any longer, because the servant does not know what the master is doing, but I have called you friends. (John 15:12-15)

Remarkably, Jesus seemed to prefer the designation friend to servant or slave, and friendship was something to which he gave himself unstintingly. Anyone who has ever seen the stage-play *Godspell* is reminded of the significant role of human friendship in Jesus' ministry. Most poignant among the scenes is the affectionate, tender, personal goodbye he offers to each of his followers as he moves inexorably toward the cross.

Whether we reflect on Jesus' attentiveness to the festive proceedings at the wedding of Cana, his honest confrontations with Mary, Martha, and Lazarus of Bethany, or his relationship with the Beloved Disciple, it seems that human friendship was critical to Jesus' own personal identity. And it is to ours, as well.

Long ago Goethe wrote: "Friendship makes all the world a garden." Yet we know that friends fail. One of the most moving aspects of the Passion narratives is Jesus' lonely struggle in the

Garden of Gethsemane. He entreated his closest friends to "watch with him," but they could not. Either they did not sense the great travail through which he was passing, or they did not care. Jesus made no pretension of not needing them; as their friend, he asked that they walk through this vale of unknowing with him, that they might offer support through their alert presence and prayer. Their failure does not issue in Jesus' abandonment of them; indeed, the most joyful scenes in the Gospels are the encounters the Risen Christ has with his friends.

Our lives are graced with friends. Without them we live an impoverished and lonely existence. We know ourselves better because of their honesty, and we are encouraged to become more fully ourselves. L. Gregory Jones wrote about what makes a good marriage partner: "someone who will challenge the vices you have come to love and affirm the gifts you are afraid to claim."[42] These seem to be good ingredients for friendship, too. The friendship we strive for must bear the same marks of vulnerability that Jesus evinces in the garden. We must be willing to speak of our need and receptivity to what others could offer as sustaining friends. If we fail, we can experience the welcome of forgiveness and the joy of restoration, as did Jesus' friends.

Once again we return to the earlier theme of *imago trinitatis:* our lives as human persons are to reflect the communing movement in the divine life in which persons become themselves through their other-oriented relations. In our lives as friends we call forth the personhood of those with whom we share life, and we embody Christ's presence where two or three are gathered together.

Experience of Godforsakenness

Jesus' normative humanity may most clearly be seen in his own experience of Godforsakenness.[43] Silence in the face of rending prayer was Jesus' experience in the garden and on the cross; it is also (perhaps to a lesser degree) the experience of countless Christians. Pouring out their hearts to God about wrenching personal circumstances of illness, death, and loss, they wonder if the one they have trusted all their lives without reserve has abandoned them. The seeming absence of God in the exigencies of life pushes faith to the edge.

The reality of Jesus' experience of Godforsakenness is a key concern in the writings of Moltmann. From almost the beginning of his contributions to systematic theology, as he likes to describe his monographs, Moltmann has probed the relevance of the God-forsakenness of Jesus for the lives of oppressed persons who feel that their lives have been abandoned by God.[44] This is a dense and weighty area of contemporary theology, and my brief summary statements will in no way give sufficient interpretation. Two summary statements give us a glimpse of the argument Moltmann proffers:

• Jesus experiences Godforsakenness on the cross as God abandons the Son to the extremity of human suffering of all those who die feeling cut off from the gracious God, that God might take death into the divine life and overcome it.

• In his Godforsakenness Jesus harrows hell, conquering its claim upon the unrighteous, thereby becoming the companion and suffering redeemer of all those whose agony prevents them from trusting in the goodness of God.

Important for our concern is the central thesis of Moltmann: Jesus' experience of feeling abandoned is what most deeply acquaints him with our grief. We are not left comfortless in the harrowing parts of life; God in human form has traversed these with us and will not let these grievous pains rob us of our significance to God or our personhood.

Indeed, Jesus' cry of dereliction, of absence, may be the clearest expression of his kinship to us. As the cadences of the old spiritual intoned, "Jesus knows all about our troubles," God has not been absent from any of the suffering that accosts human beings. God's willingness to bear not only our sin but also our suffering suggests that only in and through this companioning service can God redeem our lives fully.

It is from being in *our* likeness that God now knows the joy and anguish of being human. In God's desire to befriend humanity, God has come among us as an oppressed, first-century Galilean, full of grace and truth. While some feminists might quibble with my delineation of Jesus as "normative" humanity, believing that this paradigm further disenfranchises women, I would argue that the inclusiveness of Jesus and his own liberative solidarity with women mitigates this critique.[45]

These three expressions of Jesus' closeness to us can enrich our self-understanding. His humanity is the measure of our own; we perceive the contours of our lives through his own full faithfulness.

Toward His Likeness

"When he is revealed, we will be like him" (1 John 3:2), the epistle writer proclaimed. This is our life's work, to be formed after the image of Christ.[46] In this final section we shall consider how a dusty, fallen creature is destined for glory as one made after the likeness of Christ. Created after the likeness of God, given direction in our humanity by the one made in our likeness, we now examine the goal of our lives.

A theologian by training, in these recent years at Central Seminary I have begun to teach in the area of spiritual formation. I have made many discoveries about Baptists' need for greater intentionality in helping persons mature in faith. Baptists have not until of late used the classical terminology of spiritual formation,[47] fearing that it was either too Catholic or that it in some way threatened the Baptist affirmation of the priesthood of all believers.

> Baptists, schooled in the voluntary principle, have rightly resisted any coercive dimension of Christian faith; however, their stress on the priesthood of all believers has both exacerbated individualism and contributed to a wariness about spiritual direction or guidance from another Christian. Thus, the idea of formation as an intentional receptiveness to a set of Christian practices, guided by a more mature Christian, has not been sufficiently a part of Baptist catechetical structures.[48]

The renewed interest in Christian spirituality among Baptists is a sign of a willingness to rethink our soteriology, that is, we are coming to understand that converting the heart is a lifelong enterprise. One does not spring from the baptistery as a full-grown Christian. Rather there is a patient, formative work to do in which we cooperate with God for good in our lives. The apostle Paul described the process in this manner:

> And all of us, with unveiled faces, seeing the glory of the Lord as though reflected in a mirror, are being transformed into the same image from one degree of glory to another; for this comes from the Lord, the Spirit. (2 Cor 3:18)

Here Paul is presupposing incorporation into Christ that has already occurred in Christian baptism; he believes that this incorporation transfers glory to the believer. Indeed, Paul characterizes the pneumatic life of transformation into the resurrection likeness/image of Christ as a metamorphosis of Glory.

Transforming work is done by the indwelling Spirit of God, but we also have our part to do. By faithful, steady contemplation of the "splendor of the Lord," we come to share in that splendor. Simone Weil's perception is instructive: "One of the principal truths of Christianity, a truth that goes almost unrecognized today, is that *looking* is what saves us."[49] We become what we behold, as Nathaniel's beloved story "The Great Stone Face" reminds us.

The Eastern Orthodox Christian world has long known the power of holy images. In the icon the devout worshiper sees not a mere devotional picture or a visual representation of a significant event or person, but a divine archetype. The New Testament speaks of Christ as the true icon of God, one through whom the iconic presence of God is revealed. Once in the form of God, the eternal Christ came to share our form and make possible our participation in the divine life.[50]

Gregory of Nyssa's vision of the Christian life, in keeping with the fourth-century ethos of his time, was a vision of moving from "glory to glory." According to him, humankind was created to be made one with God. Human life was a progressive movement toward Godlikeness, a concentration on and unification with the divine. This was effected in lengthy stages of spiritual growth.[51]

Biblical theology speaks of "seeing face to face" as delighting in the fullness of presence, God's and our own. Such clarity of vision and communion occurs after a lifetime of learning to pay attention to the mode of God's presence, however elusive. It will not occur otherwise, because as Simone Weil claimed, "Attention is the only faculty of the soul that gives us access to God."

Our lives, then, must be characterized by "looking to Jesus" until the vision becomes clear and we are like him, fully belonging to God and most fully ourselves. Then we will at last know the ecstasy of communion for which human persons were created, making our home in the eternality of God's self-giving love.

Notes

[1]Douglas John Hall, *Professing the Faith: Christian Theology in a North American Context* (Minneapolis: Fortress Press, 1993) 187, writes: "There is a kind of unspoken assumption among many Christians that when we turn from the consideration of deity to humanity and the world, we are moving from matters that presuppose belief to aspects of our tradition that are more or less open to the inspection and verification of any intelligent human being."

[2]John Calvin, *Institutes of the Christian Religion*, vol. I, ed. John T. McNeill, *The Library of Christian Classics* (Philadelphia: Westminster Press, 1960) 35.

[3]A dated but still informative treatment is that of David Cairns, *The Image of God in Man* (London: SCM Press, 1953). He probes the biblical perspectives and selected major theologians (until mid-twentieth century) such as Aquinas, Luther, Calvin, Brunner, and Barth, and then compares them with the contrasting contributions of Marx, Freud, and de Chardin. A more inclusive and contemporary study is provided in the following: Douglas John Hall, *Imaging God: Dominion as Stewardship* (Grand Rapids: Eerdmans, 1986); Edmund Hill, *Being Human: A Biblical Perspective* (London: Geoffrey Chapman, 1984); Wolfhart Pannenberg, *Anthropology in Theological Perspective*, trans. Matthew J. O'Connell (Philadelphia: Westminster Press, 1985); Rosemary Radford Ruether, *Sexism and God-Talk: Toward a Feminist Theology* (Boston: Beacon Press, 1983); and Anne E. Carr, *Transforming Grace: Christian Tradition and Women's Experience* (San Francisco: Harper & Row, 1988), especially chapter 6.

[4]*Inferno*, vol. 1, 39f.

[5]Jürgen Moltmann, *God in Creation: A New Theology of Creation and the Spirit of God* (San Francisco: Harper & Row, 1985) 87.

[6]*City of God*, vol. 11, ch. 24.

[7]*Christian Faith*, rev. ed. (Grand Rapids: Eerdmans, 1986) 186. He also notes perceptively: "It must be said that man [sic] had only become fully man [sic] when he [sic] became aware of God's presence and learned to pray."

[8]William G. Rusch, trans. and ed., *The Trinitarian Controversy* (Philadelphia: Fortress Press, 1980), illustrates the process by which early Christianity reached a coherent doctrine of God as Trinity. Jürgen Moltmann, *The Trinity and the Kingdom* (San Francisco: Harper & Row, 1981), argues persuasively that the biblical material does evince a trinitarian structure throughout.

[9]*Church Dogmatics*, vol. 3/1, 191ff.

[10]Claus Westermann, *Genesis 1-11*, trans. John J. Scullion, S.J. (Minneapolis: Augsburg, 1984) 144-45, offers an overview of the interpretive options.

[11]Barth holds to a dynamic view of the *imago*; human being is always a being-in-fellowship in his analysis. Barth's treatment is found in *Church Dogmatics*, vol. 3/1, 41, pts. 2, 3. For an analysis and critique of Barth's hierarchical rendering of

the male/female relationship, see Paul K. Jewett's study, *Man as Male and Female* (Grand Rapids: Eerdmans, 1975).

[12]See Phyllis Trible, *God and the Rhetoric of Sexuality* (Philadelphia: Fortress press, 1978) 98-99. She writes: "His sexual identity depends upon her even as hers depends upon him. For both of them, sexuality originates in the one flesh of humanity."

[13]Two recent works that seek to traverse the divide between biblical perspectives and contemporary insights, but come to very different conclusions, are Stanley Grenz, *Sexual Ethics: A Biblical Perspective* (Dallas: Word Publishing, 1990) and James B. Nelson, *Between Two Gardens: Reflections on Sexuality and Religious Experience* (New York: The Pilgrim Press, 1983).

[14]*Between Two Gardens,* 121.

[15]See the article by my former doctoral student Mark S. Medley, "Becoming Human Together: Imaging the Triune God," *Perspectives in Religious Studies,* 23 (Fall 1996): 289-316.

[16]Catherine M. LaCugna, *God for Us: The Trinity and Christian Life* (New York: HarperCollins, 1991) 416, n. 72, observes: "We have seen how Augustine's view of the Trinity . . . contributed to this view of persons as a self-possessed individual whose relationship to others is secondary. In addition, given Augustine's identification of the male with the rational and female with irrational, the Augustinian contemplation of self belongs to the *ratio superior,* the masculine expression of humanity, whereas *actio* belongs to the *ratio inferior,* the feminine expression."

[17]*De Trinitate,* vol. 9.

[18]*God in Creation,* 241.

[19]*God for Us,* 400.

[20]The primary texts illustrating their constructive contributions can be found in: J. N. D. Kelly, *Early Christian Doctrines,* 5th rev. ed. (London: Black, 1977); A. Mason, ed., *The Five Theological Orations of Gregory of Nazianzus,* Cambridge Patristic Texts 1 (Cambridge: University Press, 1899); G. Prestige, *God in Patristic Thought,* 2nd rev. ed. (London: SPCK, 1952).

[21]*Trinity and the Kingdom,* 175.

[22]See Miroslav Volf, *Exclusion and Embrace: A Theological Exploration of Identity, Otherness, and Reconciliation* (Nashville: Abingdon Press, 1996).

[23]*Professing the Faith,* 82.

[24]I have been informed greatly by the perceptive study of Wendy Farley, *Tragic Vision and Divine Compassion: A Contemporary Theodicy* (Louisville KY: Westminster/John Knox Press, 1990), in which she challenges the neatness of the anti-tragic Christian myth, arguing that engaging the tragedy of radical suffering instead of the sin of "the Fall," is the only way to address the problem of evil in the world in a way that does justice to the power and goodness of God.

[25]Rosemary Radford Ruether offers a stringent critique of rampant dualism in Western thought in her feminist theology, *Sexism and God-Talk: Toward a Feminist Theology* (Boston: Beacon Press, 1983), especially chs. 3-4.

[26]Mary Aquin O'Neill, "The Mystery of Being Human Together," *Freeing Theology: The Essentials of Theology in Feminist Perspective*, ed. Catherine Mowry LaCugna (New York: HarperCollins, 1993) 143.

[27]Prominent among scholars addressing this weighty concern is Sallie McFague. Two of her volumes are especially constructive: *Models of God: Theology for an Ecological, Nuclear Age* (Philadelphia: Fortress Press, 1987) and *The Body of God* (Minneapolis: Fortress Press, 1993).

[28]*God the Spirit,* trans. John F. Hoffmyer (Minneapolis: Fortress Press, 1994) 303.

[29]See his thoughtful work so titled, *Not the Way It's Supposed To Be: A Breviary of Sin* (Grand Rapids: Eerdmans, 1995).

[30]For a stringent and scholarly critique of these implications in Augustine's thought, see Basil Studer, O.S.B., *The Grace of Christ and the Grace of God in Augustine of Hippo: Christocentrism or Theocentrism?* trans. Matthew J. O'Connell (Collegeville MN: Liturgical Press, 1997).

[31]John Hick, *Death and Eternal Life* (New York: Harper & Row, 1976) 369f., has been particularly helpful in distinguishing these two strands in Christian theology, especially with reference to constructing a theodicy. See also his *Evil and the God of Love* (New York: Harper & Row, 1966).

[32]See the detailed discussion of this part of Irenaeus' theology in G. Wingren, *Man and the Incarnation: A Study in the Biblical Theology of Irenaeus* (Philadelphia: Muhlenberg, 1959) 26-38.

[33]*Faith Seeking Understanding: An Introduction to Christian Theology* (Grand Rapids: Eerdmans, 1991) 130.

[34]Humanity's sinfulness is perhaps most clearly seen in the alienation between the sexes. See Rosemary Radford Ruether's treatment of this in *Religion and Sexism*, ch. 4. See also my article,"Family: Male and Female," *Therefore: Newsletter of the Texas Christian Life Commission*, Spring, 1985.

[35]Molly Truman Marshall, *No Salvation Outside the Church? A Critical Inquiry*, NABPR Dissertation Series, vol. 9 (Lewiston NY: Edwin Mellen Press, 1993) 126. I am citing Karl Rahner, "On the Theology of the Incarnation," *Theological Investigations,* vol. 4, trans. Kevin Smyth (London: Darton, Longman & Todd, 1966) 115.

[36]See his crowning work *The Word of Truth: A Summary of Christian Doctrine Based on Biblical Revelation* (Grand Rapids: Eerdmans, 1981) 416f.

[37]Ben Witherington, III, *The Christology of Jesus* (Minneapolis: Fortress Press, 1990) 55, says of the relationship between John the Baptist and Jesus: "John was the main human touchstone for Jesus, the one figure who helped him sort out his own sense of identity and mission."

[38]Ibid.

[39]*Jesus and the Victory of God*, Christian Origins and the Question of God, vol. 2 (Minneapolis: Fortress Press, 1996) 481.

[40]E.g., John 9:4; 10:37.

[41]See my discussion of this in *What It Means To Be Human* (Macon GA: Smyth & Helwys, 1995) 100ff.

[42]"Shaping Character," *Christian Century*, 115 (23-30 December, 1998) 1252.

[43]See the insightful study by David Emmanuel Goatley, *Were You There?: Godforsakenness in Slave Religion* (Maryknoll NY: Orbis, 1996).

[44]The following are critical to his exploration: *The Crucified God* (New York Harper & Row, 1972), *The Trinity and the Kingdom* (San Francisco: Harper & Row, 1991), *The Way of Jesus Christ* (New York: Harper Collins, 1990), and *The Coming of God* (Minneapolis: Fortress, 1996).

[45]I have dealt with the thorny issue of the male savior's relationship to women in "On a Hill Too Far Away?" *Review & Expositor*, 91, 2 (Spring 1994) 247-59.

[46]In this section I am drawing from my essay "Spiritual Formation: The Journey Toward Wholeness," *Central Thoughts on the Church in the 21st Century*, ed. Thomas E. Clifton (Macon GA: Smyth & Helwys, 1998) 121-33.

[47]For a fuller discussion of this phenomenon, see my article "The Changing Face of Baptist Discipleship," *Review & Expositor*, 95, 1 (Winter 1998) 59-73.

[48]Marshall, *Central Thoughts,* 121.

[49]*Waiting for God* (New York: Capricorn Books, 1951) 36.

[50]Some of this material is drawn from my unpublished article, "Unfinished Presence: The Spiritual Formation of Christians."

[51]*From Glory to Glory: Texts from Gregory of Nyssa's Mystical Writings* (Crestwood NY: St. Vladimir's Seminary Press, 1979) 29.

Sin

Michael G. Cogdill

A Baptist university student received an intriguing assignment from his religion professor. "I want you to visit a church of a denomination you have never visited and explore its beliefs and worship," instructed the professor. After contemplating several possibilities, the student decided to visit a Roman Catholic church. Though aware of Roman Catholicism, the student had never visited or worshiped with these fellow Christians.

Upon locating and visiting a nearby Roman Catholic church, the student became enamored with that structural part of the Roman Catholic church called the confessional,[1] a booth-like structure in which parishioners enter to confess their actual sins in the hearing of a priest who sits nearby. Thinking he was all alone, the student entered the confessional, sat quietly, and pondered its significance. Suddenly, to his surprise, there arose the intimidating voice of a priest. "Welcome, my son," voiced the priest. "What sins have you to confess today?" Totally stunned, the student panicked for a response. Finally, he blurted out, "I am sorry, sir, I am a Baptist—and we Baptists don't confess our sins!" Making a hasty exit from the confessional and from the church, the student heard uncontrollable laughter rising from the priest, only a prelude to what would be experienced in his later report to the class.[2]

While good Baptist theology about sin does not evolve well out of panic, the truth is that Baptists do take sin seriously and believe strongly in its confession, though not necessarily to a priest. Baptists generally are clear in their understanding that sin is *public enemy number one* in the Christian life. Baptists will come as close to being of one mind on this truth as any other.

Baptists have a history of being focused on the problem of sin. A fervent belief in the reality of sin and its eternal consequences has spawned among Baptists a strong evangelistic spirit, primarily evidenced by the legions of church programs, revivals, and denominational emphases aimed at reaching people with the message of salvation. Southern Baptists' most famous preacher of recent years, Billy Graham, is best known for his vigorous preaching against sin and for his worldwide efforts to win the lost to Christ. A widespread belief among Baptists in the United States is that no service of worship in a Baptist church should close without an opportunity to invite sinners to repentance.

For Baptists, sin is active and not passive. It is "the devil's work," an evil power active each day, corrupting lives, damaging families, and working against God's work in the world. Sin is the stubborn enemy of God, energized by Satan, and working always to create distance between God and human beings, and between human beings and one another. Sin is alive and strong, issuing in rebellion against God's will and established standards. According to the Bible, sin is inescapable and has no human solution. It is conquered only by the sacrificial and atoning death of Jesus Christ on the cross.

Baptists today join with other Christians in fearing that there has developed in contemporary culture a profound erosion of belief in the reality and seriousness of sin. Evidence appears abundant that such fear is justified, beginning with the general trend toward a more permissive moral and ethical climate in society. Proclamations against behaviors Baptists have traditionally regarded as sins often fall on apathetic ears in a highly individualistic society, especially of people prone to value individual autonomy over communal accountability and divine authority. Books popular today in Christian communities lament the erosion of religious authority in America.[3] Tim Keller expresses a very common belief among Christians:

> We do not live in an *immoral* society—one in which right and wrong are clearly understood and wrong behavior is chosen. We live in an *amoral* society—one in which "right" and "wrong" are categories with no universal meaning and everyone "does what is right in his/her own eyes." In America, this amoral society is now arriving in its fullness.[4]

Right or wrong, this is a perceived belief. Political correctness catches some of the blame. The push toward a politically correct society often results in recasting behaviors and attitudes long thought of as sins into different categories such as personal choices and individual rights. Suffice it to say that, among Baptists, there exists a strong consciousness of a widespread sense of ambivalence and apathy relative to the seriousness of sin.

Such consciousness of ambivalence toward sin has been noted by others. John Claypool quotes a British psychologist who indicates that this may be a worldwide problem. The psychologist writes, "Twentieth-century human beings are no longer troubled about their sins. They regard this category as a hangover from a primitive past. They have outgrown such a concept."[5]

Baptists generally would agree with such an analysis. They would add to this perspective only by saying that such apathy and ambivalence toward sin is the best evidence of its power. Sin is disobedience to God, and treating God's laws and standards with ambivalence is "Exhibit A" of the reality and presence of sin.

Baptists, as well as all Christians, would do well to engage in fresh thinking about the seriousness of sin, its terrible impact on human lives, and its consequences for the world. Perhaps such investigation can lead to renewed passion to preach and teach more frequently regarding the wickedness of sin and to proclaim the only good news there is on this subject, namely, that in Jesus Christ there is victory over sin.

A Religious Concept

The subject of sin has to be understood first and foremost as a religious concept and a theological subject.[6] Sin is understood only in its connection to God. It is not a legal, medical, or sports term. Sin is a theological term, and it carries the meaning of a personal violation against God. It cannot be understood apart from this frame of reference.

Numerous are the verses in the Bible that illustrate this truth. King David, in his confession of sin after his adultery with Bathsheba and his later confrontation before Nathan the prophet, realized this truth. His penitent words reflected his deep anguish that, though he had hurt others, he had sinned primarily against God:

> Against you, you alone, have I sinned and done what is evil in your sight so that you are justified in your sentence and blameless when you pass judgment. (Ps 51:4)

Similarly, the prodigal son, in his penitent speech before his merciful father, stated that he had sinned "against heaven" as well as his family. One begins to understand sin rightly when it is viewed first and foremost as a personal violation against God.

Understanding sin in this manner presents both good and bad news. The good news is that sin, as terrible and deadly as it is, is not stronger than God. Sin does not have to be the ultimate victor in a person's life. Sin was not the ultimate victor in the lives of King David or the prodigal son. That there can be victory over the consequences of sin through God's redemptive and saving love is the grand message of the Bible. There is no mistaking, however, that sin is the central problem of the Christian faith. Thankfully, it is not its central truth. The central truth is that human beings are created in the image of God, not as sons and daughters for sin.[7] Divine love called humanity into being, and God's purposes for humanity have not changed. Sin, however, has changed humanity. Sin distorts God's will and places humanity on a trajectory of disobedience and ungodliness.

Even though sin is not stronger than God, there is bad news. Sin is persistent and inevitable. Because of the power of sin, humanity lives in a fallen condition. Sin led to the expulsion of the first human pair from the Garden of Eden, and all life since that time has been lived with the presence of sin.[8]

Moreover, all sins are bad. There are no good sins, and there is no sin that is not a sin against God. So serious is sin, the Bible teaches that the ultimate consequence of sin is death.

Thus, sin is the great human predicament. Any solution to sin would have to come from God. Fortunately, it did. The solution to sin came in the person and work of Jesus Christ, the second Adam, whose sacrifice for sin made possible the miracle of redemption and the new person in Christ.

In addition to understanding sin first and foremost as a religious concept and theological subject, we must also understand sin as an intruder into creation rather than as a component of creation. Genesis 1 and 2 witness to God's work in creation. God shared God's self and created a perfect and permanent home for creation. In these chapters, sin is nowhere to be found. Sin was not a part of the created order and thus was not a creation of God.

With Genesis 3, however, this idealistic picture of the new creation is radically altered. Without warning, there suddenly appears a diabolical intruder into God's creation in the entrance of the serpent. The serpent sought to persuade Adam and Eve not to believe God. Unbelievably, the serpent was successful. The first pair believed the tempting words of the serpent rather than trust the promises of God. They flagrantly disobeyed God, ate of the fruit of the tree, and thus sin was born.[9] Sin is disobeying God, and deliberate disobedience highlights its ugliness. Sin involves rebellion against God and God's purposes.

Sin intruded into creation. It led to the fall of the first human pair from a state of original righteousness. Morris Ashcraft offers the excellent reminder that the serpent in Genesis 3 was not the source of sin, only its occasion.[10] The source of sin lies in the disobedient heart and will. We are the cause of our sins, not some outside source.[11]

Relative to the source of sin, Baptists focus more on the illumination of sin as opposed to its origin. This is a departure from traditional Roman Catholic theology, which has focused more on the origin of sin, as illustrated by the doctrine of original sin.[12] Put simply, original sin has been understood to mean that Adam's sin, the first and original sin, has been inherited by all other human beings. Adam's sinful nature has been passed down as a hereditary disease to all others. Persons are connected to Adam and his sin by biological descent from him.[13]

The earliest Baptist confessions of 1609 and 1610 denied original sin.[14] On the other hand, the *London Confession of 1644* strongly affirmed original sin.[15] Subsequent Baptist confessions have reflected one position or the other, depending on whether they originated in General Baptist (Armenian) or Particular Baptist (Calvinistic) circles. The *Baptist Faith and Message* statement of 1963, in the section on "Man," represents something of a mediating position, but the emphasis is on condemnation only for one's own sins.[16] Thus, a traditional Baptist interpretation of sin is that sin originates in the perverse and disobedient will of human beings, even though we are "tainted" by the presence and reality of original sin.

J. S. Whale, not a Baptist, states a perspective about the origin of sin that most Baptists would generally affirm:

> The permanent wound in human nature that needs healing is deeper than anything biology can explain. This central, typical, fatal sin is self-sufficiency or pride. . . . Man's proud unwillingness to accept the absolute authority and claim of God in whose image he has been made, is, and remains, the mystery of iniquity.[17]

John Newport, a Baptist, states a classical Baptist position on the origin of sin:

> Every Christian knows in his own experience the truth of the biblical witness that sin is his fault, not his fate. Therefore, according to the Bible, the final solution of sin is repentance, not analysis ... Try as we may to understand and explain sin, we cannot do so. We can only confess it and repent of it.[18]

Thus, Baptists disavow belief in original or inherited sin, but would affirm that humans are tainted by original sin in that we share its presence and reality. Human egocentrism rather than human biology causes sin and leads to rebellion against God. This is the nature of sin Baptists seek to understand.

The Bible and Sin

The subject of sin is not an isolated topic in the Bible. The story of sin runs like a flowing stream throughout the biblical story. Sin appears in the Bible within the parentheses of grace.[19] Just as one cannot understand sin apart from the backdrop of divine revelation, neither can one understand sin without considering its reckoning with grace. The Bible is the reporter of this dramatic story.

Because sin is dynamic and not static, the Bible describes sin more than it defines sin. Sin is most vividly defined and described when it is seen standing in stark contrast to God's love and grace. Sin has no light, and thus its essence is best seen when its darkness stands in contrast to the light of Jesus Christ.[20] Sin's darkness can never overcome the light of the incarnate Christ.

Sin is real, but it is also a mystery. Throughout the biblical story, a number of different terms, episodes, and events reveal the nature of sin. Generally, all point to the same truth. Sin is a personal violation against God, a revolt against God's will, and rebellion against God's authority. Nevertheless, even with these truths highlighted, sin is still deeper and darker than words can explain, for its roots include a perverse will and a corrupt heart. Likewise, sin has far-reaching consequences in this life and the life to come.

The most well-known biblical definition of sin is that of missing the mark or goal.[21] This meaning of sin is found in both testaments and can also mean failure, fault, or error.[22] In the New Testament the term is used more frequently to describe actions against God.[23] The truth conveyed by this term is that sin causes persons to miss the mark or goal of God's intended will for their lives. As a stray bullet misses its target or an arrow its bullseye, sin causes one to miss God's desired intention for a person's life. Paradoxically, sin seldom misses its target, striking with deadly accuracy through the power of temptation. When the Bible speaks of Jesus as one without sin, this meaning is conveyed. Jesus, though, did not miss living out God's will in his human life.[24]

Other terms used frequently in the Bible to describe sin are disobedience, rebellion, revolt, transgressions, ungodliness, and iniquity. The Bible describes sin in both religious and moral terms. Terms such as disobedience, revolt, and rebellion refer to religious understandings of sin, whereas terms such as transgressions, ungodliness, and iniquity describe more specifically the moral failures that sin causes. All terms convey the idea of offense toward God. Sin is always first and foremost an action against God. Sin causes sins.

The Bible also teaches that sin arises from a corrupt heart. The depth of evil in the hearts of human beings is not ignorance, but sin. Such evil leads to a perverted will and misdirected freedom. Sin causes one to revolt against God, to be free from God rather than being free to move toward God. Such misuse of freedom, resulting from a corrupt heart and disobedient will, comes close to describing the essence of sin.

Jesus focused more on relating to sinners than defining sin. The problem of sin and its lack of a human solution called forth the mission of Jesus, which he described as a mission to seek and to save the lost. Jesus lived out his mission by relating redemptively to sinners, not by lecturing on sin. He incarnated God's love to sinners. Sinners found a friend in Jesus and still do so today. This truth has not been lost on Baptists, as evidenced by the popularity of the hymn "What a Friend We Have in Jesus," frequently sung in Baptist churches.

The apostle Paul is the theologian of sin in the New Testament. For Paul, sin is an evil power contending against humanity. Paul believed that persons wrestle not against flesh and blood, but against principalities and powers. Sin personifies itself as an evil power that enters into one's life and subjects one to slavery.[25] Sin's power is so great that human power is insufficient to overcome it. Only God's power is adequate. Salvation from sin comes by casting oneself upon God's mercy in Christ whose power delivers us. Only in Christ can one find salvation and freedom from the power of sin.[26] Sin met its match in Christ and its defeat in the cross and the resurrection. In Christ, sin is remedied. And even though Christian believers still sin, they are freed from sin's tyranny—that is, freed not to sin—although this freedom has to be exercised. Paul never tired of proclaiming this mystery.

Key Theological Concepts

Since sin is an action and violation against God, it is theological. Certain key theological concepts stand out in describing sin. These concepts collect the essential biblical teachings concerning sin.

The four theological concepts described below are primary but not exhaustive. These concepts are sin as unbelief, idolatry, rebellion, and ungodliness. Most Baptists would affirm these descriptions of sin (and their preachers might even use them as points in a sermon!).

Sin as Unbelief

Sin can be described as unbelief. Unbelief can have multiple expressions. The most extreme form of unbelief is atheism, or no belief in God. Such unbelief denies God's reality and presence and provides no room for faith, fellowship, or relationship. Blatant denial of God's reality is a wicked expression of sin, for it is the direct opposite of the response God desires from people. Human beings are created in the image of God, a little lower than the angels. God rejoiced in the goodness of the creation of the first human pair. They were nothing short of the climax of creation.

How terrible it is, then, for human beings to turn away from God in unbelief. Unbelief is arrogant, prideful, and egocentric, trusting in human sufficiency rather than in divine sufficiency. Unbelief is the first human step into estrangement.[27]

Actually, pure unbelief in God is rare. Sociologists remind us that the great majority of persons in the world today confess some belief in God or a higher power. What Baptists often encounter is not pure unbelief in God, but practical atheism.[28] This term describes a person who gives intellectual assent to God but does not combine that belief with a lifestyle of worship, faith, and service. A person who says he/she believes in God but never follows God in discipleship actually functions like a practical atheist. Numerous are those who profess belief in God but never identify with a local body of believers. Similarly, numerous are those who have united with a local body of believers but are seldom present when the body of believers gathers for worship. Though both groups purport to believe God, in actuality, they only believe *in* God. It is much easier to believe *in* God than to believe *God*. Thus, sin as unbelief can be expressed in intellect or devotion, as blatant denial or practical atheism. Baptists tend to struggle with the latter perhaps more than the former, although the influence of a highly secular society would seem to indicate otherwise.

In the Christian life, doctrine (what one believes) and ethics (how one behaves) go hand in hand. Belief in God should result in believing God, issuing in a life of faith and obedience, worship and service. Spiritual immaturity results when belief and behavior are not complementary in a believer's life. To be sure, it is easier to believe *in* God than to believe *God*! The challenge of Christian discipleship is to believe God more than to believe in God.

Sin as Idolatry

The first of the Ten Commandments is the requirement to have no other gods before God. The second commandment is like the first, directing believers not to make any graven images or likeness that would cause them to bow before idols. Violation of these commandments is sin.

It was not long in Israel's life before these commandments were broken. Examples are numerous in the Bible where humanity, and often the people of God, lapsed into the worship of idols. First came a golden calf; later would come objects of Baalism. Still later there would be statues and idols believers had to confront, such as Nebuchadnezzar's great idol described in Daniel 3. In the New Testament, Paul came face to face with a city full of idols and saw one idol boasting the inscription "to an unknown god."

Idolatry as sin can be described as usurping the place of God in a believer's life with alien objects, allegiances, or affections. The Old Testament prophets used some of their harshest words to preach against the sin of idolatry. Typical examples are 1 Samuel 15:22-23, where sin is actually called idolatry; Jeremiah 10:1-16, where Jeremiah discusses God's stance concerning idols in the sixth to fifth century; Hosea 8:1-14, where Hosea deals with the problem of idolatry; and Isaiah 44:6-23, where Deutero-Isaiah proclaims God's judgment on the sin of idolatry.

In the New Testament, no more poignant passage describes the sin of idolatry than the following passage from Paul:

> For although they knew God they did not honor Him as God or give thanks to Him, but they became futile in their thinking and their senseless minds were darkened. Claiming to be wise they became fools, and exchanged the glory of the immortal God for images resembling mortal man or birds or animals or reptiles. Therefore, God gave them up . . . because they exchanged the truth about God for a lie and worshiped and served the creature rather than the Creator. (Rom 1:21-25)

Idolatry is sin. It is a sin because it is disobedience to the commandments of God and because it displaces God as the receiver of our ultimate faith. Some even call it the "basic sin."[29] D. E. H. Whitley calls idolatry the "primal sin," which leads to sin of every kind.[30]

Sin as idolatry has not disappeared. While humans today generally do not build images of golden calves or elaborate statues (or do we?), the reality is that other loyalties, possessions, or objects can become the receiver of our ultimate trust. False gods are as real and present in the contemporary age as at any time in the history of God's people. They are simply called by other names. Idolatry as sin is real. It is self-glorifying and blatant. Indeed, it is a sin and a serious one at that.

Sin as Rebellion

Acknowledging that human beings choose to be disobedient to God in view of divine love is indeed a mystery. But such rebellion highlights the terrible nature of sin. Some rebel against God with full knowledge of God's displeasure.

The seat of a rebellious spirit is a perverse will. Viewing sin only as outward, disobedient behavior is shallow. There is something deeper and darker that is wrong with humanity. That something is a perverse will—an inclination in the heart, spirit, and attitude to be hostile to God. Jesus saw this inner cauldron at work in people. He taught that what comes from the heart is what defiles a person, for "out of the heart come evil intentions, murder, adultery, fornication, theft, false witness, slander" (Matt 15:19).

A spirit of self-sufficiency or arrogance tends to fuel a perverse will. The belief in one's goodness as a result of self-effort can lead to a life of independence from God. Extreme self-love and belief in human sufficiency alone are often described by theologians as the sin of hubris, or pride.[31] Reinhold Niebuhr describes sinful pride as undue self-regard, vanity, egotism, and a general overestimation of virtue and power.[32] Such sinful pride leads to rebellion against God in multiple ways. Rebellion can take the form of libertinism, or outward and flagrant acts of disobedience. Rebellion can also take the form of legalism, or harsh and rigid stances toward persons and ideas without regard for new insights or grace. Rebellion against God can be lived out in multifaceted ways.

God is not content with rebellion. God seeks His lost children, ever inviting them to return to His love. If the heart and spirit never yield to God's love, God then decides whether to give one over to his/her choices or vices. Sin as rebellion is a contest between the divine will and the self will.[33] For human beings, it is a fight worth losing!

Sin as Ungodliness

Can there be a more profound expression for sin than ungodliness? The term itself captures the idea of living contrary to God's Word and will. Ungodliness is behaving in a way totally opposite from God's laws and standards.

Ungodliness is a moral description of sin. It refers to a lifestyle that dishonors God. The wrath of God, according to the Bible, is revealed against all ungodliness. The following verses describe why:

> And since they did not see fit to acknowledge God, God gave them up to a debased mind and to things that should not be done. They were filled with every kind of wickedness, evil,

covetousness, malice. Full of envy, murder, strife, deceit, crafti-
ness, they are gossips, slanderers, God-haters, insolent, haughty,
boastful, inventors of evil, rebellious toward parents, foolish,
faithless, heartless, ruthless. They know God's decree, that those
who practice such things deserve to die—yet they not only do
them but even applaud others who practice them. (Rom 1:28-32)

These four theological concepts, while not exhaustive, collect
the primary biblical descriptions of sin. Sin is unnatural, for we are
created to live in harmony with God. Sin is larger than description,
but with some description, we can understand it a little better.

The Consequences of Sin

A popular television program in years past was a game show called
"Truth or Consequences." Contestants were required to speak the
truth about questions they were asked. The host possessed prior
knowledge of what a truthful answer would be. Should the contes-
tant not tell the truth, he/she had to face the consequences, usually
humorous.

Likewise, sin has consequences. Unfortunately, none of the consequences of sin are funny. They can be deadly, either in this life or
the life to come. The church does not delight in the consequences of
sin, but does face the task of being faithful to proclaim them. The
church does so, always with a view toward reclaiming sinners
through repentance and reconciliation.

One sure consequence of sin is the reality that sins are never
harmless nor hidden. Sin is always a violation toward God and thus
damages that relationship. One powerful biblical teaching about sin
is the frightening truth expressed in Numbers 32:23: "Be sure your
sin will find you out." We cannot hide our sins or hide in our sin.

Another real consequence of sin is estrangement, or isolation
from God. Estrangement leads to lostness and leads one away from
God. Estrangement is in many ways the fundamental consequence
of sin. As a result of sin, human beings are alienated not only from
God, but also from one another, from the created order, and even
from self. Estrangement from God or others is a terrible
consequence of sin.

Still another powerful consequence of sin is guilt. It did not take
long for this consequence to surface when God confronted Adam

and Eve with their sin. They were guilty of sin and knew it. Bodily shame and anxiety about their relationship with God resulted.[34] All persons are guilty of sin. "There is no one who is righteous, not even one" (Rom 3:10), claimed Paul. There are no degrees of guilt in sin; God judges all sin. To deny one's guilt is to continue in unrepentant sin. Consciousness of one's guilt in sin can have a positive side. Guilt can be a prelude to forgiveness. When the prodigal son returned home to his forgiving father, his words reflected a consciousness of guilt over his sins. He said, "[Father] I am no longer worthy to be called your son" (Luke 15:19). Dietrich Bonhoeffer reminded Christians that repentance without confession is cheap grace. Similarly, repentance following genuine repentance and confession is costly grace.[35]

The ultimate consequence of sin is death. The Bible teaches that "the wages of sin is death" (Rom 6:23). The Bible speaks to two forms of death regarding sin. The first speaks to separation from God in this life. To the first human pair, God said, "In the day that you eat of it (the tree) you shall die" (Gen 2:17). Death in this context means separation, not annihilation. Paul expressed the same idea when he said, "You were dead through [your] trespasses and sins" (Eph 2:1). Persons in sin are not physically dead, but they are dead in sin. They are not annihilated, but they are separated from God. There are legions of persons in the world today who are physically fine but spiritually dead. Sin brings a death that is to be understood as separation from God.

The second form of death that can result from sin is eternal separation from God following the conclusion of history and the final judgment. Such finality from God is the ultimate consequence of sin. Eternal separation from God with no chance of reunion is hell. There is no humor in such a consequence, but there is deliverance! And this is the only good news there is about sin.

Victory Over Sin

"A second Adam to the fight and to the rescue came!"[36] "For I handed on to you as of first importance what I in turn had received: *that Christ died for our sins* in accordance with the scriptures" (1 Cor 15:3). "As all die in Adam, so all will be made alive in Christ" (1 Cor 15:22).

But God ... (Eph 2:4).

With these representative words, the New Testament proclaims a victory over sin. Victory is a term of conquest, declaring a hard-fought battle to have been won. Sin, present since the opening season of creation, persistent throughout the centuries, and powerful enough to have no human solution, would now be conquered by the only One capable of doing so—God. In a tremendous show of divine love, God acted in Jesus Christ to bring liberation to humanity from the bondage of sin. Victory over sin was accomplished through the person and work of God's Son, Jesus Christ, and his death on the cross to atone for the sins of humanity. As Paul so triumphantly described, God was in Christ, reconciling the world unto Himself.

Salvation from sin results only from the will and work of God. Human beings could not extract themselves from the bondage of sin. Salvation could not be achieved by human effort. Salvation could not be earned.

To atone for sin, however, would require sacrifice. The Old Testament system of sacrifice had long ago given way. Burnt offerings and sacrifices would not remedy humanity's inward dispositions of disobedience, idolatry, and rebellion. Jesus Christ had to come, incarnate of God, full of grace and truth, to effect this sacrifice. His mission led him to the cross. There, he became the sacrifice for sin, dying on behalf of humanity, giving a sacrifice for sin that was superior to any previous sacrifice. He who was sacrificed was sinless, and his sacrifice for sin was sufficient that it need never be repeated. One can hardly plumb the depths of the biblical proclamation, "while we were still sinners Christ died for us" (Rom 5:8). In addition to these objective aspects of atonement, the subjective dimension of the atonement has implications for salvation. The cross provides an example of self-giving love that, when followed, leads to victory over sin.

The salvation provided for sinners through Jesus Christ is made effective by faith. Faith in Christ's sacrificial death and subsequent resurrection brings a new standing of the believer before God and new life to the sinner. While the resurrection of Jesus may be the greatest miracle in the New Testament, the possibility of the creation of the new person in Christ must surely follow closely behind. Paul expressed this miraculous transformation with these words:

From now on, therefore, we regard no one from a human point of view. . . . So if anyone is in Christ, there is a new creation: everything old has passed away; see, everything has become new! All this is from God, who reconciled us to himself through Christ . . . (2 Cor 5:16-18)

In Jesus Christ, God acted to redeem humanity from sin. Through faith, there is victory over sin. It is no wonder Baptists never tire of proclaiming, singing, and testifying relative to the great victory over sin possible through faith in Jesus Christ.

"O happy day! O happy day!
When Jesus washed my sins away."

Summary

From this survey of selected biblical and theological teachings regarding sin, the following points may be realized:

• Sin is a religious concept and a theological subject. It cannot be understood without this frame of reference. All sins are sins against God.

• Sin was not a part of the created order. Sin was an intruder into God's creation. It did not and does not belong.

• Sin originates in the disobedient will of human beings. It is not biologically inherited, though we are tainted by the reality of original sin. Human beings are the cause of their own sins.

• Sin is described in the Bible in both religious and moral terms. Sin can be unbelief, idolatry, or rebellion. It can also be ungodliness, iniquity, or transgressions. Sin causes sins.

• Sin has no human solution. It is the universal human predicament. Only God can effect atonement for sin.

• There is victory over sin. Salvation from sin results from God's action through Jesus Christ to atone for sin. This salvation is made effective by faith. Sin does not have to be the ultimate victor in a person's life.

Conclusion

In a provocative book published some years ago, Karl Menninger, a psychiatrist, posed the question, "Whatever happened to sin?"[37] In the book, he expressed a conviction that unconfessed sin rather than psychological difficulties were the cause of many of his patients' problems. Thus, he asked, "Whatever happened to sin?"

Baptists today would likely answer "nothing." Sin has gone nowhere, and it is just as present and dangerous as ever. Sin is rebellion against God, and such rebellion is as present in the contemporary age as it was in the Garden of Eden. Sadly, cultural forces at work in society today have desensitized persons to the reality and consequences of sin. Baptists are challenged to proclaim a biblical view of sin to a world with so many competing and alternate worldviews. Ironically, the loss of intensity in awareness of sin may be striking Baptists inside their own churches. A strange paradox among Baptists is that, while espousing fervent beliefs about sin, Baptists rarely set aside time in their worship services for the confession of sin. Announcements, activities, and other items along with music and proclamation tend to fill the worship schedule. This is a mystery indeed.

The secret of sin lies in the battle between spirit and flesh, with flesh taking the lead and the spirit never successful in overtaking it.[38] We are the slaves of sin. Sin is not a defect in a person's character or a side to human nature that can be rehabilitated with human effort. Sin holds us hostage, and liberation can come only from One who is not a part of this human condition. Rehabilitation cannot set the sinner free or remedy this human condition.

Running parallel to the biblical story of sin is another story—the story of God's redeeming love for sinners. God's love for sinners has been never-ending and became ultimately incarnate in the person and work of Jesus Christ. Through his obedience to God, Jesus brought freedom from the bondage of sin. He has made possible a new creation in humanity—the new person in Christ.

The ultimate victor, then, in the battle with sin is God. God's love for sinners is stronger than the power of sin. Sin could not defeat God's love in Christ. The cross did not destroy Christ, but it did destroy the ultimate consequences of sin for the believer. In the suffering and miracle of the cross and resurrection, the truth proclaimed by the prophet Isaiah comes ringing true: "Though your sins are like scarlet, they shall be like snow" (Isa 1:18). Wonder of wonders, because we believe and trust in the atoning work of Jesus Christ, we are now "heirs, heirs of God and joint heirs with Christ" (Rom 8:17).

"Here is the Lamb of God who takes away the sin of the world!"
(John 1:29)

Notes

[1]The confessional booth has been in use by Roman Catholics since the sixteenth century. While some contemporary Catholic congregations no longer use the confessional booth, the confession of sin remains an integral part of Catholic worship.

[2]I am indebted to E. Cleve Wilkie, Kinston NC, for this story.

[3]One example is Stephen L. Carter *The Culture of Disbelief* (New York: Doubleday and Co., 1993). Popular also are a number of current books that speak to a belief in the "death" of Christian principles. Examples are *The Death of Truth* (Minneapolis: Bethany House, 1996), *The Death of Common-Sense* (New York: Warner Books, 1996), and *The Death of Outrage* (Thorndike ME: G. K. Hall, 1999).

[4]Tim Keller, "Preaching Morality in an Amoral Age," *Leadership* (Winter 1996) 112.

[5]John Claypool, *The Light Within You* (Waco TX: Word Books, 1983) 183.

[6]Gustaf Aulén, *The Faith of the Christian Church* (Philadelphia: Fortress Press, 1960) 231.

[7]Cf. Gen 1:26f.

[8]Cf. Gen 3:23f.

[9]Gen 3:1-5; 12-13.

[10]Morris Ashcraft, *Christian Faith and Beliefs* (Nashville: Broadman Press, 1984) 203.

[11]Ashcraft, 203.

[12]For an informative and fuller treatment of the doctrine of original sin, see F. R. Tennant, *The Sources of the Doctrines of the Fall and Original Sin* (Cambridge: Cambridge University Press, 1903); N. P. Williams, *The Ideas of the Fall and of Original Sin* (London: Longmans and Green, 1927).

[13]Shirley Guthrie, Jr., *Christian Doctrine* (Richmond VA: CLC Press, 1968) 214.

[14]William L. Lumpkin, *Baptist Confessions of Faith* (Valley Forge PA: Judson Press, 1959) 100.

[15]Ibid., 157.

[16]Ibid., 394-95.

[17]J. S. Whale, *Christian Doctrine* (Cambridge: Fontana Books, 1941) 47-48.

[18]John Newport, "What Is Christian Doctrine?" *Laymen's Library of Christian Doctrine* (Nashville: Broadman Press, 1984) 99.

[19]Theron Price, "Sin," *Mercer Dictionary of the Bible* (Macon GA: Mercer University Press, 1990) 827.

[20]Price, 827.

[21]This is the meaning of the term, *hamartia,* so commonly referred to in biblical studies of sin. See Walter Grundmann, "Hamartia," *Theological Dictionary of the New Testament* (Grand Rapids: Wm. B. Eerdmans, 1964) 1:267-316.

[22]Price, 827.

[23]Ibid.

[24]2 Cor 5:21 points to this truth. "For our sake he made him to be sin who knew no sin, so that in him we might become the righteousness of God." Traditional Christian orthodoxy relative to the humanity and divinity of Christ is that Jesus was fully God and fully human, two natures in one, without conflict or confusion. Thus, he could be "without sin," fully God, and still fulfill God's will in his human life.

[25]Ashcraft, 180-81.

[26]Rom 7 is one passage where Paul outlines his concept of freedom from sin. Romans 5-8 is a lengthier treatment of his views.

[27]Ashcraft, 184.

[28]Peter Rhea Jones, *The Teaching of the Parables* (Nashville: Broadman Press, 1982), 133.

[29]John MacQuarrie, *Principles of Christian Theology,* 2nd ed. (New York: Charles Scribner's Sons, 1977) 260.

[30]D. E. H. Whitely, *The Theology of St. Paul* (Philadelphia: Fortress Press, 1972) 52.

[31]Since Augustine, it has been the consistent view of Christian orthodoxy that the basic sin of human beings was pride, or self-love.

[32]Reinhold Niebuhr, *The Nature and Destiny of Man,* vol. 1 (New York: Charles Scribner's Sons, 1964) 186f.

[33]Aulén, 237-38.

[34]Cf. Gen 3:11-20.

[35]Dietrich Bonhoeffer, *The Cost of Discipleship* (New York: The MacMillan Co.) 45f.

[36]Whale, 50

[37]Karl Menninger, *Whatever Happened to Sin?* (New York: Hawthorne Books, 1973).

[38]H. R. MacKintosh, *Types of Modern Theology* (London: The Fontana Library, 1937) 86.

Scripture
R. Alan Culpepper

I was raised on Bible stories. Just as surely as I was formed by my parents' love and the family stories they gave me, I was nurtured from infancy on Bible stories at home and at church. I still have the battered childrens' Bible story book from which my parents read to me the stories of Israel and Jesus. In fact, I trace my Christian faith to the formative influence of the gospel story as mediated to me by my parents.

One evening when I was six my father was reading the story of the crucifixion. The story spoke to me of Jesus' love for the world, for me. The story of Jesus' suffering was so powerful that it altered my perception of life irrevocably. A part of my father's account of that event, written on August 26, 1952, two days after I was baptized, reads as follows:

> One night his father read the story of the crucifixion. . . . Alan's eyes filled with tears as he was visibly moved. He said, "Daddy, I just can't understand it—I try to, but I just can't." I explained to him that I did not understand all about it either, but that it made plain to us the love of God and the reality of sin. . . . A few days later he told me that he wanted to come into the room where I studied and talk to me about something. The next morning he came in and climbed up in my lap. He said, "Daddy, you know all those Bible stories we have been reading. Well, I want you to tell me the meaning of them." I began and told him the story of creation and the fall and redemption on through the meaning of church membership and the ordinances. At points he would say, "I understand that; go on." At other points he would say, "I don't understand that; explain it."

The following night I told my parents that I wanted to be baptized. So I began a pilgrimage with scripture that led through a call to ministry, professional preparation including the biblical languages, and twenty-five years of teaching the New Testament. My understanding of scripture, I am sure, is formed as surely by that early background as by anything I have learned or experienced since. This early experience was also thoroughly Baptist: it convinced me of the sufficiency of scripture for faith and the competence of the individual to understand and experience it.

The Stakes

Sadly, for at least the past twenty years, Baptists have used statements regarding the nature and authority of scripture as badges of identity and slogans for controversy. The real issues often were power and control of the denomination and contemporary social issues, but the political shorthand of the controversy was how we talk about the Bible. What is the Bible, and how should we define its authority? Now, after twenty years of wearying controversy, it is all but impossible for a Baptist to talk about the Bible without political overtones being attached to every word. Nevertheless, the Bible is central to Baptist life and faith. Baptists separated from other religious groups over the freedom to interpret scripture and follow its light as they understood it. For the early Baptists, the scripture's teaching on faith and baptism led them to practice believer's baptism. Their conviction that each individual was capable of reading scripture and discerning truth apart from the direction of church authorities led them to defend the freedom of conscience of every person both from the state and from the church.

A great deal is at stake, therefore, in the way we define the authority of scripture. I am convinced that a Baptist cannot separate the authority of scripture from two other cardinal issues: faith in Jesus Christ and what our forebears spoke of as "soul competence," or every believer's freedom of conscience and ability to be led by the Spirit to discern truth. Our affirmations of the authority of scripture are actually expressions of a heritage of faith. What we say about scripture also reflects our understanding of the Baptist heritage and our understanding of religious authority, especially the relationship between Christ and scripture. In turn, our understanding of scripture has a direct bearing on the way in which we interpret the Bible on issues that divide contemporary believers. The place to begin is with what the Bible says about the nature of scripture and with an overview of the role of the Bible in the life of the church.

The Bible Speaks about Scripture

The earliest Christians brought with them from Judaism a high regard for the written record of God's revelation in the history of Israel, most often referred to in the New Testament either as "the writings" (i.e. the Scriptures), or "the law and the prophets" (or "Moses and the prophets"). Only once, in Luke 24:44, are the three parts of the Old Testament referred to: "the law of Moses, the prophets, and the psalms." There was as yet no standard set of writings accepted as scripture by all Jews, but the Torah (the books of Moses) and the writings of the prophets were read and interpreted whenever and wherever Jews gathered in the synagogues (see Luke 4:16-28). Quotations from the Old Testament, most often from the Septuagint or Greek translation of the Hebrew Scriptures, fill the New Testament and illustrate the ways in which scripture was interpreted in the early church. Two passages speak specifically of the authority and interpretation of scripture, 2 Timothy 3:15-16 and 2 Peter 1:20-21.

In 2 Timothy 3:15-17 Paul charges Timothy to continue in what he has learned, remembering

> ... how from childhood you have known the sacred writings that are able to instruct you for salvation through faith in Christ Jesus. All scripture is inspired by God and is useful for teaching, for reproof, for correction, and for training in righteousness, so that everyone who belongs to God may be proficient, equipped for every good work.

These verses have often been interpreted out of context as though their emphasis was on the inspiration of the Bible. First, Paul is here speaking of the Torah or the Jewish Scriptures since there was as yet no New Testament. Second, the emphasis is not on the inspiration of the sacred writings, which was undisputed, but on their function in the life of a believer such as Timothy. Paul has been reminding Timothy of the source of his instruction and guidance. Timothy has learned from Paul himself and from childhood instruction in the Jewish Scriptures. Remarkably, the law and the prophets are able to point beyond themselves to "salvation through faith in Christ Jesus." The Greek here may be translated variously: "All scripture is inspired by God," "Every scripture is inspired by God," or "Every inspired scripture is useful." The alternatives arise from the ambiguity as to whether Paul means all scripture, every book of scripture, or every passage of scripture. Moreover, there is no verb "is" in this verse; the emphasis falls on the functions of scripture that follow. The best rendering is probably the standard translation, as long as one recognizes that "inspired by God" and "useful" are joined very closely by the Greek conjunction, almost as one idea. The affirmation of the inspiration of scripture says nothing about the means of inspiration; God as spirit, who breathed life into humankind and breathed the Holy Spirit into the disciples, also "inspired" the Scriptures. Functionally, the Scriptures provide guidance for teaching, for the conviction of sinners (see the reference to "wicked people and impostors" in v. 13), for correction of false beliefs and practices, and for educating and nurturing believers in righteousness. The result of such correction and education (*paideia*) is that everyone who belongs to God may be ready and prepared "for every good work." Scripture, therefore, serves to lead those who are responsive to God to faith in Christ Jesus and instruct them in how they are to live.

Second Peter, like 2 Timothy, was probably among the latest of the books of the New Testament. In the context of debate over predictions of the coming judgment, 2 Peter affirms that no prophecy in scripture is subject to one's individual explanation or interpretation.

> First of all you must understand this, that no prophecy of scripture is a matter of one's own interpretation, because no prophecy ever came by human will, but men and women moved by the Holy Spirit spoke from God. (1:20-21)

The point of verse 20 is different from that of verse 21. Verse 20 does not say that no prophecy ever arose from one's own interpretation. It says that no one is authorized to offer his or her own interpretation of scriptural prophecy. Scripture is not subject to one's own interpretation because it was given by God. The alternative, apparently, is to follow the authorized interpretation found in the tradition of the apostles' teaching. This verse is particularly troublesome for Baptists, not because of its affirmation of the authority of scripture, but because it is an early indication of how the interpretation of scripture would become controlled by the church. These verses from 2 Peter should at least serve as a caution for Baptists that individual interpretations need to be tested in the community of faith.

Two other references affirm the priority of Jesus over the Scriptures, John 5:39 and Matthew 5:17-18. In the context of Jesus' debate with the religious leaders about his claim that God was his father, Jesus cites various witnesses that support his claim, among them the Scriptures. "You search the scriptures because you think that in them you have eternal life; and it is they that testify on my behalf" (John 5:39).

The Scriptures have no power to give life; their function is to point us to Christ through whom we have the promise of eternal life. This verse should serve as a caution about making great claims for the Scriptures apart from their role in pointing to the Lordship of Christ. The religious leaders who opposed Jesus had a high regard for the Scriptures, but they failed to see that the Scriptures themselves point to Jesus.

Again, in the Sermon on the Mount, Jesus claims authority over the Scriptures. He came in fulfillment of the Scriptures, and he alone could say that they had heard the commandments, such as "You shall not murder," but he brought a new standard of righteousness: "Don't even be angry with your brother or sister." At the same time, he affirmed the continuing authority of scripture:

> Do not think that I have come to abolish the law or the prophets; I have come not to abolish but to fulfill. For truly I tell you, until heaven and earth pass away, not one letter, not one stroke of a letter, will pass from the law until all is accomplished. (Matt 5:17-18)

While other verses might be cited, these are the primary passages that deal with the authority of scripture. The principal subject of the New Testament, clearly, is not the Bible but Jesus. Its concern is not that we have a correctly articulated doctrine of scripture, but that we have faith in Christ. The inspiration and authority of scripture is assumed, and the Hebrew Scriptures are quoted throughout the New Testament. They are not an inviolable code because Jesus gives a new standard of righteousness, and the food laws and cultic laws of Israel are set aside as no longer binding on the early Christians. Christ himself is the center and focus of scripture. Ultimately the Scriptures derive their authority from him. The Scriptures are true and reliable because they point us to salvation in Jesus Christ.

It is tempting for a Baptist to skip from the Bible to Baptist confessions (and debates) about scripture, but Baptist understandings of scripture are also shaped by the translation, use, and interpretation of the Bible in the history of the church. A brief survey of the Bible in the history of the church is essential if we are to appreciate both the ways in which Baptist thought is distinctive and the areas in which Baptists and other believers hold convictions in common.

The Bible in the Early Church

The history of the Bible in the early church confirms the priority of Christ over scripture, while at the same time showing how the church received and over the centuries shaped the Bible as we know it. Significantly, the early controversies were not about scripture but about the Trinity and the nature of Christ. Quietly, though, the Spirit was leading the church to set apart the writings of the New Testament.

During the first century, early Christians relied on the Hebrew Scriptures, at least the Law and the Prophets, and a variety of writings used by various Jewish groups. They also recalled the teachings of Jesus. They were led by prophets who spoke under the leadership of the Spirit and by the apostles who founded and guided individual churches. From the early church we have quotations from various books that were used as authoritative, discussions about which books should be regarded as scripture, and manuscripts that collected the New Testament books, sometimes along with other writings.

Second Peter 3:16 refers to Paul's letters and "the other scriptures." By the end of the second century, the four Gospels, the book of Acts, the letters of Paul, 1 John, and 1 Peter were well established. Other writings—such as the Didache, the Shepherd of Hermas, and 1 Clement—were used along with the books of the New Testament and in some instances copied along with them in the early biblical manuscripts. This situation prevailed until the fourth century, when efforts were made to distinguish the biblical writings and fix the "canon" or list of the books of scripture.

A list called the "Muratorian Canon," which was once thought to date from the end of the second century but is now given a later date by many scholars, includes the four Gospels, the book of Acts, the thirteen letters of Paul, Jude, 1 and 2 John, the Wisdom of Solomon, Revelation, and the Apocalypse of Peter.

Eusebius of Caesarea, the great fourth-century historian of the early Church, compiled three lists: acknowledged books, disputed books, and heretical books. In the first list he places the four Gospels, the book of Acts, fourteen letters of Paul (counting Hebrews as a Pauline letter), 1 John, 1 Peter, and in some communities Revelation. Eusebius himself, and many of the churches in the East, did not accept Revelation. Among the "disputed books" Eusebius lists: James, Jude, 2 Peter, 2 and 3 John, Revelation (for some), and five other writings that were eventually rejected. The first list of the twenty-seven books of the New Testament, with none others, is found in the Easter letter of Athanasius, bishop of Alexandria, in AD 367. Thereafter, his list was accepted by the North African Councils in 393 and 397.

The New Testament was formed slowly, therefore, over a period of several centuries. It arose from the daily life and use of writings in the church, as it gradually sifted the writings, determining which ones were apostolic (written by an apostle or one closely associated with the apostles), catholic (speaking to the whole church), orthodox (teaching true doctrine), and held by tradition and use to be scripture. The core of the New Testament was well established by the end of the second century, while other writings remained in debate through the fourth century. The New Testament, therefore, is the church's book, formed by generations of believers who sought to discern the authentic ring of truth in the writings they had.[1]

In AD 386 Augustine (AD 354–430), the greatest scholar of the fifth century, experienced a dramatic conversion while reading Romans 13:13-14 and later founded a monastery in Hippo and wrote his Confessions, The City of God, and other works that shaped Western Christian thought. On the subject of biblical authority, Augustine contended that the Bible is about salvation and faith. Its purpose is to bring us to faith. As Clifton Black put it so articulately:

> In his sermons on 1 John, Augustine boldly proposes that, when we approach the Bible as scripture—when we inquire after God through assiduous reading of the biblical text—it is there we encounter the God who is relentlessly inquiring after us.[2]

According to Polman, the Bible's purpose is not to speak authoritatively in other areas: "Although our authors knew the truth about the shape of the heavens, the Spirit of God who spoke by them did not intend to teach men these things, in no way profitable for salvation."[3] Augustine accepted the Bible as authoritative beyond any of the councils or pronouncements of the church. Nevertheless, it is the work of men who were at one and the same time inspired by God but still limited in their understanding. Augustin Pea commented:

> I venture to say, brethren, that not even John himself has presented these things just as they are, but only as best he could, since he was a man who spoke of God—inspired, of course, but still a man. Because he was inspired he was able to say some things; but because he who was inspired remained a man, he could not present the full reality, but only what a man could say about it.[4]

The Bible in the Middle Ages

A new era was introduced by the translation of the Bible into Latin. The formation of the Latin Vulgate began when, in 382 or 383, Pope Damascus commissioned Jerome to produce a Latin Bible. Jerome began a revision of Old Latin manuscripts, correcting them from a text of the Greek Septuagint, but he soon abandoned this approach in favor of producing a Latin translation based on Hebrew and Greek manuscripts. In the process he advocated that the writings contained in the Septuagint but not in the Hebrew Bible should be considered apocryphal. Popular sentiment prevailed, however, and the books of the Apocrypha were added to the Latin Vulgate, and therefore the Apocrypha was part of the Bible for the next eleven hundred years—until the Reformation.

In the fourth century Latin was the common language for the Western church, but over time Latin increasingly became the language of the church and the educated. Few ordinary believers had access to the Latin manuscripts, so the Bible became an official document interpreted by priests rather than common believers. The work of Thomas Aquinas (d. 1274), the great systematizer of medieval theology, shows how, under the influence of Aristotelian philosophy, theology was based on reason. The Bible was used to prooftext the pronouncements of the Church councils and authorities. William of Occam (d. 1349) prepared the way for the Reformation by arguing that faith precedes reason, and the Bible is the ultimate authority for faith, not the Pope or the ecclesiastical councils.

The Bible in the Reformation

The sixteenth century was an era of sweeping change. A renaissance of learning and culture, distrust of ecclesiastical leadership and authority, and competition among national and territorial groups swept over Europe. The invention of the printing press brought the innovation of printed money, banks, a growing merchant class, and a rise in literacy. Fascination with Greek and Roman culture led to a revival of the study of Greek and Hebrew. The humanists Jacques Lefevre and Erasmus laid a foundation for the Reformers by their work on the Hebrew and Greek texts. Erasmus collected six Greek manuscripts of the New Testament and started the process of recovering the earliest text (textual criticism). Attention to language and texts fueled the move away from traditional exegesis toward the plain and literal meaning of scripture.[5]

The Reformation marked a shift in the Church's concept of authority. In the Roman Catholic Church, authority has always been balanced between scripture and the Pope as Christ's representative on earth, and hence between scripture and tradition. The great slogans of the Reformation were *sola scriptura, solus Christus,* and *sola fide,* thereby opposing the established balance of scripture *and* tradition, Christ *and* the Church, and faith *and* works. Scripture became the sole basis of authority. Later, during the Enlightenment, reason would emerge as the basis for rationalism, and experience would become important especially among the Pietists and Wesleyans.[6]

Martin Luther (1483–1546) began the study of law in 1505. Shortly thereafter he was caught in a severe thunderstorm and struck by lightning. Terrified, he vowed to become a monk and entered the Augustinian monastery at Erfurt. His piety deepened, but his struggle of soul intensified. After he became a professor of scripture in 1513, he discovered Paul's writings—"he who through faith is righteous shall live"—and later wrote, "Here I felt I was altogether born again and had entered paradise itself through open gates."[7] In the Scriptures he found that faith alone, not works, was the basis of salvation. Any Christian could hear confessions, so he moved to affirm the priesthood of all believers. At the Diet of Worms in 1521 Luther refused to recant his beliefs, saying that his conscience was bound to scripture: "Here I stand. I can do no other."

Luther later translated the Bible into German, to give the people access to scripture in their own language. He removed the Apocrypha from the Old Testament and separated Hebrews, James, Jude, and Revelation to the end of the New Testament as not belonging to the primary witnesses to Jesus Christ. For Luther, John, Paul, and 1 Peter were the center of the canon. Luther abandoned excessive allegorical interpretations of scripture in favor of its literal meaning.[8] The authority of the Bible is in its subject, not its form: "Holy Scripture possesses no external glory, attracts no attention, lacks all beauty and adornment. . . Yet faith comes from this divine Word, through its inner power without any external loveliness."[9] Appealing to the illumination of the Spirit, Luther's exegesis of scripture remained fresh and free of critical conventions. By holding together the spirit and the letter, Luther transcended time. He saw his experiences in the biblical text, and the biblical events in his own experience. He could therefore "see, feel, participate, and believe in that which God once spoke by the mouth of Moses, the prophets, the evangelists, and the apostles."[10] With Luther there was no sense of distance that had to be bridged between our time and the biblical era, as would emerge as a result of the historical consciousness of the Enlightenment. Luther chose the meaning that best conformed to the literal sense, the historical conditions, and his own theological perspective, while at the same time acknowledging that one never fully understood a text and that the interpretations of others were true also. The text was illuminated by the interpreter's experience, but one should also pray for the illumination of the Spirit. In a sense, the text was not fully interpreted until it "encountered and illumined the life of the addressee."[11]

John Calvin (1509–1563) received a classical education, studied for the priesthood, and excelled in Latin. He also studied law, Greek, the classics, and Hebrew. Later he moved to Basel and became friends with several of the Reformers. In 1536 he published his *Institutes of the Christian Religion*. He was then persuaded to help reform the city of Geneva. During the rest of his life Calvin transformed Geneva into a Christian theocracy. Calvin's theology emphasized the sovereignty of God: total depravity of humans, unconditional election, limited atonement, irresistible grace, and the perseverance of the saints.

Calvin was a master exegete. He dealt carefully with texts and language in pursuit of the author's meaning. He produced lectures and commentaries on Genesis, a harmony of the four remaining books of the Pentateuch, Joshua, Psalms, the Major and Minor Prophets, and all the books of the New Testament except 2 and 3 John and Revelation.[12] T. D. Parker noted five characteristics of Calvin's interpretation of scripture:

• He has a greater interest in historical and critical matters than Luther.
• Calvin is more careful in stressing the text's plain meaning.
• Calvin is more likely to state the text's meaning rather than discuss theological issues.
• He is more cautious about letting his own experience intrude on the exposition.
• Calvin seeks for practical expositions dealing with his readers' common life.[13]

Calvin regarded the issue of the authority of scripture as self-evident, following Augustine. The purpose of scripture is to lead us to salvation. The Bible clearly shows us God. Yet, its authority is based on its testimony to Christ rather than its form. In his commentary on Hebrews 10:6, Calvin notes that scripture achieves its saving purpose in spite of inaccuracies in its quotations:

> They [the apostles] were not overscrupulous in quoting words provided that they did not misuse Scripture for their convenience. We must always look at the purpose for which quotations are made . . . but as far as the words are concerned, as in other things which are not relevant to the present purpose, they allow themselves some indulgence.[14]

From the Reformers, therefore, Baptists inherited the Protestant canon (which omits the Apocrypha), a renewed commitment to translating the Scriptures into the everyday language of the people —which grew out of the conviction that every believer should be able to read and interpret the Bible—a passionate insistence on the principle of the authority of scripture over tradition, and a distinction between the essential purpose and message of scripture on the one hand and its "creaturely" form on the other.[15] The latter became a regular feature of the articles on scripture in Baptist confessions of faith.

Biblical Authority in Baptist Confessions

Baptists have often agreed to issue confessions or statements of faith, but they have always been reluctant to invest much authority in such statements or make them binding on other Baptists. The introductory statement of the *Baptist Faith and Message* (1925, retained in 1963) clarifies the role of confessions among Baptists in five succinct points:

> That they constitute a consensus of opinion of some Baptist body, large or small, for the general instruction and guidance of our own people . . .
> That we do not regard them as complete statements of our faith, having any quality of finality or infallibility.
> That any group of Baptists, large or small, have the inherent right to draw up for themselves and publish to the world a confession of their faith whenever they may think it advisable to do so.
> That the sole authority for faith and practice among Baptists is the Scriptures of the Old and New Testaments. Confessions are only guides in interpretation, having no authority over the conscience.
> That they are statements of religious convictions, drawn from the Scriptures, and are not to be used to hamper freedom of thought or investigation in other realms of life.[16]

The introductory statement also affirms that "the sole authority for faith and practice among Baptists is Jesus Christ whose will is revealed in the Holy Scriptures" and that "Baptists emphasize the soul's competency before God, freedom in religion, and the priesthood of the believer."[17] The history that led to these declarations begins with John Smyth and a small community of dissenters from the Church of England.

Persecuted as nonconformists, John Smyth and his group sailed to Holland, where in 1608 or 1609 Smyth baptized himself and then

administered believer's baptism to about forty others. They constituted the first Baptist congregation, affirming believer's baptism,
regenerate church membership, separation of church and state, and
the soul competence of the individual believer. In 1611 or 1612
Smyth and some of his followers requested membership in the
Mennonite church. Thomas Helwys, a lawyer educated in London,
separated from Smyth, led a group back to England, and there
formed the first Baptist church on English soil.[18]

In 1608, as part of his exchange with the Mennonites, Smyth
wrote "Differences of the Churches of the Separation," which is the
earliest confession of the English Baptists. In a series of statements
on the Scriptures, Smyth held that "the holy Scriptures viz. the
Originalls Hebrew and Greek are given by Divine Inspiration and in
their first donation were without error most perfect and therefore
Canonicall."[19] Elements of this early statement are influential in later
confessions. Smyth held that the authors of scripture were inspired,
but not the translators.

> Holy Scripture (as all other writings whatsoever,) consist of two
> partes: of the tong [tongue] & character & of the substance or
> matter signified by the character. The tong or character hath
> apertaining to it the grammar & the Rhetorick whereof the tong
> or character is the subject. The matter or substance of the Scrip-
> ture hath in it, Logick, History, Cronology, Cosmography,
> Genealogy, Philosophy, Theologie & other like matter. The
> principall parte of the matter is the Theologie.[20]

Smyth esteemed translations into the common tongue, but maintained that "no translation can possibly express all the matter of the
holy originalls."[21] Translations, therefore, were no better than expositions, resolutions, or sermons and should therefore not be used as
aids for the eye or memory in worship. Smyth's theology of scripture employed two distinctions that would become crucial for the
nuances of later confessions. He distinguished the originals ("without error most perfect") from translations ("humane," the work of
"ordinary men"), and he distinguished the "character" (or "tong,"
form) from the "matter" ("substance," principally theology). Not all
of the early confessions had separate articles on scripture, however.
In 1610 John Smyth wrote his "Short Confession of Faith in XX
Articles," but there is no article on scripture in this confession.[22]

The sequence of topics in the Baptist confessions of faith is significant also. The confession Thomas Helwys (ca. 1570–ca. 1615) wrote shortly after he separated from John Smyth contained twenty-seven articles, and the article on scripture is number 23, placed after the statements on the Trinity, Christ, salvation, the church, and other topics. Moreover, the statement emphasizes the function of scripture and its witness to Christ, echoing 2 Timothy 3:16-17 and John 5:39: "The Scriptures off Old and New Testaments are written for our instruction" and hence "wee ought to search them for they testifie off Christ" and should be used "withall reverence, as conteyning the Holie Word off God, which onlie is our direction in al thinges whatsoever."[23] The "Holie Word off God" is apparently a reference to the gospel or the preaching of Jesus Christ. *The Standard Confession* (1660) of the General Assembly of General Baptists also places the article on scripture late in the sequence (article 23): the Bible "is the rule whereby Saints both in matters of Faith and conversation [conduct] are to be regulated."[24]

It was not until the *Second London Confession* (1677, 1688) of Particular Baptists (influenced by the Westminster Confession) that the term "infallible" appeared in reference to scripture, and there it is not used in reference to the inspiration of scripture but describes the function of the Bible in guiding us to salvation. The *Second London Confession* was written as a response to persecution of dissenters from the Church of England. Because the Presbyterians had escaped the brunt of this persecution, the Particular Baptists followed the *Presbyterian Westminster Confession* wherever they could. The latter began not with the nature of God, as had previous Baptist confessions, but with ten articles on scripture. These the Baptists adopted, adding as an introduction to the first article of the statement that "the Holy Scripture is the only sufficient, certain, and *infallible* rule of all saving Knowledge, Faith, and Obedience."[25] Later in the statement on scripture, the "matter" of the Scriptures is the first of eight reasons why the Bible is the Word of God: "We may be moved and induced by the testimony of the Church of God, to an high and reverent esteem of the Holy Scriptures; and the heavenliness of the matter."[26] The *Second London Confession* placed scripture references in the margins "for proof of what is asserted by us" in the hope that all who read the confession might follow the example "of the noble Bereans, who searched the Scriptures daily that they might find out whether the things preached to them were so or not."[27]

Early American Baptists reflected the mix of General and Particular Baptist convictions of the English Baptists. Confessions were slow to gain widespread acceptance among the early American Baptists. The *Philadelphia Confession* (1742) preserved the language of the first article of the *Second London Confession*. During the revivals of the Great Awakening, new converts often separated from the established churches and required conversion prior to baptism. The Separate Baptists of the Sandy Creek tradition returned to the pattern of Baptist confessions prior to the *Second London Confession* by devoting the first article to God. The second article of the *Principles of Faith of the Sandy Creek Association* (1816) dropped the term "infallible," declaring "that the Scriptures of the Old and New Testament are the word of God, and the only rule of faith and practice."[28]

By 1830 the views of Baptists in New Hampshire had shifted from the Calvinism espoused by the *Philadelphia Confession*, and the New Hampshire Convention commissioned the drafting of a more acceptable statement of faith. The poetic language of the New Hampshire "Declaration of Faith" (1833) insured that it would become the most influential of the eighteenth and nineteenth-century Baptist confessions. It again placed the statement on scripture first and the statement on God second, following the order of the Reformed confessions. The article on scripture set the pattern for the *Baptist Faith and Message* statements of 1925 and 1963, affirming:

> We believe the Holy Bible was written by men divinely inspired, and is a perfect treasure of heavenly instruction; that it has God for its author, salvation for its end, and truth, without any mixture of error, for its matter; that it reveals the principles by which God will judge us; and therefore is, and shall remain to the end of the world, the true centre of Christian union, and the supreme standard by which all human conduct, creeds, and opinions should be tried.[29]

Close comparison with earlier statements will show that the *New Hampshire Confession* omits the term "infallible" that was used in the *Second London* and the *Philadelphia* confessions. Instead, it echoes the insistence of John Smyth on the inspiration of the human authors of scripture and the distinction between form and matter.

G. Hugh Wamble, in a definitive exposition of the article on scripture, traced the affirmation that the Bible "has God for its author, salvation for its end, and truth, without any mixture of error, for its matter" back to a letter written by John Locke (1632–1704), the English philosopher. Although Locke was an Anglican, he was sympathetic toward the Protestant dissenters. In a letter dated August 25, 1703, commending the study of scripture, especially the New Testament, to a young clergyman named Richard King, Locke wrote:

> Therein are contained the words of eternal life. *It has God for its author; salvation for its end; and truth, without any mixture of error for its matter.* So that it is a wonder to me, how any one professing Christianity, that would seriously set himself to know his religion, should be in doubt what to employ his search, and lay out his information; when he knows a book where it is all contained, pure and entire; and whither at last, every one must have recourse, to verify that of it, which he finds any-where else.[30]

Emphasis on matter as distinct from form, a distinction rooted in English philosophy, reaching back to Plato, and mediated to Baptist confessions by the language of John Locke, thereby became an enduring feature of Baptists statements on the nature of scripture.[31]

The influence of the *New Hampshire Confession* is a remarkable story in itself. J. Newton Brown, the primary author of this confession, added articles on "Repentance and Faith" and "Sanctification" and published it in *The Baptist Church Manual* in 1853. Because it lacked a statement on the universal church, the *New Hampshire Confession* was popular among Landmark Baptists, and J. M. Pendleton published it in his *Church Manual* in 1867. The *New Hampshire Confession* was also printed in early Bulletins of the Southwestern Baptist Theological Seminary. In 1933 the General Association of Regular Baptist Churches adopted the confession.[32]

The Abstract of Principles of the Southern Baptist Theological Seminary (1858), written primarily by Basil Manly, Jr., reflects the influence of the *Second London* and *Philadelphia* confessions, but substitutes the term "authoritative" for "infallible": "The scriptures of the Old and New Testaments were given by inspiration of God, and are the only sufficient, certain, and authoritative rule of all saving knowledge, faith, and obedience."[33]

In 1925, responding to the controversy over evolution and building on recent initiatives to build fraternal relations with Baptists around the world, the Southern Baptist Convention adopted the *Baptist Faith and Message*. The committee that prepared the statement, chaired by E. Y. Mullins, used the *New Hampshire Confession* as its basis, adding ten articles, omitting two, and modifying others. Only one significant change was made in the article on scripture—the first article. The *Baptist Faith and Message* (1925) added the adjective "religious" to affirm that the scope of biblical authority is limited to "religious opinions," or concerns of faith and practice, rather than the whole range of human knowledge:

> We believe the Holy Bible was written by men divinely inspired, and is a perfect treasure of heavenly instruction; that it has God for its author, salvation for its end, and truth, without any mixture of error, for its matter; that it reveals the principles by which God will judge us; and therefore is, and shall remain to the end of the world, the true centre of Christian union and the supreme standard by which all human conduct, creeds, and *religious* opinions should be tried.[34]

The lack of significant change in this article reflects the fact that there was little debate among Baptists about the nature of scripture. Attention was focused on other issues, and the implications of debate over the teaching of evolution had not yet been translated into differences in the ways in which factions articulated their views of scripture.

Responding to the controversy over the publication of *The Message of Genesis* by Ralph H. Elliott, the Southern Baptist Convention in 1962 commissioned the drafting of an updated confession of faith. The *Baptist Faith and Message* (1963) retained the introduction to the 1925 statement and reduced the number of articles from twenty-five to seventeen. The article on scripture was broken up into three sentences, and two significant statements (italicized below) were added.

> The Holy Bible was written by men divinely inspired and is *the record of God's revelation of Himself to man. It is* a perfect treasure

of *divine* instruction. It has God for its author, salvation for its end, and truth, without any mixture of error, for its matter. It reveals the principles by which God judges us; and therefore is, and shall remain to the end of the world, the true center of Christian union, and the supreme standard by which all human conduct, creeds, and religious opinions should be tried. *The criterion by which the Bible is to be interpreted is Jesus Christ.*[35]

The 1963 additions move the emphasis away from making the Bible the ultimate revelation. The Bible is "the record" of God's revelation, and Christ is the ultimate norm by which scripture is to be interpreted. Both added statements, therefore, serve to subordinate the authority of scripture to God's revelation in history and ultimately in the person and work of Jesus Christ. Once again, Baptists avoided attributing infallibility to the Scriptures, recognizing that the Bible was written by inspired but human writers and is "the record of God's revelation," a "perfect treasure of divine instruction." Baptists have therefore adopted a balanced statement that expresses their historic affirmation of the reliability, sufficiency, and purpose of scripture, using language that is rooted in the New Testament and in Baptist statements of faith reaching back to John Smyth.

Issues Related to Biblical Authority

Baptist confessional statements set a historical context for a Baptist theology of scripture, but taken by themselves they are inadequate. First, they are inadequate because these statements have always been set in the context of confessional statements about the sovereignty of God and the revelation of God in Jesus Christ. Second, a distinctively Baptist theology must relate the authority of scripture to the freedom and competence of the believer. The early Baptists dissented from the established church and separated from other groups over believer's baptism and the freedom of each person to read the Scriptures and pursue the truth as he or she saw it. The state could not dictate in matters of faith, and no believer should be bound by another's creed. Theologically, Baptists have held in tension two divergent emphases: a Calvinist emphasis on the perfection of God's self-revelation in scripture, especially evident in the *Second London* and *Philadelphia* confessions, and an Armenian emphasis on the "soul competence" of the believer guided by scripture and the illumination of the Holy Spirit.

The Baptist confessional statements also show that Baptists have regularly distinguished the form (or expression, or in John Smyth's language, the "tong") and the matter (or essence and meaning) of scripture. The more elevated Calvinist confessions almost led Baptists away from this important distinction. It remains important, however, because it frees Baptists from the futile exercise of attempting to maintain the truth of every geographical, cosmological, historical, or mathematical reference in the Bible. The Bible is authoritative in all matters of faith and doctrine, but not necessarily in other areas.

The distinction between form and matter and the insistence on emphasizing the inspiration of human authors rather than the infallibility of the text of scripture also free Baptists from the necessity to defend the perfection of hypothetical "original autographs." We may assume an "original autograph" for a Pauline epistle, for example, but it is much more difficult to define what an "original autograph" would mean for a book like Genesis or Psalms that is the end result of the compilation and revision of earlier documents, codes, and collections. The argument that inconsistencies and inaccuracies in our earliest manuscripts must not have been there in the "original autographs" undercuts the reliability of the text we do have. In fact, discoveries of more and more early manuscripts and advances in textual criticism mean that we can have great confidence in the reliability of the modern Greek and Hebrew texts of the Bible and the contemporary translations that are based on these texts.

The practical result of the strong, positive affirmations of the authority of scripture for faith and practice, the distinction of "truth for its matter," and the competence of the believer is that Baptists define and defend their beliefs on the basis of scripture. Differences of conviction on such issues as whether God created the world in seven twenty-four-hour days or through the process of evolution, or whether women can be ordained as deacons and ministers quickly expose differences in the ways in which Baptists of different persuasions interpret the Scriptures. Given the weight of different texts, we may ask: Are the texts understood to be literal descriptions or symbolic interpretations? Do the biblical accounts reflect accommodation to contemporary perspectives and under-standings (for example, the roles of husbands and wives), or do they set forth codes and rules for every time and culture? On questions such as these Baptists always have and always will differ. The differ-ences do not necessarily mean that one group has a higher regard for the authority of scripture than another, only that they read and interpret it differently. Here, the Baptist emphases on freedom of conscience, autonomy of the local church, and the importance of being open to correction by the community of believers are vital. The study of scripture, openness to the guidance of the Spirit, and fellowship and dialogue with other believers are all important in the quest for truth.

The Scriptures draw us to faith in Jesus Christ, but at various points all of us need to confess, "I just can't understand it—I try to, but I just can't." The perfection and illumination of scripture, on one side, are balanced by our sinfulness and lack of understanding on the other. The confession of the believer is always "This is a won-der. Once I was blind, but now I see!" Yet there is always more truth, some of which we cannot yet grasp or bear. In Christ and in com-munity, the Bible will continue to guide us in the journey of faith until we see not dimly but clearly and the "conviction of things not seen" becomes glory in the fellowship of God.

Notes

[1]For more detail, see Harry Y. Gamble, "Canon: New Testament," *The Anchor Bible Dictionary* (New York: Doubleday, 1992)1:852-61.

[2]C. Clifton Black, "Serving the Food of Full-Grown Adults: Augustine's Interpretation of Scripture and the Nurture of Christians," *Interpretation*, 52, 4 (1998) 347.

[3]Jack Rogers, ed., *Biblical Authority* (Waco TX: Word, 1977) 21-22, citing A. D. R. Polman, *The Word of God According to St. Augustine*, trans. A. J. Pomerans (Grand Rapids: Wm. B. Eerdmans, 1961) 59-60.

[4]Rogers, 22, citing Augustin Pea, *The Study of the Synoptic Gospels*, English version ed. Joseph A. Fitzmyer (New York: Harper & Row, 1965) 59.

[5]Eric W. Gritsch, "The Cultural Context of Luther's Interpretation," *Interpretation*, 37 (1983) 266.

[6]Thomas D. Parker, "The Interpretation of Scripture: I. A Comparison of Calvin and Luther on Galatians," *Interpretation*, 17 (1963) 61-75.

[7]"Preface to the Latin Writings," *Luther's Works*, 34:337.

[8]Scott H. Hendrix, "Luther Against the Background of the History of Biblical Interpretation," *Interpretation*, 37 (1983) 234.

[9]Willem Jan Kooiman, *Luther and the Bible*, trans. John Schmidt (Philadelphia: Muhlenberg Press, 1961) 237.

[10]Roland Bainton, "The Bible in the Reformation," *Cambridge History of the Bible*, vol. 3, *The West from the Reformation to the Present Day*, ed. S. L. Greenslade (Cambridge: Cambridge University Press, 1970) 3:37.

[11]Hendrix, 236.

[12]Basil Hall, "Biblical Scholarship: Editions and Commentaries," *The Cambridge History of the Bible*, 3:88.

[13]Parker, 74-75.

[14]John Calvin, *Hebrews and the First and Second Epistles of St. Peter*, trans. William B. Johnston, ed. D. W. and T. F. Torrance (Grand Rapids: Wm. B. Eerdmans, 1963) 136, cited by Rogers, 28.

[15]T. H. L. Parker summarized Calvin's view of the nature of scripture as follows: "The creatureliness of the Bible is no hindrance to hearing God's Word but rather the completely necessary condition." *John Calvin: A Biography* (Philadelphia: Westminster Press, 1975) 77, quoted by Rogers, 29.

[16]H. Leon McBeth, *A Sourcebook for Baptist Heritage* (Nashville: Broadman, 1990) 504.

[17]Ibid.

[18]Robert G. Torbert, *A History of the Baptists* (Valley Forge PA: Judson Press, 1963) 35-37.

[19]John Smyth, *Differences*, ch. 7; McBeth, 16.

[20]Ibid., ch. 8; McBeth, 16.

[21]Ibid., ch. 8; McBeth, 17.

[22]For the text, see William L. Lumpkin, *Baptist Confessions of Faith*, rev. ed. (Valley Forge PA: Judson Press, 1969) 100-101.

[23]Thomas Helwys, "A Declaration of Faith of English People . . ."; Lumpkin, 122.

[24]Lumpkin, 232.

[25]James Leo Garrett, Jr., "Biblical Authority According to Baptist Confessions of Faith," *Review and Expositor*, 76, 1 (1979) 45-46; Lumpkin, 248.

[26]Lumpkin, 250.

[27]Ibid., 246.

[28]Ibid., 358.

[29]Ibid., 361-62.

[30]Leter, Locke to Richard King, August 25, 1703, *The Words of John Locke, in Ten Volumes*, 11th ed. (London: W. Otridge and Son, 1812) 10:306, cited by G. Hugh Wamble, "The Background and Meaning of the 1963 Southern Baptist Articles of Faith on the Bible," *The Proceedings of the Conference on Biblical Inerrancy 1987* (Nashville: Broadman Press, 1987) 339.

[31]See further William L. Hendricks, "The Difference Between Substance (Matter) and Form in Relationship to Biblical Inerrancy," *The Proceedings of the Conference on Biblical Inerrancy 1987*, 481-89.

[32]William R. Estep, Jr., "Biblical Authority in Baptist Confessions of Faith, 1610-1963," *The Unfettered Word*, ed. Robison B. James (Waco TX: Word, 1987/Macon GA: Smyth & Helwys Publishing, Inc.,1994) 173.

[33]McBeth, 312.
[34]Ibid., 505.
[35]Ibid., 505.

Salvation
Brad Creed

The burden of being a Baptist falls on the issue of salvation. In numerous ways the theme of salvation permeates and defines the Baptist witness as a comprehensive expression of the new life in Christ. It seems as if all roads that run through the Baptist domain eventually lead back to the subject of salvation. The centrality of salvation to the Baptist identity is a key to understanding how a minority group of religious dissenters before the Revolutionary War could eventually become the largest denomination in America. It also explains, in part, the fervor and passion with which Baptists approach almost anything, including their conflicts and disagreements.

The doctrine of salvation is connected to all of the other major beliefs that define Baptists. The Baptist accent on salvation is linked inextricably to their view of the church. Baptists are tenacious in their commitment to a believer's church comprised only of those who freely and personally profess their faith in Jesus Christ. Since Baptists believe that the saved are called out of the mass of humanity into a covenant relationship with other believers in the church, they contend that Christian identity and citizenship are not coterminous. Baptists have been in the forefront of the struggle for religious liberty for all people. This witness for freedom is as much a concern for the salvation of sinners as it is a courageous stand for human rights. Religious faith, if it is to be genuine, is predicated upon a person's ability to make a free, uncoerced commitment to Christ.

The ordinance of baptism, which for Baptists is a prerequisite to membership in the believer's church, reflects the drama of salvation. Baptismal candidates are immersed beneath the waters and raised back up as a testimony to the death and resurrection of Jesus Christ. This mode of baptism is more than an act of covenant faithfulness. It also is a witness to the power of salvation that ushers the new Christian from the spiritual bondage and death of sin into the newness of life in God's kingdom. The burden of salvation among Baptists is the spark that has lighted many fires of revival and ignited a passion for proclaiming the gospel and winning the lost to Christ. It has been the impetus for the zeal in sending and supporting foreign missionaries in unparalleled numbers to distant lands and foreign cultures where people have never before heard about the gift of abundant and eternal life through Jesus Christ.

The burden of being a Baptist somehow returns repeatedly to the subject of salvation. This was the essence of the faith I learned as a child growing up in a Baptist church and the heart of the Christian faith that I continue to affirm today as an adult.

As children in the Baptist church, we talked about it among ourselves, memorizing verses for Bible drill contests that outlined the plan of salvation. We were also keenly aware of those among us who had and had not yet made their professions of faith. For those of us who had not, we approached the semiannual revival meetings with both longing and dread. This could be the year when those who had not yet made their professions of faith might be saved. The evangelists who held the meetings were spellbinding, impassioned orators. With mere words fervently spoken, they opened the glories of heaven to their listeners and drew us into the stark gravity and sobering reality of human sinfulness. When they preached of the judgment awaiting the lost, hell was so hot you could feel the flames licking at your heels. Even after I had made my profession of faith and knew that my salvation was secure—for most Baptists believe in "once saved, always saved"—I gripped the back of the pew during the invitation time of those revival meetings until my knuckles turned white. I hoped that somehow I would have the strength to hang on and not fall into the fiery abyss that was so vividly being described. Saturday nights of the revivals were when the evangelist customarily preached on the second coming of Christ. More people gave their hearts to the Lord on those nights than any others. These revivals were main events in the Baptist life of my childhood and youth. All other local church activities throughout the year were either preamble or postlude. Our mission as a church was to seek and save the lost.

There were many other ways in which salvation was portrayed as the soul of the Baptist faith. The majority of the hymns we sang were about salvation. Among the more popular were "Amazing Grace," "At Calvary," "Nothing But the Blood," and "Saved, Saved," In Vacation Bible School every summer we all knew that the most important day was not Monday, the day on which Bible School began, but Thursday, when the preacher would share with all of the older children how they could be saved. As a youth, I was taught how to present the plan of salvation and witness to my lost friends.

Missions always occupied a hallowed place in my Baptist consciousness. Missionaries were heroes for Baptists. Since Baptists do not have saints, missionaries were about as close as we would come to canonizing anyone. We respected our preachers, but we revered our missionaries. They had given all, forsaking comfort and security, to travel to distant lands and live in strange cultures for the sole purpose of winning the lost to Christ.

The Baptist worship services I knew were strong on preaching and rich with spirited music, but we all knew that the time of the service when the power and blessing of God was most likely to be evident was the invitation. The invitation to come to Christ was the apogee of the worship service. This was the time when the Spirit would convict people of sin, touch the hearts of the lost, and prod sinners to take the step of faith that, for Baptists, was a literal step taken in walking down the aisle to grip the hand of the preacher as you gave your heart to Jesus.

The burden and blessing of being a Baptist for me is still about salvation. Two-week revival meetings are now rare, and we sing a greater variety of hymns (and praise choruses) that reflect other dimensions of Christian worship and living. Salvation has a life, so to speak, beyond the moment of conversion. The subject of salvation is still heart and soul about what it means to be a Baptist. My own understanding of salvation has not varied, only broadened and hopefully deepened. Since my own conversion at Royal Ambassador camp when I was eleven years old, I have grown in my understanding that salvation is not just a crisis experience at a fixed point in time. It is a comprehensive experience that affects the totality of human existence. Salvation is about our life in Christ.

While Baptists throughout their history have often stressed the climactic moment of decision that ushers a lost soul into the Kingdom, salvation has past, present, and future dimensions. Salvation is both individual and communal in its outcome. It influences specific and holistic aspects of life, and is both particular and cosmic in its ramifications. Salvation is one, unified, redemptive action of God from eternity, throughout time, and unto eternity. There are various aspects of salvation that can be examined specifically in order to gain a greater understanding and appreciation for

God's work in our world and lives. Discussions of salvation usually move towards the order of salvation (*ordo salutis*), which is the systematic arranging of the personal elements of salvation. This approach addresses such questions, for example, as how regeneration, justification, sanctification, and glorification are related to each other. The liability of this method of examination is that isolating one element could minimize the fullness and richness of salvation and force an artificial framework of understanding upon a marvelously dynamic and ultimately mysterious reality. While such a drawback should be pondered, it is almost impossible not to think about salvation in an orderly and considered fashion. This does no injury to our experience and understanding of salvation as long as we insist that the disparate elements of the order of salvation find their center and coherence in Christ. Examining phases or stages of salvation is helpful in our attempts to describe and understand something so grand and lofty in terms of everyday human existence.

Salvation is God's gracious gift of forgiveness. It is God's loving solution to the ongoing and insidious predicament of human sinfulness. Jesus Christ, through his death and resurrection, makes available God's forgiveness to the repentant sinner who turns from his former patterns of living and embraces the gift of new life in Christ. This new life, once accepted and received, initiates a renewal of all things and brings about regeneration. In the Baptist understanding of salvation, this renewing, regenerating work of the Spirit is often recognized as the experience of conversion.

The agent for regeneration is the Holy Spirit who brings us into a saving relationship with God through the work established by Jesus Christ the Son. The Spirit's application of this regenerating work is often portrayed through the image of the new birth (John 3:1-8). Just as a physical birth brings us into a new family as children, our spiritual birth means that we become sons and daughters of God. This new and miraculous beginning of spiritual life marks our inclusion into the family of God and enables us to enjoy a restored relationship with the one who created us. Whereas sin had alienated us from God our Creator, salvation brings us into a renewed understanding of God and how we are to relate to God. Formerly, we were God's enemies. Through the miracle of regeneration, we are now members of God's family. The Spirit applies the reconciling work of Christ to transform our enmity towards God into fellowship with God.

Just as God brings us into a new relationship through regeneration, God also grants us a new standing. We are justified through salvation so that God declares or considers us as righteous. This new standing through salvation is not achieved by our obedience to the law of God. There is nothing that can earn or merit this new standing given to us. Justification is not a reference to our virtue or quality of character or the respectability we have earned in being good, civil people who keep our word and perform our duties admirably. There is no prerequisite requirement that we may or must complete in order to be considered as candidates worthy of being in good standing with God. The Bible, in fact, states that all of our righteous acts are like filthy rags when compared to the righteousness God offers to us in Christ (Isa 64:6; Rom 3:10-12).

Justification is God's response to the predicament of human sinfulness. God is most righteous, not in condemning us for being sinners, but in justifying us in spite of our being sinners. God declares us to be righteous and credits the righteousness of Christ to our benefit. As violators of God's law and those who fall painfully and miserably short of God's holy standards, we are guilty and deserving of condemnation. But as we respond through faith to God's gracious reaching out to us, our guilt and condemnation are replaced with acquittal and acceptance.

Salvation is a great message of freedom. Human sinfulness results not only in alienation and condemnation, but also in enslavement or bondage. Sin is a degenerating and dehumanizing force that mars the image of God in humans and lowers their dignity. It brings guilt, anguish, remorse, and unrest. Like the terrible effects of an addiction, sin also shackles persons to a force they cannot shake. This bondage enslaves people, destroying their potential and usefulness, causing untold suffering and pain. It also ruins relationships with others and exacerbates human misery. This predicament is indeed a desperate and dismal one from which no apparent rescue or relief is readily available. Depravity means that each person inevitably chooses to rebel against the way of life established by God. Diabolical and hostile forces under the superintendence of Satan are at work to thwart every attempt we make for good and to defeat us. To intensify the dilemma, we are

ultimately unable to conquer these powers or to change the forces
of sin we have unleashed in our own lives or to avoid the consequences of those forces. There must be a rescue from this sin and a
liberation from the evil powers that seek to destroy us.

The good news of salvation is that Jesus Christ is victorious over
the forces of sin and evil. By conquering sin, death, and Satan, he
releases those who are in bondage. Conversion mediates this liberation, and the indwelling Spirit counters the control of sin in our
lives and enables us to reject sin and choose God's will. This freedom is a gift, just as our new relationship and new standing are gifts
from God.

The freedom of salvation is liberty from bondage and the ways
of death. It is also a freedom for obedience to God. Christ not only
releases captives, but also points them in a new direction, toward
God. Through salvation there is another way to live and realize our
destinies. God's freedom allows us to fulfill the purpose for which
we are created, namely, to manifest the love and embodied reality of
Christ in our daily lives. Salvation removes the tyranny of evil and
establishes a new orientation so that we might fulfill our destinies as
believers. Salvation also provides the resources and means for following Christ and living as his servants. In salvation we are given
spiritual power to do what God calls us to do. Jesus promised this
power to his disciples with the coming of the Sprit (John 14:15-31).
The apostle Paul stated that the same power that raised Christ from
the dead is living in us and giving life to our mortal bodies (Rom
8:11). This empowering is not just freedom to achieve new levels of
accomplishment and personal feats we never experienced prior to
salvation. It is the free empowering of the Spirit to pursue the purposes of God for God's people. Paradoxically, the freedom that
Christ grants us is a new form of slavery. As saved people, we are
now slaves to righteousness and are free only to the extent that we
live in bondage to Christ. Our freedom is not the liberty to do as we
please; it is the freedom to follow Christ wherever he leads us.
Christ's freedom is the freedom for discipleship.

The ongoing experience or process of salvation in the life of the
believer is often referred to as sanctification. Beyond conversion, or
the inauguration of salvation, salvation is the living out of the
reality of the new relationship to God established through the
regenerating work of the Spirit. It is living in the freedom for service

bestowed through Christ's liberating death and resurrection. Sanctification describes the dynamics and dimensions of discipleship as we grow in God's grace and seek to fulfill the purpose for which we were created and saved by God.

Baptists have tended to emphasize the inauguration of salvation, stressing heavily the justification aspect of the salvation experience. In so doing, they have often neglected a proper focus on the ongoing reality of salvation, which is sanctification. This unbalanced emphasis is due, in part, to the strong revivalist tradition in Baptist life with its attendant stress on conversion and winning the souls of the lost. The neglect of sanctification also reflects a theological dilemma in Baptist life over the work of God and the role of the believer in salvation. From their very beginnings, Baptists exhibited somewhat of a split personality over this issue. The General Baptists, who believed in a general atonement, or that Christ died for the sins of all people, stressed the freedom of the human will in salvation. Their counterparts and contemporaries, the Particular Baptists, whose Calvinistic views of the atonement asserted that Christ's death was limited or particular to the elect, magnified the sovereignty, power, and initiative of God in salvation.

Baptists have agreed that salvation is by grace alone and received through faith, which is obedient trust in Christ as God's provision for salvation. Baptists have also further agreed that no human accomplishment or effort earns salvation or makes salvation contingent. Where they have disagreed is over the role of the human will and the human response to salvation. These differences are not relegated to questions about the election, foreknowledge, and foreordination of God. They also impact considerations of sanctification. Sanctification is impossible without the continuing assistance and operation of grace in the life of the Christian. The Christian is also responsible for working out his/her salvation in fear and trembling—which is not the same thing as working for one's salvation. If the initiative for salvation rests with God prior to any human response, what, then, is the proper human response in cooperating with the Spirit so that we grow in Christlikeness as disciples?

Both divine and human aspects are inseparable in comprehending sanctification. Salvation is life, specifically, life in Christ. Sanctification is the process by which the believer daily wins the battle with sin over his life by yielding himself to God's grace in the power of the Spirit. It is the process of becoming more like Christ and being able to know and to do the will of God.

There are several aspects of sanctification that give it meaning and integrity. Fundamentally, sanctification is rooted in the holiness of God. God as the Holy One is distinct from His creation and uncontaminated by sin and imperfection. The admonition for Christians to be holy is rooted in the nature and purpose of the God who entrusts His people to reflect His reality in the world where they live. As a corollary to holiness, sanctification means to be set apart for a distinctive and special purpose. Christians have been saved for a mission. Like the "saints," or believers, in the New Testament, Christians are set apart. They have a new standing in Christ, which they received by faith. As Christians, they will grow in grace and bear the fruit of the Spirit. In brief, being one of God's saints entails a new quality, character, and conduct of life.

Sanctification is the ongoing experience of salvation in the believer's life. In writing to the Christians at Philippi, the apostle Paul admitted that he had not yet obtained all of the Christian life to which he aspired or that he had already been made perfect. He described his experience as pressing on "toward the goal to win the prize for which God has called me heavenward in Christ Jesus" (3:12-13). Baptists have generally resisted the impulse to perfectionism as a goal for the Christian life. In contrast to the Wesleyan doctrines of entire sanctification and the insistence that sanctification can conceivably culminate in this life, Baptists consistently declare that the process of sanctification is ongoing and unfinished until we complete the race that Paul describes. The ultimate fulfillment of salvation awaits the believer's glorification when he is in the presence of God.

Dallas Willard, a Baptist, wrote in his book, *The Divine Conspiracy*, of the "golden triangle" of spiritual growth.[1] Three interdependent and interlocking factors are involved in the transformation of Christians in their growth into Christlikeness. The activity of the Holy Spirit (John 3:5; Rom 8:10-13; Gal 5:22-26) empowers us to do the kinds of works Jesus did and to grow the kind of inward character that manifests itself in the fruit of the Spirit in our outward living. The ordinary events of life or "trials" (Jas 1:2-4; Rom 5: 1-5) form the second angle of the correlation.

Sanctification occurs nowhere if it does not occur in the midst of daily life where we dwell with God and neighbors. We learn to accept the circumstances of life as the places where we can experience the reality and blessings of God's kingdom. The last angle is the efforts we make in our own transformation (Col 3:12-17; 2 Pet 1:5-10). These are spiritual disciplines designed to help us to be effective in the spiritual realm of the heart, now spiritually alive by grace, in relation to God and his kingdom.

Willard's approach to the ongoing process of salvation is to emphasize both the action of the Spirit and our accompanying response. Mere confidence in what the Spirit is doing within us is inadequate for bringing the transformation of life God desires. The Christian life does not occur in a vacuum, and our engaging response to the presence of God's active grace is indispensable for faithful discipleship. Salvation is a life, and salvation has no essential or experiential meaning unless it is an embodied experience beyond a divine decree issued before the foundation of time.

Sanctification is a divine work and an active human response that yields our "growing in the grace and knowledge of our Lord Jesus Christ" (2 Pet 3:18). Our striving on this journey of faithfulness is a compelling pursuit that will not relinquish us and a magnificent obsession that will never be fully possessed in this life. Progress is often difficult and sometimes painful, but it is possible as we are empowered by the indwelling Holy Spirit to complete the course set before us.

Salvation also entails incorporation, specifically the believer's incorporation into a new community. The salvation of lost people is a strategic means for God accomplishing the encompassing purpose of creating a new people. The gospel is a message of hope and salvation for creating new persons in Christ. It is also a message of salvation for creating a new people in Christ. A redeemed community is the goal of salvation, so that we who are in Christ are no longer foreigners and aliens to one another, but instead are "fellow citizens with God's people and members of God's household" (Eph 2:19). In Christ, God chooses us to be incorporated into a royal priesthood, a holy nation, a people belonging to God (1 Pet 2:9).

According to Baptist theologian Stanley Grenz, the proper orientation for understanding God's plan and purpose in salvation is not the unfathomable past of eternity. Instead, the primary emphasis for this purpose "is the choseness we enjoy as a people in Christ to participate in God's program in history."[2] Central to our understanding of salvation is incorporation into the people of God.

Baptists champion the believer's or gathered church. The church as the people of God is comprised of baptized believers who profess their faith in Christ and join with other professing believers in a covenant relationship for worship, ministry, and service. While Baptists do not link church membership or the rite of baptism to the act of salvation, they hold that the natural, necessary, and expected progression in the witness to God's great salvation is incorporation into a community of believers who are bound together in a covenant relationship of love and faithfulness. The practice of believer's baptism is not just the next practical step required for being received into the membership of a local congregation. It is a witness to the authenticity of salvation, an important and necessary step in God's purpose of creating a new community of redeemed people who bear witness to the eternal reality of God's kingdom.

God's creation of a new people is yet another reflection of the righteousness of God in salvation. This is not solely the righteousness that comes from a right standing with God. It is the righteousness of living in communal faithfulness through a right relationship with others, thus fulfilling the intention of the Great Commandment (Matt 22:37-40). Incorporation enables the believer to participate in the Great Commission with other believers in faithful witness thus extending the offer of God's salvation to all nations (28:18-20). Incorporation as a dimension of salvation is a trinitarian reality. Our covenant with the redeemed people of God reflects the undisturbed and heavenly communion of the Godhead that lives eternally in relationship as Father, Son, and Holy Spirit. Incorporation into the community of saints is a foretaste in time of the full fellowship that we will enjoy in the new creation and with the saints from all ages at the end of time.

Salvation will reach its completion in the experience of glorification. Those whom God justifies, God will glorify (Rom 8:30). God's eternal and unfolding plan in history will triumph, and the saints of God who persevere to the end through the trials, tribulations, and testings of time will be saved. Those who are in Christ will finish the course, complete the race, and receive the crown of righteousness promised by God (2 Tim 4:8). The experience of glorification will bring a comprehensive transformation of our existence and of all of creation. On the day that is assured by God, the journey of salvation will be finished, and when we see Christ, we shall be like him (1 John 3:2).

The transformation will encompass our character and nature entirely. Sin will be completely rooted out and extinguished, and our desire will be one of perpetual praise and worship before the heavenly throne of God. The physical and emotional dimensions of our lives will be changed. In glory, there will be no more pain or decay, no more sadness or loneliness. The greatest human enemy, death, will be defeated utterly. We will be in the presence of Christ along with the angelic hosts and all of the saints, an eternal fellowship in Christ throughout time and across the ages.

In our human undertaking to describe salvation, we usually focus on how we experience salvation in our pilgrimage as the people of God. Describing the various stages or phases is helpful in our attempts to bring lofty and inspiring concepts into the realm of our everyday experience. In so doing, we catch a glimpse of the wonder and majesty of salvation. The salvation of the Lord gives us great hope and assurance in the living of our days. We look forward with eager expectation to the end of time when salvation will be fulfilled ultimately and finally. From the standpoint of eternity, however, salvation is a unified movement, holistic and comprehensive in its operation and unfolding. It is a gift beyond measure from the initiative of the Triune God—Father, Son and Holy Spirit.

Notes

[1]Dallas Willard, *The Divine Conspiracy* (San Francisco: Harper & Row, 1998) 346-48.

[2]Stanley Grenz, *Theology for the Community of God* (Nashville: Broadman & Holman, 1994) 591. See also Grenz's article "Salvation and God's Program in Establishing Community," *Review and Expositor*, 91,4 (1994) 505-20.

The Church

T. Furman Hewitt

What is the church? We think we know, but are we aware of how many possible answers there are?

The bank officer who was finalizing my house loan asked my occupation. I replied that I am a minister. "What denomination?" she asked. "Baptist." She then wrote on the form: "minister of the Baptist church." Clearly, her understanding of Baptists was that we comprise some large, inclusive organization labeled as a "church" that has numerous offices in local communities. Understandably, but wrongly, she assumed that my Baptist version of the "church" was similar to that of the Lutheran Church, the Episcopal Church, the Roman Catholic Church and others so organized. A church, in this view, is a national or international body, highly organized and having specific doctrines, standards for admission, and the power to ordain the clergy who are in charge of that church.

The radio announcer breaks in with a bulletin: "The church on the corner of Main and Elm is burning. The fire department asks that you stay away from this area." The announcer, like most people in our culture, equates the term "church" with a particular building, a structure capable of burning. Haven't we all seen buildings with signs in front identifying them as the First Baptist Church or Trinity Episcopal Church? A church is a building.

Are there other ways of viewing the church? There is a way more characteristic of the Baptist community that this particular Baptist will outline. I do not claim that all Baptists would agree with this Baptist, but I do hope that what follows is faithful to the larger Baptist history and tradition.[1]

Definition

In 1611 a group of the earliest Baptists led by Thomas Helwys described their understanding of the church.

> [T]he Church of Christ is a company of faithful people … separated from the world by the word and Spirit of God … being knit unto the Lord and one unto another by Baptism … upon their own confession of the faith … and sins ….

[T]hough in respect of Christ, the Church be one ... yet it consists of different particular congregations ... [each] of which
congregation[s], though [the members] be but two or three, have
Christ given to them, with all the means of their salvation ...
[Each of which] [is] the Body of Christ ... and a whole Church.[2]

So, according to these early Baptists, what is the church? It is a
"company of faithful people" who have been called apart by God
and who have confessed their faith and sins.

In 1611 this was a somewhat radical perspective put forward by
early Baptists, for they were projecting a very different understanding of the church from the church then in position of authority and
influence in England or even on the continent. A lot is packed into
this understanding of the church.

We should note that in this understanding of the church, it is
not a building and not really an organization—certainly not an
organization on a grand scale. Equally important, we must add, is
the fact that the church is not to be identified with its clergy. Not
that clergy are unimportant; all tasks in God's church are important. It is just that the church goes on even if there are not clergy.
Thomas Helwys said that the church community ought to come
together to pray, hear the word preached, and administer the ordinances even if they have no clergy ("officers") or if their clergy are
in prison.[3] Therefore, the ordained ministry is useful but not
essential to the Baptist community

What is the church? *The church is God's creation. The church
exists not of its own accord but at the initiative of God.* The church is
a company of faithful believers whose reason for being is that they
have been called apart by God. The church is the result of God's
gracious acts on behalf of the people whom God has chosen. This
initiative began with the selection of the community of Israel and
the covenant made with them. Most of all, however, the church is
the result of God's initiative in the life, ministry, death, and resurrection of Jesus of Nazareth. His life ushered in the hoped-for
kingdom of God. Those who responded to the meaning of his life
and who identified in faith and trust with his death and resurrection were given eternal life—more accurately, the life of the ages or
the age-to-come. They live with one foot in the kingdom, and life is
different because of God's initiative. As the writer of 1 John said, it

is "not that we loved God but that he loved us and sent his Son to be the atoning sacrifice for our sins" (4:10).

As the creation of God, the church is God's people in the same way that Israel had been God's people. As Paul wrote to the church in Galatia, "If you belong to Christ, then you are Abraham's offspring, heirs according to the promise" (Gal 3:29). However, Israel had seemingly forfeited its place as the people of God, so they became the new Israel, partners with God in the new covenant made in and through the life, death, and resurrection of Jesus the Christ (cf. Luke 22:20; 2 Cor 3:6; Heb 9:15).

As God's new people, the church becomes the place and perhaps even the engine of encounter between God and God's people. In other words, the church is the new temple, replacing the temple that dominated the skyline of Jerusalem. As Paul wrote to the church in Corinth: "You are God's temple and . . . God's Spirit dwells in you" (1 Cor 3:16) and "We are the temple of the living God; as God said, 'I will live in them and move among them, and I will be their God, and they shall be my people'" (2 Cor 6:16).

Another way of saying that the church is the place where God and humankind meet is to follow up the implication of the familiar imagery that describes the church as the "body of Christ" (Rom 12:5; 1 Cor 12:27; Eph 4:12). According to John, it was the "temple of [Jesus's] body," not Herod's grand edifice, that "dwelt ('tented' like the tabernacle in the wilderness) among us" and would survive death to become the place where God's glory is seen and felt and known (John 1:14; 2:21-22). If Jesus, the meeting place between the divine and the human, now dwells in his church so that the church can be described as the "body of Christ," does it not make sense to look at the church as a "temple"? Here the risen Christ is encountered. It is because of Christ's living presence in the church that the church is gathered and empowered and that God is glorified.

As the body of Christ and as the new temple, it is evident that the church truly exists only when the Spirit of God is present. The presence of the living Christ is the necessary ingredient that makes a merely human organization into the body and temple of the living God. The church must be more than a place that preserves the memory of God's acts. It must be a place alive and vibrant with the power of God in its midst.

The church as created by God and empowered by the Spirit of God exists for one primary purpose: glorifying the God who brought it into being. To be more accurate, the church does not exist to perpetuate itself or to exalt its human members. It exists to glorify God through its worship and through its service to others.

Second, the church is a "company of faithful people." The church is a company; that is, the church is a gathering or community. The English word "church" is derived from the Greek word *kuriakos*, which means something "belonging to the Lord." From this Greek word comes, for example, words for church such as the German *Kirche* and the Scottish *kirk*. An equally profound concept of the church is found in the use of another Greek word, *ekklesia*, the primary meaning of which is an "assembly" or gathering of persons. This Greek word was used in the Septuagint to translate Hebrew terms describing the gathering of the people of Israel (e.g., Deut 9:10, where God spoke to Israel on the "day of the assembly"). *Synagoge* is another Greek word that translates the idea of Israel's assembling itself together, but for obvious reasons the New Testament writers did not want their new community identified with the Jewish synagogue. So the Christians used *ekklesia*, with its connotation of people gathering themselves together in a community for religious and social purposes, to describe the new assembly or community of the church.

A "company" means a gathering or a community that has been called together by God. That is what the church is. Buildings, if any, can be destroyed. The church as community continues. The church is really a community of people. This is why one Baptist church is right on target with a sign in front that reads: "THE CALVARY BAPTIST CHURCH MEETS HERE." It is clear that this church meant for the term "church" to equate the assembly or community of persons while the term "here" refers to the building. Typically, particularly in Paul's epistles, this word *ekklesia* is used to denote a specific group or groups of believers in an area or even in a household, such as the "church [*ekklesia*] of God that is at Corinth" (1 Cor 1:2) or the "churches [*ekklesiais*] of Galatia" (Gal 1:2). Occasionally, the same word can be used to denote the entire Christian community in a very large area, such as "the church throughout Judea, Galilee, and Samaria" (Acts 9:31). Here the community is not really a physical community—the people could not easily have known one another—but it is nevertheless a community in that they share something in common. They have the same experience with the risen Lord.

The more extensive use of *ekklesia* noted above means that the New Testament writers and our Baptist ancestors recognized that there was a sense in which the church transcended local boundaries. The biblical writers understood that the church was a local community, but there was also a sense in which the church was everywhere that believers were and included all believers. The writer of Ephesians implied that the church is more than a local entity when he spoke of God as having "put all things under [Christ's] feet and has made him the head over all things for the church" (1:22) and of Christ who "loved the church and gave himself up for her" (5:25). Paul had something more inclusive in mind than a local community when he advised Christians in Corinth not to give offense "to Jews or to Greeks or to the church of God" (1 Cor 10:32). Surely it was more than a local community that Jesus had in mind when he said, "You are Peter, and on this rock I will build my church, and the gates of Hades will not prevail against it" (Matt 16:18).

The *Second London Confession* of 1677 attempted to explain these two perspectives on the church by distinguishing between a universal church and particular congregations. The "invisible" or universal church is composed of the entire number of God's elect[4] —past, present, and future. The "visible" church is composed of persons now in the world who profess their faith in the gospel and are obedient to God. Of these "visible saints" is constituted "all particular congregations."[5]

What is it that transcends the local community of believers? Is it some larger, more inclusive and more powerful organization? When we speak of the church in universal terms, are we speaking of a large organization that is uniform in its doctrine, worship, and polity?

There are some whose dream of a worldwide ecumenical church includes some form of such a uniform organization. The Bible, however, does not speak of organizations, but of the reality of believers who happen to exist in widely separated areas. Our Baptist ancestors, in some instances, picked up the language of an "invisible" church composed of all believers from all time and a "visible" church composed of living believers who are gathered into several distinct congregations. No mention is made by Baptists of any organization of the larger "visible" church that would supersede the prerogatives and powers of the local congregation.

Thus, while we Baptists are quite prepared to talk of the priority of the local congregation, and even refer to it as a "church," we do so with the realization that there is a larger community of believers— not necessarily an organization, however—that also deserves the designation of "church."

Third, the church is a company of faithful people who have been baptized "upon their own confession of the faith and sins." In other words, the church is composed of persons who have sufficient maturity and awareness to have confessed "their own" faith and thus have been baptized. *The church is composed of mature believers.* Infants are not a part of the church because they are not and cannot be believers in any real sense of that word. Membership awaits the individual's personal decision to respond to the offer of God's grace and mercy by her own confession of her sins and her faith and trust in God's mercy. This cannot be done for the individual, even by parents. Confession and trust cannot be done by proxy.

This Baptist rejection of infant baptism/church membership and corresponding insistence on a personal response of faith was not understood or well-received in the seventeenth century. Insistence on baptism as a believer meant that many persons baptized as infants joined a Baptist congregation by undergoing baptism a second time, although they might well have argued that they were actually being truly baptized only for the first time. This second baptism was threatening to the state-approved church and the ceremony linked seventeenth century Baptists with the worst excesses of the radical Anabaptist regime at Munster in the 1630s. Moreover, the general public did not understand this Baptist rejection of infant baptism. It seemed to opponents that denying baptism to infants imperiled the salvation of the souls of those infants—a logical conclusion if one believes that baptism saves by virtue of the saving rite having taken place—and it seemed to opponents that rejecting infant baptism also threatened the stability of the state—a logical conclusion if one believes that church and state must be linked for the protection of each and that baptism is the expected entrance into and linkage with that church and state.

In response, Baptists insisted that church and state are best left apart (one could be a good citizen without a particular religious affiliation), that the eternal destiny of children is well-handled by the grace and mercy of God, and that a vital and meaningful church must of necessity be composed of persons who choose to be a part of that community. Baptism goes with that choice. As John Smyth said in 1609, baptism is the "external sign of the remission of sins, of dying and being made alive, and therefore does not belong to infants."[6]

Baptists, therefore, have from the beginning spoken of the necessity of regenerate church membership. Membership in the church is neither automatic nor inherited. It is by personal choice and upon demonstration of a life in which one attempts to live as a penitent, faithful person, as one who has been "separated from the world by the word and Spirit of God."

Sadly, it should be noted that the insistence on regenerate church membership has been applied with less and less vigor in the twentieth century as Baptists have, in the words of James Leo Garrett, "abandoned in practice what we have formerly advocated in principle."[7] How has this principle been abandoned?

First, by the lamentable practice of accepting into membership and baptizing younger and younger children. With the encouragement of concerned but ill-informed parents, pastors and evangelists pad their baptismal statistics with ever-younger subjects. It is not unusual to see children seven or eight years of age or even younger who are accepted into the church on the pious pretext that they truly understood what they were doing when they confessed their sins and spoke of trusting in the grace of God in Christ! This is not to say that such children do not have a childlike love of Jesus that has been cultivated in the home and in the church. It is very questionable, however, if such young children have any real comprehension of their lives and their need of divine grace.

Second, the principle of "regenerate church membership" has been abandoned by a failure to apply any examination of evidence of "regeneration" to individuals—children or adults—before admitting them to membership in the church. Persons who come forward to join a church or confess their faith are usually voted on and received into church membership at that hour. Even if they are voted upon at a later business meeting and even if their baptism is postponed to a more convenient time, it is very rare for such a vote or baptism to take into account a report of the candidate's character and spiritual striving. Typically, there is not a structure in the local church for making such an examination! The result is that Baptist churches are filled with the spiritually immature, with absentee members, and with persons whose moral standards reflect the ever-lowering standards of society at large.

The Mission of the Church

The church, the community of believers, has the overall task of praising God and of being salt and leaven within the world. The early church in Jerusalem was described as follows:

> They devoted themselves to the apostles' teaching and fellowship, to the breaking of bread and the prayers. Awe came upon everyone, because many wonders and signs were being done by the apostles. All who believed were together and had all things in common; they would sell their possessions and goods and distribute the proceeds to all, as any had need. Day by day, as they spent much time together in the temple, they broke bread at home and ate their food with glad and generous hearts, praising God and having the goodwill of all the people. And day by day the Lord added to their number those who were being saved. (Acts 2:42-47)

First and foremost, there is the necessity of believers' focusing collective attention on the praise of God. *Worship* is a priority.[8] Without common worship directed to the God who called the church into being, the church shrivels and dies because its reason for being is no longer the focus of the community, and the energy that such focus gives is lost. Worship of God for God's sake, not for what God will do for us, is the source of any additional activities the church may undertake.

As the text from Acts 2 indicates, the early church gave serious attention to the various facets of worship. Recognizing their links with the Israel of old, they attended the Temple services—note that they did so together—and were reminded of their ties to God's history of love and grace along with the promises that had been fulfilled. They prayed, perhaps, the prayers taught them in the Temple or in the synagogue. They studied the word of God by giving attention to the teaching of the apostles, listening to their accounts of the life and teaching of Jesus and to their interpretation of the sacred texts of Israel necessitated by the life, death, and resurrection of their Lord. They participated in "breaking of bread," which is probably a reference to a common meal that included a celebration of the Lord's Supper.

The renewal of church life in our time will take place only insofar as the membership of the church takes seriously the need for a collective life of worship and prayer.

The early church also reached out to its own membership and to the community around them. The sharing of their possessions with one another and the "signs and wonders" done by the apostles (perhaps including the wonder of healing as recounted in Acts 3:1-10) are hints of a community that found itself caught up in a larger mission both internally and to the world.

A second mission of the church is, therefore, the internal obligation of *education or edification.* The writer of Ephesians pointed to the varied gifts given to the church as having the purpose of equipping the saints and building up the body of Christ (4:12), while Paul notes that all things, including the spiritual gift of tongues, should be done for edification (1 Cor 14:26). This building up of the body of Christ through education and assisting the process of spiritual maturation could be done in several ways.

One approach to edification is through simple instruction. Jesus' disciples were to "teach" other converts to observe all the things Jesus had taught them (cf. Matt 28:20). Typically, this instruction was done by those recognized as pastors or teachers in the community of faith.[9] Instruction through sermons and through church education programs must still be a priority. Sermons, for example, should be measured by the extent to which they teach the congregation rather than whether or not they merely excite the congregation to new levels of feel-good emotion. Preachers should grow in the process of preparing to preach, with the success of their sermons measured by the number of persons who say, "I never realized that . . ." or "You made me think. I do not know if I agree, but you made me look at _____ in a new light." The sad picture of too many church communities is that of an earnest but poorly informed membership. The competition is keen for time and opportunities to educate both the young and the old in our congregations. But it is certain that the church must find a way to instruct, to move ourselves from milk to meat, to move ourselves beyond the level of mere emotion to the level of thoughtful maturity.

Edification also takes place through discipline. The discipline of an immoral individual noted in 1 Corinthians 5:1-13 was for the purpose of saving the immortal soul of the erring individual as well as for teaching the community as a whole lessons of moral behavior and the dangers of association with immoral persons. Again we must note with some sadness that the practice of discipline has virtually disappeared from church life. While one would not wish to reinstate an arbitrary or narrow-minded discipline, still it is clearly the case that the maturity of the church community and the reputation of the church in the nonbelieving world is hindered when discipline does not exist. A true church is a disciplined church!

Finally, edification takes place in the enriching and supportive matrix of the community itself. In the community, Christians bear one another's burdens by rejoicing and suffering together (cf. Gal 6:2; 1 Cor 12:26). "How they love one another," marveled those on the outside of the early church. Those inside knew, and still know, the grace of love. It is in the love and support of the fellowship—the community, the *koinonia*—that believers find the strength to endure and the courage to persevere. Edification and education and maturation take place when we are least aware, in the give and take of the community. The potential power of the community is precisely why the modern church must be wary of losing such a gift in a headlong rush to ever larger congregations. Bigger is not always better. Thomas Helwys was aware of this problem as far back as 1611. "Members of every . . . congregation ought to know one another, that so they may perform all the duties of love one towards another." That being the case, "a church ought not to consist of such a multitude as cannot have particular knowledge one of another."[10] If we were to take that advice seriously, it would revolutionize the trend of the modern church toward size. Ever larger size may seem to be efficient, but it is entirely possible that there is a point of diminishing returns with size. One of the things that is lost in size is community. Let us be clear that merely calling ones' congregation a "family" or building a "family life center" does not make community a reality. A church is a fellowship where the level of community is indicated by the fact that individuals truly know and care for one another with the result that they also lift the level of maturity for one another.

One external mission of the church was, and is, to *be evangelists, or proclaimers of the good news* of the grace of God. The early church regarded itself as under orders. "You will receive power when the Holy Spirit has come upon you; and you will be my witnesses in Jerusalem, in all Judea and Samaria, and to the end of the earth" (Acts 1:8). The church is the community of those who are expected to be witnesses to the good news of what God had done in Christ. They would have help, of course, the power of the Holy Spirit. But witness they must, even if it meant going great distances or among despised people—for example, the Samaritans. Evangelism does not depend on whether we like the other persons, but whether they, like the wounded man on the Jericho road, are neighbors who need our assistance and witness.

The history of missions movements in various Christian communities is a testimony of the power of this call to be witnesses even in situations requiring the highest level of sacrifice. I remember visiting the Protestant cemetery in Macau and marveling at the faith and courage and commitment of eighteenth- and nineteenth-century missionaries whose simple gravestones indicated they and their families had traveled thousands of miles only to die of disease in a strange land. Why endure such hardship? It is because of the obligation the church has to be evangelists.

The writer of 1 Peter said of the church:

> You are a chosen race, a royal priesthood, a holy nation, God's own people, in order that you may proclaim the mighty acts of him who called you out of darkness into his marvelous light. . . . Conduct yourselves honorably among the Gentiles, so that . . . they may see your honorable deeds and glorify God when he comes to judge. (2:9, 12)

The church, God's people, is to "proclaim the mighty acts of him who called you out of darkness." Who is it who is to declare this wonderful news? Preachers? No. It is the "people (*laos*) of God." It is everyone who is a part of this new people of God who bears the obligation of missions and evangelism. Just being a part of the church is sufficient to lay upon us all the collective task of missions. It has always been thus. New Testament scholar T. W. Manson once described the spread of the gospel in the first three centuries. It was not done, he said, by great preachers or eloquent propagandists who swayed mass audiences, but by the common people. Converts were won by "domestic servants teaching Christ in and through their domestic service, workers doing it through their work, small shopkeepers through their trade, and so on."[11]

It should be noted that the writer of 1 Peter expected that gentle and reverent apologies for the faith often might be in response to the questioning of unbelievers who called believers "to account for the hope" they had for the future (3:15). No doubt this happened more than once. If opportunities for sharing the faith seem scarce today, perhaps the problem is that there is not enough evident difference in the community of believers to warrant interest or inquiry from the outside. Perhaps the church must recover its sense of hope and expectation about what God can and will do before outsiders will pay us much attention.

It should also be noted that 1 Peter considered at times that the ignorant attacks of foolish persons were to be silenced not by words but by "doing right" (2:15). Whether by articulation of the faith or by just doing what is right, the task of being a witness belongs to all believers, and it is a task that can be done by even the most unlearned! The issue is not the level of training of the people of God, but the level of hope, the vision of what can be done with God's leadership, and the understanding that the ministry of evangelism belongs to the entire laity.

Another task of the church in mission is to *reach out to the world in service,* to be in the world as a healing and preserving element. This is not an obvious or easy task, for it requires balancing the ideals of remaining "separated from the world," as Thomas Helwys suggested in 1611, with the need for involvement. How do we remain holy while at the same time running the risk of dirtying our hands in the world as we attempt to serve?

Admittedly, Baptists have, in general, been better at being separated from the world than in being salt in the world. In 1651 Baptists in the Midlands of Great Britain spoke of the need for contributions "for the relief of those that cannot help themselves with food and raiment . . . especially those that are of the household of Faith."[12] The *Second London Confession* stated that the saints in the community of faith are under obligation to maintain the fellowship, to make efforts at mutual edification, and to "[relieve] each other in outward things according to their several abilities and necessities."[13] But nothing was said of the need to serve those outside the community of faith. Involvement in the larger community was not a priority in a Baptist community in the seventeenth century. Understandably, Baptists sometimes went out of their way to say that they were not involved in the affairs of this world, as when a group of Baptists in 1660 denied the report that certain Baptists in London were collecting knives and other arms with the intention of cutting the throats of anyone who was not a Baptist. The restoration of Charles II was imminent and it was in their best interests that Baptists not be seen as enemies of the state.[14] In other situations the very powerlessness of the Baptist community as well as the dominant focus on saving souls has tended to keep Baptists out of the public arena.

Since the seventeenth century, however, there have been exceptions to this early and ongoing Baptist aversion to profound social involvement. Martin Luther King, Jr., Walter Rauschenbusch, Mary Bonney, and Amelia Quinton[15] stand out as Baptists who attempted to be salt to the world they knew.

The dominant history of Baptists notwithstanding, Baptists ought to hold to a view of the church that runs the risk of involvement in the name of love and for the sake of service. How can the church be salt and leaven without contact and the risk of involvement? Dietrich Bonhoeffer, while not a Baptist, is an example of a person whose early tendencies toward noninvolvement could shift to the point of profound involvement. In Bonhoeffer's case, he shifted from the position of nonviolence to the point of involvement, at considerable risk, in an abortive attempt on Hitler's life. From prison prior to his execution, Bonhoeffer reflected on the "worldliness" that characterized his life. Rather than being shallow and self-indulgent, Bonhoeffer's view of worldliness meant abandoning attempts to make a righteous person of oneself. Instead, it meant embracing life with all "its duties and problems, its successes and failures, its experiences and helplessness." It is in such a life, said Bonhoeffer, that "we throw ourselves utterly in the arms of God and participate in his suffering in the world and watch with Christ in Gethsemane."[16]

If true to its calling to be the people of God, the church will find itself on the side of the poor, fighting for justice, questioning the powerful, demanding that the disenfranchised be heard. This will not, of course, be a popular stance. Nevertheless, one of the missions of the church is that we take up our crosses in order to follow the Lord of the church who carried his own cross.

Church Polity and the Role of Clergy

We have already indicated a preference for viewing the church as a community of believers, all of whom are called out and even gifted for some form of ministry to themselves and to the world. Yet we in the Baptist community have clergy just as do other Christian communities. What is or should be the role of clergy? And what part do clergy play in the governance or organization of the church? This question is often labeled as the question of church "polity." We will deal first with the question of polity, or organization.

Baptists have consistently opted for what may be called a democratic or congregational approach to organization. In the history of the church, three major approaches to organization have made an appearance. The "episcopal" approach finds continuity in the line of bishops and, to some degree, vests authority in those bishops. Typically, bishops have the power to ordain clergy and may have considerable influence on the matching of minister and parish. The "presbyterian" approach has come to refer to communities, such as the Presbyterian Church, that vest authority and power in clergy (teaching elders) and laity (ruling elders)—"elder" being a translation of the Greek *presbuteros*. But the power is vested more in groups than in individuals. The lay elders exercise authority at the local congregational level (the session), but groups of lay and clergy elders (the presbytery) exercise power at the regional level. Local congregations contribute to the power structure of the presbyterian systems, but local congregations also give up considerable autonomy to higher levels of the organization.

Baptists, by contrast, have opted for the more democratic approach. This approach to church polity emphasizes the autonomy of the local church, including the right of each congregation to call its own clergy and to elect its own leadership. Such a congregation may well cooperate with like-minded congregations elsewhere in such causes as missions and social service, but each congregation is independent. As Thomas Helwys wrote in 1611, because the word of God comes uniquely to each congregation, "no church ought to challenge any prerogative [of] any other."[17] Baptist congregations are autonomous and self-governing. Such autonomy is sometimes misused, and congregations sometimes make terrible mistakes—for example, in the calling of a given person as pastor—but Baptists have generally decided to live with the risks of local misuse rather than submit to the equal possibility of misuse by higher authorities. Autonomy means that not all congregations will agree on any particular issue, nor must they. Some Baptist congregations have now exercised their right to call women to leadership in their congregations. Responding to what is interpreted as the will of God, individual congregations are free to bypass centuries of tradition and give women the places of service to which God has called them. Autonomy makes this possible.

Congregations in the Baptist tradition operate in a democratic manner. Each member has a vote on matters of importance to the congregation, especially on the election of leaders and clergy. This democratic participation is grounded theologically in the commitment of Baptists to voluntary church membership, to recognition of the importance of the gifts given to each member of the congregation (cf. Rom 12:6ff.; 1 Cor 12:4ff; Eph 4:11ff), and to the implications of the doctrine of the priesthood of all believers. Each believer can approach God on his or her own; each has the power to understand the will of God as well as any other. Clearly, such endowed persons may not be denied a voice in the governance of a local congregation.

The role of clergy in Baptist circles follows from the commitment to the priesthood of all believers and to a democratic community. Both commitments eliminate the possibility that the clergyperson can be regarded as an authority wielding incontestable power over his or her Baptist brothers and sisters. Members of the clergy, like members of the diaconate, are prayerfully set aside by the community in order to perform certain tasks, for example, the task of preaching and exercising pastoral care. Authority is only a moral authority, the authority that comes with the power to persuade. Authority does not reside in the clergy person by virtue of the fact that a rite of ordination has taken place. Baptist clergy are servants, not chief executive officers or infallible theologians imposing their will on a congregation.

Baptists have differed through the years on the issue of reserving the conduct of the Lord's Supper and baptism to ordained clergy. If we are to be consistent with the principle that each congregation must decide for itself, we must allow that there is no final answer to this question, only a commitment to following God's leadership in a particular body of God's people.

Baptist Congregations and the World of Churches

We have noted that the term "church" may be applied to local groups of Christians as well as to the collective community of the faithful throughout the world and even throughout time. How are individual churches related to the larger church?

As proof of the assertion that the church is by nature one, some persons cite Jesus' high priestly prayer that his disciples "may be one, as we are one" (John 17:11). References to "maintaining the unity of the Spirit" and to "one body and one Spirit, . . . one Lord, one faith, one baptism, one God and Father of all" in Ephesians 4:3-6 are often taken to mean that the church is or ought to be one and that various expressions of the church ought to be united. But what does such unity mean? Unity may be nothing more than a recognition that all Christians share a common allegiance to Jesus Christ and, therefore, recognition that all are equals in the larger family of God. Millard Erickson refers to this lowest and vaguest level of unity as "spiritual unity."[18] Unity may mean a cooperative alliance of distinctive churches or denominations in which distinctions and unique convictions are not removed. Finally, unity may be viewed as a truly organic bond in which previous distinctions are lost. Such organizational unity may be limited to church bodies that share a common tradition—for example, the United Presbyterian Church —or it may be a negotiated union of diverse church bodies with a resulting loss of previous distinctions—for example, the United Church of Canada, which includes Methodists and Presbyterians.

Perhaps there is widespread, although not unanimous, recognition of a kind of "spiritual unity" based on common allegiance to Jesus Christ. Beyond that, however, what is certain is the fact that division and even divisiveness is more characteristic of the church at large than is unity.

One form of division between congregations and between denominations follows the well-known lines of socioeconomic stratification. Individual congregations tend to be made up of persons from similar racial and social backgrounds. Denominations may also be oriented toward specific ethnic, racial, and economic communities. To the extent that this is true, it reflects "moral failure" and the "victory of the world over the church."[19] It is sad to remember that many Baptist denominations—bearing the same name but having a very different appearance—had their origin in the defense of slavery, in racial identity, or in ethnic heritage. This much can be said: the church will not be truly the church until such human divisions are no longer a factor.

Another form of division between denominations is more theologically based. The church community is divided into Roman Catholics and Baptists, Methodists and Lutherans, Presbyterians and Pentecostals, and so on. The modern ecumenical movement of the twentieth century began as an effort to remedy these divisions by searching out ways of cooperating across denominational lines and by identifying those things that either unite or divide the separate church communities. Many Baptists, however, fearful of attempts to create a single monolithic church within which Baptists' dearly-bought distinctives would be lost, have maintained an arm's length relationship with the ecumenical movement.

How should Baptists then seek to relate to the ecumenical movement? It will help to recall our definition of the church. It is foremost "a company of faithful people" who have confessed their sins and faith; it is not primarily an organization. Focus on organic unity should, therefore, not be the agenda. In any case, organic unity will not be favorably received among Baptists due to an historic Baptist reluctance to yield authority to those who do not share the same commitments on polity or theology. Baptists need not feel guilty or heretical for not wanting to endorse organic union.

Baptist churches can, however, express their unity with the rest of the Christian community by genuine expressions of love and goodwill. Then, Baptists should go beyond the notion of "spiritual unity" to a cooperative alliance with the rest of the Christian community at local, national, and international levels. Such unified efforts are pragmatic—the cause of Christ is served more efficiently when Christians are not duplicating efforts or working at cross purposes—and they may be seen as a part of the mission of the church to share its understanding of the gospel, even with other Christians! Baptists, a dissenter community from the very beginning, must be careful to protect their commitments to freedom for individuals and churches. Such protection does not, however, preclude living and working "as one" in the larger body of Christ.

The Measurement of Success

How will we know if we have been successful in being the church of Jesus Christ? Will we know because we have remained faithful to a set of doctrinal statements? Because we have preserved a certain conception of the authority of the Bible? Because we have collectively upheld certain moral standards? Because we have organized the church along democratic lines that preserve the idea of the priesthood of all believers? Because we have baptized persons in the proper way by properly authorized ministers?

These are important issues, to be sure. However, as Elton Trueblood once pointed out, tests such as these are "too easy" and too prone to the "oversimplification which makes a small and easily distinguishable mark the crucial one."[20] The church is more complex than we recognize, and criteria for its faithfulness are less adequate than we could ever imagine. Trueblood suggests, therefore, that we consider again the measurement of success proposed by Jesus. "By this everyone will know that you are my disciples, if you have love for one another" (John 13:35).

The test of a true church is not baptism properly administered (as our "Landmark" Baptist brothers might have put it), nor is it the details of what we believe. The real test of church is whether or not we have become a community where love abounds. Love, *agape*, is the outpouring of life on behalf of another without regard to what that person can do for us. Love is patient and not self-centered; it does not harbor resentment. Love is hopeful when reasons for hope are in short supply. Love endures all that evil or the randomness of life can throw at it. For all these reasons, love is superior even to ecstatic worship, to grand preaching, and to the most profound thinking. When all is said and done, and this imperfect world has seen its last, it will be the attitude and acts of love that stand supreme (1 Cor 13)!

Orthodoxy means nothing if love is not present. Crusades for social improvement, important as they might be, are meaningless if they are done in an unloving way. In the final analysis, the measure of the church is the measure of its love. The early church in Jerusalem was a community where members loved others as themselves and thus were willing to share everything with them (Acts 2:44f). Tertullian's famous words demonstrate how the church retained this priority.

> It is our care for the helpless, our practice of lovingkindness, that brands us in the eyes of many of our opponents. "Only look," they say, "look how they love one another. . . Look how they are prepared to die for one another."[21]

What is the church? Most of all, it is a fellowship of persons, called out by the grace of God, who trust the grace of God and who love each other.

Notes

[1] Readers may wish to study the doctrine of the church as it has been formulated by Baptist theologians such as W. T. Conner, *The Gospel of Redemption* (Nashville: Broadman, 1945); Millard J. Erickson, *Christian Theology* (Grand Rapids: Baker, 1996); Duke K. McCall, ed. *What Is the Church? A Symposium of Baptist Thought* (Nashville: Broadman, 1958); James W. McClendon, Jr., *Doctrine: Systematic Theology*, vol. 2, (Nashville: Abingdon, 1994); Stewart A. Newman, *A Free Church Perspective: A Study in Ecclesiology* (Wake Forest NC: Stevens Book Press, 1986). Other helpful treatments include J. Robert Nelson, *The Realm of Redemption* (London: Epworth, 1951); Elton Trueblood, *The Company of the Committed* (New York: Harper, 1961); R. Newton Flew, *Jesus and His Church* (London: Epworth, 1943).

[2] "A Declaration of Faith of English People Remaining at Amsterdam in Holland" (1611), articles 10-11, William Lumpkin, ed., *Baptist Confessions of Faith* (Philadelphia: Judson Press, 1959) 119-20. Spelling and some wording have been modernized, and scripture references have been omitted.

[3] "A Declaration . . . ," article 11, Lumpkin, 120.

[4] The *Second London Confession* reflected a Calvinistic understanding that emphasized the priority of God's election from all eternity of some to salvation while leaving of others to condemnation.

[5] "*The Second London Confession*," (1677), ch. 26, Lumpkin, 285. Cf. a similar distinction in the *General Baptist's Orthodox Creed of 1679*, articles 29-30, Lumpkin, 318.

[6] "Short Confession of Faith in 20 Articles by John Smyth," article 14, Lumpkin, 101.

[7]James Leo Garrett, "Seeking a Regenerate Church Membership," *Southwestern Journal of Theology,* 3 (April 1961) 25.

[8]W. T. Conner wrote, "The first business . . . of a church is not evangelism, nor missions, nor benevolence; it is worship." *Gospel of Redemption,* 277.

[9]Note, however, the example of lay leaders such as Aquila and Priscilla who clearly functioned as teachers (Acts 18:26).

[10]"A Declaration . . . ," article 16, Lumpkin, 121.

[11]T. W. Manson, *Ministry and Priesthood: Christ's and Our* (Richmond VA: John Knox, 1959) 21.

[12]"The Faith and Practice of Thirty Congregations," (1651), Lumpkin, 184. Spelling modernized.

[13]"*The Second London Confession,*" ch. 27, Lumpkin, 290. The writers of the *Second London Confession* were quick to add in this section that assistance to other saints does not infringe on the title "which each man hath in his goods and possessions."

[14]"A Brief Confession or Declaration of Faith," (1660), article 25, Lumpkin, 234.

[15]Bonney and Quinton were Baptist women from Philadelphia who were instrumental leaders in the fight to preserve the rights of American Indians.

[16]Dietrich Bonhoeffer, *Prisoner for God: Letters and Papers from Prison* (New York: Macmillan, 1953) 169.

[17]"A Declaration . . . ," article 12, Lumpkin, 120.

[18]Cf. Erickson, 1135.

[19]H. Richard Niebuhr, *The Social Sources of Denominationalism* (New York: Henry Holt, 1929) 22.

[20]Trueblood, 96.

[21]Tertullian, *Apology,* XXXIX, cited in Trueblood, 101. Our Baptist ancestors had a vision of this same standard. Remember Thomas Helwys' recommendation that congregations should be small enough that members might have knowledge of one another and therefore "perform all the duties of love one towards another, both to soul and body." "A Declaration . . . ," article 16, Lumpkin, 121.

Ministry
M. Vernon Davis

William Hordern wrote of a minister who said: "I love flowers, but I hate botany. I love religion, but I hate theology."[1] In our culture, which places high value on action, feeling, and experience, many people resonate with such candid testimony. Serious and systematic theological reflection does not appear to be high on the "to do" list of many outside the academic community and the keepers of theological orthodoxy. The spiritual hunger of this generation is most frequently expressed as a hunger for experience rather than a quest for intellectual understanding of that experience.

Although we may see the value in disciplined and clear thinking about the mysteries of the faith and its central theological affirmations, we still may ask, "Why theologize about ministry? "Why not, in the words of the ubiquitous Nike™ commercial, "Just do it"? Surely this is an area where the mandate and model for action are clear. After all, we know at some deep level in ourselves that our basic problem here lies not in our lack of understanding, but in our reluctance to obey. As my father often said, "It's not the parts of the Bible that I don't understand that give me the most trouble; it's the part that I do understand and don't do anything about."

If theological reflection becomes mere detached speculation or an occasion to avoid taking responsible action, it is obviously irrelevant at best and destructive at worst. We can easily become like the disciples who seemed much more interested in discovering the theological explanations for blindness than in helping a man who could not see. Jesus' impatience with unproductive theological speculation is clear as he focused the attention of his disciples then and now on the urgency of making a redemptive difference: "We must work the works of him who sent me while it is day; night is coming when no one can work" (John 9:4).

To set theological understanding and Christian obedience over against one another, however, is to err and deny ourselves the contributions that each can make to the other. Authentic Christian theology grows out of the experience of faith and in turn guides the believer into more responsible ways of being a follower of Jesus Christ. Christian experience tests the adequacy of our theology and points the way to unsolved issues and deeper insight.[2]

A theology of ministry can be helpful in enhancing our experience of the Christian way of life, but to be authentic it must be developed at the intersection of action and reflection. Ministry can more readily be pointed out than defined. In thinking of the characteristics of authentic ministry, we call to mind stories and symbols more easily than abstract words and explanations. The theology of ministry discovers its source in narrative, in the stories of a people and individuals who sought to take seriously the difference their experience of God makes in the context of their daily lives. A theology of ministry is a theology of incarnation, the Word becoming flesh, uniquely in Jesus the Christ, but also in the experiences of all the people of God in order that the redeeming love of the living God might be embodied in the church and revealed to the world.

Foundations

The foundation of a theology of ministry lies in the nature and purpose of God as discovered in the witness of Scripture. A clear theme of biblical faith is that people inevitably become like the God they serve. The purpose of the living God who acts in the history of the covenant people is that they reflect God's redemptive power and purpose among themselves and in the world.

A theology of ministry begins with the formation of a covenant people. The God who created in love was not defeated by the rebellion of humans, who were created in God's image and given dominion in the created order. Through grace God made a covenant with a people in which they would receive blessings of restored relationship and through which they would bless the nations (Gen 12:1-3). God's election of a people was for the purpose of service. They were to be a ministering and missionary people, "a priestly kingdom and a holy nation" (Exod 19:6), through whom all could come to know and serve the living God. In the prophecy of Isaiah the missionary mandate is clear: "I have given you as a covenant to the people, a light to the nations" (Isa 42:6). Ministry is integral to the identity of the people of God.

Within the life of Israel, priests were appointed and prophets called to embody the covenant faith and provide leadership in the lives of the people. They functioned not only to preserve and extend the way of life called for by the covenant, but the prophets also called the people to remember and repent when they had forgotten who they were as the people of God and had distorted the meaning of their election for service. The prophet railed against a perversion of religion that sought to please God through ritual correctness rather than in ethical responsibility. The words of Micah are a classic summation: "He has told you, O mortal, what is good; and what does the Lord require of you but to do justice, and to love kindness, and to walk humbly with your God?" (Mic 6:8).

A basic key to the biblical understanding of ministry is found in the Old Testament concept of "the Servant of the Lord." In Isaiah 40–55 extended descriptions of the nature and work of God's Servant provide language in which Jesus understood his mission and believers discover the ideal of their service. Addressed to Israel as God's servant people, the descriptions of the Servant of God go far beyond what the nation had embodied. The images point to the faithful covenant partner whom God would bring forth.

Jesus understood his mission in terms of the Servant of the Lord. From the time of his baptism until his death on the cross, Jesus consistently interpreted his work in servant terms. He identified with suffering and sinful people and acted in love for their good. The beginning of his ministry in Nazareth set the tone of his life and work. He went to the synagogue on the Sabbath and read from Isaiah 61:1-2:

> The spirit of the Lord is upon me, because he has anointed me to bring good news to the poor. He has sent me to proclaim release to the captives and recovery of sight to the blind, to let the oppressed go free, to proclaim the year of the Lord's favor." When he had completed the reading, he proclaimed: "Today this scripture has been fulfilled in your hearing." (Luke 4:16-21)

After years in the company of Jesus, the disciples persisted in thinking of their place in the Kingdom in terms of status rather than service. In an especially contentious time he spoke unmistakable words to clarify their role and his: "Whoever wishes to become great among you must be your servant, and whoever wishes to be first among you must be slave of all. For the Son of Man came not to be served but to serve, and to give his life a ransom for many" (Mark 10:43-45). If the disciples needed any evidence that Jesus was serious, they would soon receive it as Jesus in the upper room took a towel and basin and washed their feet (John 13:1-17).

In a post-resurrection encounter after breakfast by the sea, Jesus asked Peter that piercing question: "Simon son of John, do you love me more than these?" In the exchange that followed, Jesus made it clear that the proof of love would be demonstrated in service to the community. He left no doubt that such a way of life would be costly.

Paul provided a defining statement of the character of the minister and the work of ministry in 2 Corinthians 4:1-18. Ministry is seen as *diakonia*, humble service rendered personally to another. The original sense of the word is "waiting at table" or "providing for bodily sustenance." It is also used in the New Testament for any "discharge of service" in genuine love. "A decisive point for understanding the concept is that early Christianity learned to regard and describe as *diakonia* all significant activity for the edification of the community" (Eph 4:11ff.).[3] Note Paul's affirmation that ministry is given to us "by God's mercy" (2 Cor 4:1). It is because of this conviction that he does not "lose heart," despite the difficulty of the ministry to which he was called. He describes himself as "your slave for Jesus' sake" (2 Cor 4:5), a remarkable witness to the conviction that we serve Christ by serving others.

A theology of ministry informed by the story of the covenant people of God and the fulfillment of that covenant in Jesus Christ goes beyond the prescription of the kind and scope of specific activities appropriate for Christian ministry. It explores the believer's motivation for all of life. What brings a person to serve another human being? And what gives one the sustaining power to persist in such a way of life? An authentic theology of ministry sees serving as a comprehensive way of life. It does not consist of a certain way of doing special things; it is a special way of doing everything. Ministry becomes the life-response of persons to the God who is both creator and redeemer, the Lord of life in its totality.

Paul admonished the Colossian Christians: "Whatever you do in word or deed, do everything in the name of the Lord Jesus, giving thanks to God the Father through Him" (Col 3:17). In similar words he instructed the Corinthians to "do everything for the glory of God" (1 Cor 10:31). Because every action we take in relation to our fellow human beings is to be seen as done unto God, it is clear there can be no neat division of life into the categories of sacred and secular. Boyd Hunt states:

> Ministry, then, in this sense of selfless service to God and to others in Christ's name, is to characterize the life-style of all believers. This is what is intended in the claim that the church *is* ministry ....The church exists to serve. It has no authentic existence apart from service. Ministry is its mission![4]

Ministry is essentially how all followers of Jesus are called to act in the world in response to the radical difference Christ has made in their lives. The challenge of such a comprehensive understanding of life in terms of ministry is not only difficult to understand but also to accept.

The understanding of Christian ministry as "selfless service to God and to others in Christ's name" is informed by the biblical witness and shaped by expressions of ministry in the life of the church that have developed throughout its history. The essence of ministry is clear from the biblical precedents and the historical development. The form of ministry is constantly changing as believers grow in their understanding of life in Christ and as their faith is planted in new soil and cultivated in varied cultural contexts. At times the people of God have lost the perspective of biblical faith and have been shaped more by the prevailing culture than by the gospel. At other times recovery of biblical truth and renewal of commitment to Christian discipleship have led to revival within the church and effective witness in the world. Thus the task of theology is unending and must be done in every time and place where people seek to hold together faith and life, theological reflection and servant ministry.

Perspective

Ministry is selfless service given to others as a response to the grace we have received through Christ, the call we have heard from Christ, the gifts we have been given by the Spirit of Christ, and the example we have witnessed in the life of Jesus. Ministry is the means through which God's redemptive love is made visible, believable, and desirable in the church and in the world. Ministry becomes the means by which the believer both gives and grows. There is a receiving that can be experienced only in giving. There is a blessing that comes to the one who blesses. The expression of ministry is both individual and corporate, as the disciple grows in understanding and motivation in the context of a community of faith, the body of Christ.

The message of the church of Jesus Christ ultimately becomes believable through the authentic expression of serving love—not the exercise of institutional power, the celebration of cultural status, or the force of rational argument. For the church as a whole and for individual believers ministry as a distinctive and comprehensive way of life is possible only through a relationship with the living Christ that is being constantly renewed. Several dominant themes can be observed in such a life of ministry.

Response to Call

The Christian does not simply choose to minister from among the many options presented in life. Whether we are receptive or resistant to life as ministry, we cannot claim that it is our own idea. In the community of faith we are nurtured, nudged, and/or nagged by an inescapable necessity to become fully who we say we are—servants of the Servant Christ. In the discovery of our own gifts, in the response to human need, and in the arresting word that comes to us through the Scriptures and the lives of others, we hear a call from God to reflect God's life and love through our own.

In the models of ministry taught in the Scriptures there is a consistent witness to ministry as life in response to an inescapable call. It is heard in Jeremiah's words: "If I say, 'I will not mention him, or speak any more in his name,' then within me there is something like a burning fire shut up in my bones; I am weary with holding it in, and I cannot" (Jer 20:9). The reality of call is clear in Paul's confession: "If I proclaim the gospel, this gives me no ground for boasting, for an obligation is laid on me, and woe to me if I do not proclaim the gospel! For if I do this of my own will, I have a reward; but if not of my own will, I am entrusted with a commission" (1 Cor 9:16). Again, Paul identifies this "obligation" in his affirmation that "the love of Christ urges us on" (2 Cor 5:14).

Most compelling is the experience of Jesus, especially as seen in the writings of Luke. He repeatedly uses the word *dei* to convey Jesus' sense of divine necessity and urgency throughout his life. The term "expresses the character of necessity or compulsion in an event." As Luke uses the term, he "thinks of God in terms of the will which personally summons man and which fashions history according to its plan. . . .This will of God claims man in every situation of life and gives goal and direction to life on the basis of its saving purpose."[5]

Jesus moves through his life and ministry as a man under divine constraint. He *must* be in his Father's house. He *must* move on to preach the Kingdom of God to other cities. He *must* journey on to Jerusalem. He *must* go to the house of Zacchaeus. He *must* suffer many things. He *must* be delivered unto death. He *must* be numbered among the transgressors. The Scriptures *must* be fulfilled. This divine *must* of Jesus' ministry is in some sense unique, but it is not unlike the experience of every disciple who knows that the mission of our Lord must truly become our own. However it comes to us, the *must* of our ministry is the divine call that draws us into the life of service and keeps us there.

The late George Balanchine was the premier choreographer and master teacher of American ballet. The demanding teacher frequently pushed students to their limits in the maximum development of their skills and their disciplined understanding of the ballet. When questioned about his demanding approach to teaching, Balanchine answered: "I don't want people who want to dance. I want people who *have* to dance."[6] At the heart of the disciple of Christ is the divine sense of call, the *must* of the will of God. We *have* to minister, for it is the only authentic expression of our new nature in Christ, who "came not to be served but to serve and to give his life a ransom for many" (Mark 10:45). Such commitment is our only way to make the message of the reconciling gospel visible, believable, and desirable in a culture so distracted from things eternal.

Gratitude for Grace

Ministry is the disciple's response to grace received. The motivation for ministry is not a desire to attain merit or favor with God. It is not a response born out of anxiety and insecurity in our relationship to God. Rather, it is the believer's attempt to pass on what can never be paid back. One ministers freely in gratitude for new life in the security of grace, God's undeserved favor and unattainable gift. Any other motivation is a delusion of ourselves and results in a distortion of the reality of grace we are seeking to make a reality in the lives of others.

Wendell Berry notes the significance of motivation for our work. "Good work," he says, "finds the way between pride and despair. It graces with health. It heals with grace. It preserves the given so that it remains a gift." In contrast, much of our work proceeds out of our pride or our despair. Either we think too much of it or not enough. "There is the bad work of pride. There is also the bad work of despair—done poorly out of the failure of hope or vision. Despair is the too-little of responsibility, as pride is the too-much."[7]

Too much effort in the name of Christian service is expended out of pride or despair. We either work diligently in the futile effort to gain our own salvation or work without a sense of hope that our effort will really make any difference. In either case we serve with the illusion that our own effort is the substance of our service and the condition of our status with God. What we would have others see as love is too often the need-love that we have for ourselves rather than the gift-love freely given in our concern for another.

The verses that introduce the account of the Passover meal Jesus shared with his disciples before his crucifixion reveal much about the kind of service that proceeds from the security of a life in grace (John 13:1-5). Jesus, who knew that "his hour had come," was confident also that his relationship with God would not be broken by the impending cross. Although it appeared that events beyond his control were moving quickly to his appointment with tragedy, Jesus viewed them as an opportunity to continue in character. Having acted in gift-love for his disciples throughout his life, he did not view this crisis as an occasion to become preoccupied with his own welfare. He knew himself to be in concert with the eternal will of God. He knew his destiny was secure. In that confidence he arose from the table, took a towel and a basin, and performed the menial service of washing his disciples' feet that one would have expected to be done by a slave.

The disciples did not understand what Jesus was doing before them. They could not grasp the significance of the example of Jesus for their own future relationship with him and each other. They were being challenged to serve one another freely in the most humble of tasks confident in the reality of grace they knew in relationship to their Lord.

Stewardship of Spiritual Gifts

What is the content of this serving that Christ has given us to do? In many ways it is shaped by the need we discover in another—the pain of injustice, the agony of poverty, the terror of alienation, the weight of guilt, the isolation of despair, the numbness of meaninglessness. In response to these many-faceted needs, what does the Christian have to give? Ultimately, we can only bear witness to what we have seen and heard for ourselves and give out of the grace we have received.

In the particularity of our own circumstances each of us experiences the call to minister, and each of us receives gifts of grace that equip us for ministry. Each of us in our own uniqueness has been gifted for service—to meet some need, not all needs. We are called to be good stewards of the gifts we have received in the service of grace. We are called as members of the body of Christ, who together have been gifted for the whole ministry to which God has called his servant people. In the words of Stanley A. Nelson, "God has richly gifted his people, empowering them for Kingdom service and enabling them in attitude and action to minister in Jesus' name."[8]

The entire biblical story portrays the life of the people of God as one of stewardship, not only for what they have been given in creation but also in redemption. The people of faith become convinced that what God does for us and in us will be done for others through us. In the unique ways the individual believer has been gifted by God and in the circumstances where one becomes the key witness to another, we hear the instruction, "Like good stewards of the manifold grace of God, serve one another with whatever gift each of you has received" (1 Pet 4:10). Thus, in ways of marvelous diversity and creativity, Christians become forgiven forgivers, loved lovers, reconciled reconcilers, helped helpers, receiving givers. In such ways the people of God are engaged in the redemptive purpose of God. "The whole church lives from Christ's self-giving and in self-giving for the reconciliation of the world."[9]

The holy God called the covenant people to be holy. The people who received divine blessing were to become the means through which the blessing comes to others. "I will make of you a great nation, and I will bless you, and make your name great, so that you will be a blessing; . . . and in you all the families of the earth shall be blessed" (Gen 12:2-3). To the inheritors of that covenant in Christ came the reaffirmation of its blessing and the renewal of its challenge: "But you are a chosen race, a royal priesthood, a holy nation, God's own people, in order that you may proclaim the mighty acts of Him who has called you out of darkness into his marvelous light. Once you were not a people, but now you are God's people; once you had not received mercy, but now you have received mercy" (1 Pet 2:9-10).

Controlled by Love

The thread of this theme has been woven through the fabric of the previously developed characteristics of Christian ministry and in effect holds them together. Love stands at the heart of the meaning of Christian service. The Christian minister faces the probing questions: "Why do you live like this? What makes you do these things?" The response of the authentic disciple can only be that expressed by Paul: "The love of Christ urges us on" (2 Cor 5:14). John take us further: "We love, because he first loved us" (1 John 4:19).

In the aftermath of Jesus' washing the disciples' feet at the Passover meal, he said to them: "I give you a new commandment, that you love one another. Just as I have loved you, you also should love one another. By this everyone will know that you are my disciples, if you have love for one another" (John 13:34-35). Ultimately, the infallible evidence of the reality of our discipleship is discovered in the quality of our love. "They will know that we are Christians by our love"; or perhaps in spite of all our pretensions and efforts to convince the world, they will sense we are not authentic followers of Jesus because of our lack of it.

Jesus not only challenged his followers to make love the central motivation of their lives, but he also claimed the right to define the kind of love he had in mind. Love is not defined for the disciple by cultural usage or personal feeling. Love is defined by the actions of God in Christ. Jesus said to love one another "just as I have loved you," and that leaves little doubt as to what he expected of us. Into the word *agape* is poured the content of God's covenant love. In the cross of Jesus the climactic revelation of that love is displayed for all eternity.

Jesus clearly needed nothing from us; nevertheless, "having loved his own who were in the world, he loved them to the end"

(John 13:1). His actions in taking up both the towel and basin and the cross portray the scope and depth of his caring. Jesus' life and ministry define forever the meaning of gift-love. His love was unqualified and unending.

In the Old Testament God's covenant love is often expressed through the word *hesed*, frequently translated as "steadfast love." Throughout the Psalms rolls the magnificent refrain: "For His steadfast love endures forever." The Old Testament bears witness to the integrity of God's commitment to the covenant people and the tenacity of God's love that would not let the people go in spite of their turning away to follow other gods and pursue their own self-interests. The picture of God as a patient parent in Hosea 11 reflects the character of the God who comes as the Holy One in the midst of the people, not to destroy but to save.

Jesus as the faithful covenant partner embodied this kind of love. In his life and ministry he demonstrated *agape* as an attitude that considers others of inestimable value and acts for the lasting good of the other in spite of the cost to oneself. *Agape* values another not because of that one's accomplishments or capacity to do anything to enhance the one who loves in return. The value comes because of every person's being created in God's own image and in God's commitment to redeem them even at great cost. The Christian is to view all human beings as persons for whom Christ lived and died.

The *agape* that is defined most clearly in Christ's death is demonstrated also in his acts of ministry throughout his life. T. B. Maston saw the cross as "the unifying symbol" not only of Christ's life but also of those who would follow him. "Jesus not only died on the cross, he also lived the cross-like life, and in that way as well as by his death he revealed God and was a redemptive influence among men."[10] The life of Jesus demonstrated that the way of *agape* is the way of a cross in a world like ours. In his life and death he acted *for* us, doing on our behalf what we could never accomplish for ourselves. Yet he acted *before* us, providing a model for those who would take up the cross and follow him. The minister in Christ's name cannot be under the illusion that the call to serve in love as a faithful disciple will result in an easy way.

Paul prayed that believers would be "rooted and grounded in love" and that we would "know the love of Christ that surpasses knowledge" (Eph 3:17-19). He prayed for us to be stretched in our understanding and embodiment of this love. In 1 Corinthians 13 he writes of no less challenging but far more specific expressions of the love that is to characterize our relationships in the church and the world. The meaning of Christian ministry is measured by the degree to which we are willing to love like that.

God's Creative and Redemptive Purpose

A theology of ministry takes seriously two fundamental theological affirmations. First, the God whom we serve is both creator and redeemer, the God of Genesis 1:1 and John 3:16. Second, humans are created as unitary beings, body and spirit in a continuing, interpenetrating relationship. A person cannot be defined in terms of one without reference to the other. Ministry that grows out of these convictions addresses the needs of the whole person, body and spirit. It does not emphasize one order of concerns at the expense of the other. To do so would be ultimately to invalidate the effectiveness of the service rendered.

The church has too often created a false dichotomy that sets the concerns of the body against the needs of the spirit. Many have set social action and evangelism over against each other as either/or options for the fulfillment of the mandate to minister. Although historically Baptists have been deeply involved in holistic ministry involving both creative social action and effective evangelistic proclamation, many give priority to the saving of the soul as having eternal consequences over against the ministry to the physical and social hurts of humanity, which has only temporal benefits. Stanley Grenz has stated:

> We propose that the involvement of the church in social action is crucial regardless of its relationship to evangelism. It is a natural extension of Jesus' own ministry as entrusted to us. . . . Our Lord did not describe his task as proclamation in isolation but as proclamation in the context of service.[11]

The Christian witnesses to the presence of the creative and redemptive love of God in every human relationship. Christian ministry has as its purpose to join the living Christ in the commitment to complete what is not yet finished and restore what has been broken and distorted.[12] Such service refuses to separate life into neat categories of sacred and secular, eternal and temporal. Boyd Hunt expressed this understanding of ministry well:

> The church's mission is *holistic* or comprehensive in scope. God's redemptive purpose in Christ is to sum up *all things* in the Son (Col 1:20; Rev 21:5), a purpose broad enough to include the cultural mandate of Genesis 1:26-30: "Fill the earth and subdue it" as well as the sweeping redemptive mandates of Matthew 22:37-40 and Matthew 28:18-20. The concerns of the kingdom, while emphasizing the ultimacy of redemptive issues, are as wide as creation itself.[13]

Service of Hope

Acts of Christian ministry to others are signs of hope for persons who face the future with fear, anxiety, or despair. They are acts of love that express partially in the here and now what will be perfectly experienced only in the eschatological future. Living between God's "already" and "not yet," the Christian servant ministers today toward the future. In the power of what is coming to be, the believer dares to light a candle in the face of overwhelming darkness. With a realistic understanding of personal inadequacy, the disciple of Jesus acts in confidence of the certain triumph of the Kingdom of God. Stanley Grenz has put it this way:

> Service arises out of an awareness of the "not yet" status of the world in every current form. The arrival of the fullness of God's kingdom awaits the future eschaton. In the meantime the vision of that great future day provides both the motivation and the blueprint for Christian service.[14]

Thomas Jackson captures this understanding of Christian life and ministry in his hymn, "We Are Called To Be God's People." As the people of God, we are called to be "signs of hope for all the race." Doing the work of God's servants and God's prophets, we are challenged to be faithful, confident of the fulfillment of God's future. In the line, "Let us share our lives together as we shall around His throne,"[15] we are summoned to provide a foretaste of what we will experience only in God's eschatological future.

This approach toward our responsibility in ministry is modeled by the courageous act of Jeremiah in buying the field at Anathoth as a sign of hope in a time of desolation. For the prophet there was the assurance that, in the words of the gospel song, "God's tomorrow will be better than today." Jeremiah demonstrated the faithfulness of one who is obedient even when the act is difficult to understand and the future is impossible to see.

Christian ministry embodies the spirit of Jesus, "who for the sake of the joy that was set before him endured the cross, disregarding its shame, and has taken his seat at the right hand of the throne of God" (Heb 12:2). In the face of Jesus set toward Jerusalem and the certain death that awaited him there is not the symbol of the brave victim, but of the confident victor. He did not minimize the cost of redemption, but he bore it in the confidence that death was not to be the last word. In the power of the living God, the last word would be life. It is this confidence that impels the people of God's Kingdom to be faithful in the ministry of word and deed.

Ministry in the name of the crucified and risen Christ is thus an eschatological act, an act of hope. It demonstrates irrepressible faith in God's future by acting redemptively in God's world today. As Jürgen Moltmann has said:

> Individual anticipations of what is to come can only prove themselves as such through intervention and self-giving for the future of others. True hope is lived in the giving of oneself to the future of the hopeless. Anticipated liberty is practiced in the liberation of the oppressed. Faith is manifested in love for those in need.[16]

The Ministry of Every Christian

Is there a distinctive way Baptists think about and do ministry? Although the foregoing study reflects primarily the perspectives of Baptist scholars, the understanding of ministry it presents is shared widely across the lines of confessional traditions. Doing the work of ministry together has often become the way Christians have discovered their common experience in Christ even though they persist in diverse ways of worship, church polity, and theological understanding. Regrettably, however, this is not always the case. Some Baptists insist that theological agreement in great detail is a necessary condition for ministering together with other Christians. At times some Baptists find it easier to join cause with persons of other confessional bodies who share particular theological and ethical concerns than to work together in the mission of Christ with those who share a common heritage of faith and practice. The Baptist story in this regard has both a bright and shadow side.

To perceive how Baptists approach ministry, one must consider seriously the way Baptists have historically shaped their understanding of faith and practice. The Baptist way has been formed by taking the Bible seriously, by trusting the competency of the individual in matters of faith, by reacting to thought and practice that insert any human being or institution between the individual and God, and by resisting any dilution or distortion of the conviction that salvation is by grace through faith alone. These convictions are essentially nonnegotiable in the Baptist heritage, and they have a significant impact on the mind of Baptists in regard to ministry.

Baptists affirm the ministry of every Christian. The doctrines of the priesthood of every believer, the competency of the individual soul before God, and religious liberty form a triumvirate of ideas that express the sometimes fierce individualism of Baptists. Often Baptists have championed the priesthood of all believers with greater emphasis upon an affirmation of the right of direct access to God and individual interpretation of Scripture than upon an acknowledgment of the responsibility to become priests to one another in the name of Christ. When Baptists are at their best, they recognize that the freedom we have in Christ always brings with it a radical responsibility we cannot delegate to another. The priesthood of all believers stands against every attempt to define the Christian life in terms of power and privilege rather than love and service.

Henry Cook, a British Baptist, has stated well the Baptist conviction that every Christian is called to minister and gifted for the ministry to which Christ leads. He emphasizes that the individual's gifts and calling will be in the service of the church's ministry and not independent of it.

> The gift will vary with the need the Lord has in mind to meet, but to every believer in some form or other the call will come, in the perception of the gift and in the realization of the need, to engage in the church's ministry somewhere, that so, by the consecrated use of the God-given capacity whatever it is, the church may be strengthened in its witness and Christ's redemptive purpose for the world advanced.[17]

A Baptist view of ministry will see it as an expression of one's experience of salvation rather than as a means of obtaining it. At their best the activistic Baptists will regard what they do in outreach to one another and to those outside the church as bearing witness to what they have seen and heard of the redeeming love of Christ. They are committed to the ministry of the good news both in the word of proclamation and the deed of mercy.

Because of their advocacy of the ministry of every Christian, Baptists will always experience tension between the responsibility of every believer and the role of those who are called to leadership in the body. The inability to deal with this tension constructively has often resulted in conflict and division in local congregations and in larger Baptist bodies. When the primary consideration of the issue is framed in terms of power and authority rather than love and servanthood, it is difficult to come to a resolution in which members of the family of faith can live in peace and fulfill the mission God has given them.

The Ministry of Leadership in the Church

Baptists acknowledge the biblical precedent for official leaders in the church. For example, *The Baptist Faith and Message* of 1963 states without elaboration: "Its [the church's] Scriptural officers are pastors and deacons." The New Testament is clearer in its insistence on what kind of persons the leaders of the church are to be than in what specific duties they are to perform. Stewart Newman said,

> A ministry of "servants," recognized for the services they rendered rather than for the position they occupied, represents the purest forms of the ministry in the early church. This is the only form of ministry which is consonant with the essential character of Christian faith.[18]

Dale Moody provided a detailed study of the developing ministry of the New Testament church in which he presented the evidence not only for a ministry of service based upon spiritual gifts (*charismata*), but also an official ministry in the early church that was recognized by ordination (*cheirotonia*). Moody developed the evidence for the authority of the ministry in the New Testament that is often seen in Baptist theologies.[19]

The New Testament reflects the church in its early stage of dynamic development. The developing role of the official ministry is evident. In the succeeding centuries the form of the ministry reflected not only its basic biblical function, but also cultural influences and secular structures. Nelson notes that the church was moving from simplicity to elaborateness.

> This can be seen by comparing the New Testament idea of a servant to the view in the concluding days of the Patristic period, where the bishop served a church wearing a crown. Does that reflect a change? It is a change of great magnitude.[20]

From their beginnings Baptists have reacted to this kind of development in the role of the minister in the church. A hallmark of the Baptists was the belief that their leaders should be *of* them rather than *over* them. According to H. Wheeler Robinson, "Such authority as these men naturally came to exercise in their office was derived from the community which (acting as it believed under the guidance of the Holy Spirit) called them to exercise it."[21] John Smyth, the first English Baptist, wrote:

> We maintain that the power of the Eldership (i.e., the ministry) is a leading, directing, and overseeing power, ministry, or service, in the Kingdom and Priesthood of the Church, and that the negative voice, the last definite determining sentence, is in the body of the Church whereto the Eldership is bound to yield, and that the Church may do any lawful act without the Elders, but the Elders can do nothing without the approbation of the body or contrary to the body.[22]

Baptist thought with reference to the meaning and practice of ordination reflects no consensus. A Baptist view would reject the understanding that the laying on of hands conveys divine power and authority. Generally, Baptists see ordination as a recognition by the church of the inner call and the spiritual gifts for ministry that an individual has experienced. Ordination also expresses the belief of the church that the individual has been led to a specific ministry in the life of the church, and the congregation sets the person apart for the work of the gospel and commends the person to the body with prayer. Although the service of ordination is symbolic, it is a serious expression of the way in which the individual and the congregation see their mutual responsibilities in the service of Christ.

H. Wheeler Robinson commended the practice of observing the Lord's Supper for inclusion in a service of ordination to the ministry.

> This is the more fitting, because the primary conception amongst Baptists is that it expresses the fellowship of believers. It is within, not above, this fellowship that the minister is set apart for the service of all. His best work will be done through ordinary human intercourse with his fellows; he must draw his motive for it from that high motive of constraining love which the Lord's Table sets forth; he must live on that high level of spiritual life which is made possible alone by the nurture of the Holy Spirit, symbolized in the elements; he must find his primary evangelical message in the Cross which the Table commemorates.[23]

Persons who are set apart for leadership in the ministry of the church must give evidence of their calling and their readiness for the work. Men and women from every walk of life and with diverse gifts have heard the inner call of God and responded in obedience. Churches have recognized these gifts and affirmed these callings in ordination.

Baptists in the twenty-first century will experience considerable confusion in the theology and practice of ordination. Several factors have contributed to the confusion: the biblical precedents are few and the instruction meager. Baptist history itself reflects a variety of expressions in ordination practice. The increasing specializations in professional ministry raise the question of whether or not every staff member of the church or every para-church minister should be recognized by ordination. The lay renewal movement with its emphases upon the priesthood of every believer and the blurring of the distinction between clergy and laity has resulted in many people's questioning whether official ordination is appropriate for anyone. The influence of the government in defining a ministry for purposes of taxing status has caused some to decide the issue on pragmatic rather than theological grounds.

The rapid rise in the number of women who are experiencing a call to ministry and seeking ordination has stirred controversy in local churches and denominations. Today there is conflict among Baptists concerning who is a proper candidate for ordination. Seeing the issue as one of appropriate authority and proper interpretation of scripture, many churches have denied ordination to persons on the basis of gender or marital status. Other congregations, exercising their belief in the autonomy of the local church under the leadership of the Holy Spirit, have celebrated God's call to an ever-growing number of women in ministry and affirmed it through ordination.

Baptists today experience the painful phenomenon of many women who have come to faith in Jesus as the Christ in a Baptist congregation, heard the call of God on their lives in Baptist worship services and missions organizations, and prepared themselves for the ministry to which God has called them in Baptist institutions only to face the reality that they are all too often denied a place of ministry in the family of faith that nurtured them. The fierce conflict that has resulted has divided Baptists from one another. The resolution of this tension and the affirmation of the freedom of the living Christ to call anyone to serve him in any capacity He chooses in the church and the world is in the minds of many a key to the integrity of the Baptist witness in the days ahead. In a lost and hurting world the task of the church increases, and all those whom God has chosen for ministry need the affirmation and encouragement of God's people as they respond to God's call.

Conclusion

When Carlo Maria Giulini was the conductor of the Los Angeles Philharmonic Orchestra, an interviewer asked him: "Maestro, what is your primary responsibility as music director of the Philharmonic?" Giulini replied: "First, to serve the music the best I can; second, to serve the orchestra the best I can; third, to serve the audience the best I can. That's it."

The maestro's response can be a helpful analogy for understanding the nature of the minister's task. By God's mercy we have this serving to do. We are engaged in the service of God's glorious music of creation and redemption. We are members of the body of Christ who are given the responsibility of displaying the wonder of Christ's reconciling love in our own relationships. We are entrusted with the message and ministry of reconciliation that is good news for all the world. In the company of the people of God let us serve the music of God's grace and power for the sake of the world. Let us serve the music; and let us serve it well.

Notes

[1]William Hordern, *A Layman's Guide to Protestant Theology* (New York: Macmillan, 1957) 1.

[2]John Claypool has aptly stated that "theological activity that does not eventually express itself in concrete action is a perversion of reality. By the same token, activistic ministry that never seeks for the foundation of its efforts is little more than mindless frenzy that will eventually 'run out of gas' and suffer the fate of any 'cut-flower' enterprise. The truth of the matter is that the fruit of good theology is the authentic practice of ministry, and for the practice of ministry to stay healthy and true to its essential nature, there must be constant theological reflection." "Theology of Ministry," *Southwestern Journal of Theology*, 15, 2 (Spring 1973): 3.

[3]Gerhard Kittel, ed. *Theological Dictionary of the New Testament*, vol. 2 (Grand Rapids: Eerdmans, 1964) 87.

[4]Boyd Hunt, *Redeemed! Eschatological Redemption and the Kingdom of God* (Nashville: Broadman and Holman, 1993) 200.

[5]Kittel, 23.

[6]*Forbes* (11 May 1992) 224.

[7]Wendell Berry, *What Are People For?* (San Francisco: North Point Press, 1990) 10.

[8]Stanley A. Nelson, A *Believer's Church Theology*, rev. (Taejon, Korea: Widow's Mite Computer Products, 1996) 272.

[9]Jürgen Moltmann, *The Church in the Power of the Spirit* (New York: Harper and Row, 1977) 97.

[10]T. B. Maston, *Why Live the Christian Life?* (New York: Thomas Nelson, 1974) 157. In a significant chapter, "Its Unifying Symbol: The Cross" (pp. 157-73), Maston develops this theme and explores its application to the life and ministry of the Christian.

[11]Stanley J. Grenz, *Theology for the Community of God* (Nashville: Broadman and Holman, 1994) 660.

[12]Claypool, 9.

[13]Hunt, 196-97.

[14]Grenz, 663.

[15]Thomas A. Jackson, "We Are Called To Be God's People," *The Baptist Hymnal* (Nashville: Convention Press, 1991) 390.

[16]Moltmann, 195.

[17]Henry Cook, *What Baptists Stand For* (London: Kingsgate Press, 1958) 100.

[18]S. A. Newman, "The Ministry in the New Testament Churches," *What Is the Church?*, ed. Duke K. McCall (Nashville: Broadman, 1958) 61.

[19]Dale Moody, *The Word of Truth* (Grand Rapids: Eerdmans, 1981) 448-58.

[20]Nelson, 211.

[21]H. Wheeler Robinson, *The Life and Faith of the Baptists* (London: Kingsgate Press, 1946) 105.

[22]Quoted in Robinson, 105.

[23]Robinson, 106.

Baptism

R. Wayne Stacy

I still recall the shocked look of disbelief and betrayal on her face. "I have to be what?" Julie was a rather sophisticated, urbane Episcopalian who had been attending our Baptist church for about two years when she finally decided to "take the plunge," shall we say, and convert to the Baptists. But when I told her that she would have to be immersed, she balked. "You mean, I have to be dunked in a tank of water in full view of the whole church with my hair streaming down my face and my makeup running and without benefit of so much as a shower cap or anything . . . you mean, before God and everybody?" I said: "Yes, Julie, that's what I'm saying. You see, the one thing we Baptists all have in common is wet hair." She said: "But it's so . . . so . . . inelegant!" And I said: "Precisely."

> This is the one thing that Baptists stand for against the great mass of modern Christians. The Greek Church, the Roman Catholic Church, the Lutheran Church, the High Church Episcopalians, and the Sacramental wing of the Disciples attach a redemptive value to one or both of the ordinances. It is just here that the term "Evangelical Christianity" comes in to emphasize the spiritual side of religion independent of rite and ceremony.[1]

With these words the great Baptist linguist and Greek scholar, Professor A. T. Robertson, opened his address to the 1911 convocation of the Baptist World Alliance in Philadelphia, titled "The Spiritual Interpretation of the Ordinances." In it he delineated what he regarded as the quintessential Baptist theology of baptism: baptism of believers only, by immersion, and most important of all, as a symbol (not a sacrament) of one's participation in Christ's death, burial, and resurrection. With his statement few Baptists would disagree. And so that, as they say, would seem to be that.

But with Baptists, that is rarely ever "that." When you get two Baptists together to discuss any subject, you'll have at least three opinions. One of them, it seems, won't be able to make up his/her mind. Not surprisingly, Walter B. Shurden, in whose volume Robertson's address is cited, begins his book with the caveat: "These people [whose addresses are printed herein] did not speak for the Baptist World Alliance (BWA) any more than they spoke for their individual Baptist communions or local Baptist churches. They spoke as Baptist individuals."[2]

Baptists, like other Protestants, affirm the autonomy of the individual soul and the priesthood of all believers. But unlike other Protestants, we Baptists are not just autonomous; we're belligerently autonomous! And so even though believer's baptism by immersion in a nonsacramental sense is perhaps the *sine qua non* of Baptist theology, Baptists, it seems, are even willing to argue about that! Go to some Baptist churches, and you'll likely hear Baptists "discussing" baptism rather loudly—everything from whether or not baptism "takes" in a "tank" to alien immersion. [For the record, I want to make it clear that I, personally, have never witnessed an "alien immersion"—though I once saw an alien autopsy on the TV show "X-Files"—but I have my doubts.]

In any case it is notoriously difficult to speak with authority on any issue of "Baptist theology." For, indeed, there is no such thing as the "Baptist theology." There are only Baptists' theologies. Even given Baptist diversity, however, one can find some common features to Baptist thinking.

Since Baptists, like other Protestants, affirm the Protestant principle of *sola scriptura*, they anchor their belief about baptism in the Scriptures rather than in any authoritative tradition, as, for example, in the Roman Church. For Baptists, if it cannot be demonstrated from the Scriptures, it is not authoritative, regardless of custom, tradition, or contemporary church practice. Therefore, I begin by discussing the origins of Christian baptism in terms of its antecedents in late second-temple Judaism and in the emergence and meaning of baptism in the New Testament. Then I will describe in broad parameters what I deem to be the Baptist consensus on the meaning of baptism. Finally, I will state my own theology of baptism, with the caveat that such constitutes only one individual Baptist's theology of baptism, nothing more and nothing less.

Baptism in the New Testament

Antecedents to Christian Baptism

There is considerable debate among New Testament scholars about the origin of Christian baptism. Part of the problem lies in the fact that the New Testament never addresses the issue. Rather, baptism is introduced as something familiar to the reader, already part and parcel of the believer's experience.

Etymology offers some help. The New Testament word for baptism is *baptizo*, which means "to dip." As the late Baptist humorist Grady Nutt once observed, that makes Baptists "dippers," and our denomination the "Southern Dip Convention." The president of the Southern Baptist Convention, then, would be, he quipped, "the Big Dipper." The origin of the word, however, does provide some clue as to its meaning. The verb *baptizo* comes from the root *baph*, from which we get, by means of aspirated metathesis, our English word bath, from the Greek root *bath*.[3]

In the Septuagint *baptizo* translates the Hebrew, *tabhal*, to dip or immerse. From this root derives the word for Jewish proselyte baptism (*tebilah*), about which more will be said later. In the New Testament *baptizo* is used exclusively in the technical sense of immersion as an act of incorporation into Christ and his death.[4]

But when we move from etymology to antecedents, problems proliferate. Chief among them is the issue of origin. That Christianity began in the piety of second-temple Judaism is undeniable. That second-temple Judaism practiced baptism is also beyond dispute, But among the various expressions of Jewish "baptism" in the first century AD, to which does Christian baptism owe its primary origin: the Jewish *mikvah*, the baptism of John the Baptist, Jewish proselyte baptism, or the baptism practiced among the Essenes at Qumran?

One possibility is the Jewish *mikvah*. It is an important part of Jewish law to immerse oneself for purification.[5] In Jewish theology one immerses oneself when life and death meet. In Judaism there is nothing more important than life; and when life and death meet in one's body, one becomes spiritually, that is, essentially, out of balance. The sense of *shalom*, the spiritual regularity of the world, is violated and must be restored. In Judaism, only living water can do that. You immerse yourself in a pool, a *mikvah*, to restore the *shalom*. A Jewish man will go to the *mikvah* when he feels a spiritual need for it; for example, before the Sabbath, before feasts or festivals, or some other time when he feels the need. A Jewish woman must go to the *mikvah* when life and death have met in her body, and that means either at the end of her monthly cycle or when she gives birth. Some believe that the Christian rite of baptism has its roots in this Jewish immersion ritual. Christian baptism, the ritual purification through living water, is the Christian counterpart to the Jewish *mikvah* in which life and death meet in the waters of baptism so that the believer dies to an old life so as to be born to a new life.

Most New Testament scholars, however, would trace Christian baptism, at least to some extent, to that practiced by John the Baptist in the wilderness around the Jordan. That there was some overlap between the ministries of John and Jesus is clear from the New Testament record.[6] John, as did Jesus, had disciples who practiced baptism.[7] Both the baptisms of John and of the early church were eschatological rites in anticipation of the messianic age. Both were by immersion. Both were initiatory rites marking induction into a new community. And, of course, the New Testament affirms that, despite the overwhelming desire that surely must have been present to suppress it, Jesus himself was baptized by John in the Jordan. But what were the antecedents of John's baptism?

The answers have been two: Jewish proselyte baptism (*tebilah*) and the baptisms (*mikvaoth*) of the Convenanters of Qumran. Those who would argue for Jewish proselyte baptism as the background for John's practice point to the once-for-all nature of Jewish proselyte baptism, the initiatory status given to it in which a Gentile was incorporated into the people of Israel, and the fact that it involved immersion in water.[8] Problematic for this view is the fact that proselyte baptism appears to have been self-administered, while John served as the prophetic agent for his baptism. Moreover, John baptized Jews, not Gentile proselytes. For John's baptism to have been based on proselyte baptism, it would have been necessary for John to have abandoned the people of God as the people of God, for which there is no evidence in the Gospels. Other scholars point out that Jewish proselyte baptism was primarily a "covenant ceremony" in which Gentiles, "strangers to the covenant of promise," were brought under the "yoke of the Torah," an emphasis largely missing from John's eschatological rite.[9]

Gaining ground is the notion that the baptism of John owes its origin to the ritual baths the Covenanters of the Qumran community practiced daily.[10] More than a dozen *mikvaoth* were found at Qumran, serving a community of only about 200 Essenes. Moreover, the *Rule of the Community* contains regulations regarding the practice of ritual purification among the Covenanters. Evidently, the Essenes were a messianic "baptist," reformation sect of Jews who had protested the corruption of the Jerusalem temple cultus by retreating to the northwest shore of the Dead Sea there to immerse their community in preparation for the coming of the messiah. John the Baptizer, as the Fourth Gospel refers to him, also had apparently retreated to the wilderness to form a messianic "baptist," reformation sect immersing the people of God in preparation for the coming of the Messiah. The fact that his movement was centered only about a mile or so from Qumran makes it difficult to believe that there should have been no connection between them.

But overriding all these antecedents is the baptism of Jesus, both his water baptism performed by John in the Jordan and his "baptism of death" on the cross.[11] These events more than any others provided the specific content of the early church's understanding of baptism. That Jesus was baptized by John is beyond dispute, vouchsafed by the fact that the early church found it necessary to explain it.[12] That Jesus would number himself with repentant Israel was problematic for the early church. But Jesus was apparently willing to risk misunderstanding at that point in order to identify himself with the sinners he came to save. His intention, apparently, was to create a new people of God out of just such ones as these. That God affirmed Jesus' chosen identity and mission is clear from the message declared by the heavenly voice, a conjoining of two Old Testament messianic texts affirming both Jesus' sonship and servanthood. Sonship was to be the shape of his unique identity, servanthood the shape of his mission. He would be the Son who accomplished his mission through serving and dying.

In Matthew's account of Jesus' baptism (3:13-17), christology and ecclesiology virtually merge into one. He begins by closing what he considers to be a crucial gap in the Markan account; namely, the implication that Jesus, along with all the other "sinners," came to John in the Jordan to be baptized. Matthew will have none of that. And so he has John demur by protesting to Jesus: "I have need to be baptized by you, and you come to me?" The inference is clear: Jesus did not submit to baptism as a sinner. Then, Matthew makes explicit what was implicit in John's protestation when Jesus responds by saying: "Do it now, for in this way it is appropriate for us to fulfill all righteousness." That is to say, Jesus' baptism was an act of obedience to the righteous will of God.

As confirmation of the Son's obedience, the heavens open, a voice is heard, and the Spirit descends. Jews of Jesus' day would have regarded all of these phenomena as portents of the advent of the messianic age of the Kingdom. In the wake of divine silence in the Exile, Judaism's theodicy had relegated God to the sidelines of history. To them, God spoke only through the Torah. But among Jews of Jesus' day there was hope held out that in the last days God would once again become active in history with the appearance of the Messiah whose presence would be accompanied by divine manifestations such as the ones accompanying Jesus' baptism. As in Mark, the nature of the message declared by the heavenly voice is that Jesus is both God's Son and Servant. But whereas the Markan account emphasizes the former, Matthew's account emphasizes the latter.[13] Though Jesus is Son, he is baptized as God's obedient Servant, thus modeling for the church the nature of authentic discipleship.[14]

What was implicit in Jesus' baptism became explicit in his teaching: there is a "baptism" that is not water baptism to which water baptism merely points. Jesus himself seems to have joined the ideas of baptism and death together when he said: "A baptism I have with which to be baptized, and how I am in anguish until it be completed."[15] Moreover, Jesus made it clear that this "baptism" was not his alone, but would also be demanded of his followers, a necessary death through which he must bring his own in leading them to life.[16] This other "baptism" became the object of much theological reflection as the early church began to articulate its theology of baptism. This is especially true of the apostle Paul.

Baptism in the Acts of the Apostles

When we come to Luke's account of the rise of the earliest church in the Acts of the Apostles, one thing becomes immediately clear: the first Christians understood themselves to be an eschatological community of the Kingdom that had dawned, they believed, in the events surrounding the life, death, resurrection, and ascension of Jesus of Nazareth.

The eschatological character of the early Christians' preaching as recorded in Acts is evident from the first sermon Peter preached at Pentecost. Following the outpouring of the Spirit at Pentecost, Simon Peter stood up to interpret the associated phenomena by announcing that the ecstatic speech that onlookers had witnessed when the Holy Spirit descended upon the assembled, praying Christian community was not the result of drunkenness, but was rather the fulfillment of the prophecy of Joel who had predicted that in the last days God's Spirit would be "poured out upon all flesh, and your sons and your daughters shall prophesy, and your young men shall see visions, and your old men shall dream dreams"[17]

As Peter made clear in that sermon, the earliest Christians believed that the manifestation of the Spirit at Pentecost, enabling them to fulfill Jesus' commission to them to be his "witnesses in Jerusalem, Judea, Samaria, and the ends of the earth," signaled the advent of the messianic age. The appropriate response to such an event, said Peter, is to "repent, and be baptized every one of you in the name of Jesus Christ for the forgiveness of your sins; and you shall receive the Holy Spirit," one presumes, as an ensign that they, too, have entered the messianic age.[18]

In Acts, baptism, invariably associated with the proclamation of the advent of the messianic age, constitutes, along with repentance and faith, the appropriate response to the good news that the new age had dawned.[19] Beyond that, however, it is difficult to identify any particular pattern in Acts. For example, at Pentecost the sequence was preaching, conviction, repentance, baptism, and the gift of the Spirit. But in Samaria (Acts 8:12ff.) the sequence was preaching, faith, baptism, laying on of hands, and the gift of the Spirit. For the Ethiopian eunuch (8:26ff.), the pattern was the reading of the Scriptures, preaching, and baptism, apparently with no laying on of hands and no mention of the coming of the Spirit. With Cornelius (Acts 10:44ff.) the sequence was preaching, the gift of the Spirit, the manifestation of tongues, and baptism. For the disciples of John at Ephesus (Acts 19:1ff.), the sequence was corrective teaching, baptism, laying on of hands, the gift of the Spirit, tongues, and prophecy. It is fair to say, then, that baptism in Acts is an eschatological act closely associated with preaching/teaching, repentance, the gift of the Holy Spirit, and the forgiveness of sins, and functions as a response indicating one's faith and signifying one's acceptance of the gospel. That is to say, baptism is a sign, or indication, of conversion. But more than that the evidence will not support.

Baptism in the Letters of Paul

Paul's theology, too, is thoroughly eschatological.[20] He believed that in Jesus Christ the new age had dawned. The new thing that Paul adds to this fundamentally eschatological perspective that seems to have permeated the early church's theological reflection about the significance of Jesus is the idea of "Christ mysticism." For Paul, the advent of the Kingdom of God heralded by Jesus and his immediate followers had become virtually identified with the Risen Christ. For Paul, to be in the Kingdom is to be in Christ. Through union with Christ we are delivered from this evil age and here and now participate in the powers of the new age to come.[21]

For Paul, this union with Christ involved a transformation of the profoundest sort. So countercultural and catastrophic was this metamorphosis that Paul likened it to death to an old way of life and birth to an utterly new way of life:

> Do you not know that as many of you as have been baptized into Christ Jesus were baptized into his death? We were, therefore, buried with him through baptism into death in order that just as Christ was raised from the dead through the glory of the father, so also we in newness of life should walk.[22]

Baptism, then, functions for Paul, even as it did for Luke in Acts, as a sign of a conversion so profound that only it will prepare one adequately for life in the new age. The death that the believer dies, s/he dies in union with Christ. It is not just a death to aspects of one's self, it is a death to self, a yielding up of one's life to another. For Paul, this baptism into the death of Christ is overtly expressed in water baptism but is never to be confused with water baptism.

In Galatians 3:27 and elsewhere, Paul's Christ-mysticism is extended beyond union with Christ in his death to union with Christ in his life: "For whichever ones of you were baptized into Christ have put on Christ." The imagery is that of putting on Christ as one puts on a robe. Elsewhere Paul extends this metaphor to "taking off" the old life and "putting on" the new life in Christ.[23] Here, too, baptism may be the metaphorical symbol of the spiritual transformation occurring in the believer in that typically the baptizand would strip off his/her clothes before being baptized as a symbol of stripping off the old life and following his/her baptism would put on a new robe as a symbol of new life in Christ.

Perhaps the most remarkable analogy Paul employed for baptism was that it was the Christian's circumcision:

> In whom also you were circumcised with a circumcision made without hands in the putting off of the body of flesh, in the circumcision of Christ, having been buried with him in baptism, in whom also you were raised together through faith which is energized by God who raised him from the dead.[24]

Paul seems to pick up the idea that circumcision in Judaism involved "putting off" a part of the body as a sign that one belonged to God and attaches it to the Christian rite of baptism as a "putting off" of the entire body of flesh in a "circumcision not made with hands." Baptism, in this analogy, functions as the *sine qua non* of the Christian's identity just as circumcision had functioned as the *sine qua non* of the Jew's identity. Just as circumcision was the initiatory rite of entry into the community of the people of God, Israel; so now baptism is the initiatory rite of entry into the new people of God, the Church.

Although baptism is not discussed in the passage, Romans 5:12ff. is significant for any discussion of baptism in that it is the biblical *locus classicus* for the doctrine of original sin, the dogmatic presupposition underlying the practice of paedobaptism, or the baptism of infants or small children.[25] Biblically, the concept of original sin "originates" with the Vulgate's mistranslation of this passage when it rendered verse 12 from the original Greek into Latin as follows: "Therefore, just as through one man sin entered into the world and death through sin, even so death spread unto all men [through the one man] in whom [*en quo*] all sinned."[26] The assumption was that the reference was to Adam, and that Paul had in mind some notion of original sin biologically transmitted from one generation to another.

That interpretation subsequently became the official dogma of the Roman Catholic church, and, abetted by Calvin's concept of total depravity, has also become the dominant view in much popular Protestant theology. Scholarly opinion, however, is virtually unanimous that the key Greek phrase, *eph ho*, is idiomatic Greek for "in that," "inasmuch as," or "because."[27] The correct translation, then, is: "Therefore, just as through one man sin entered into the world and death through sin, even so death spread unto all men inasmuch as all sinned." Paul's point is that we are sinners not because of something Adam did, but because of what we all, as a matter of course, in fact do.

In good Jewish fashion Paul is composing a midrash on the Genesis account of Adam's fall in which he, consistent with the Jewish theology of his day, stresses the tension between the inescapableness of human sin on the one hand, and the recognition of human responsibility and accountability for sin on the other. It is the Jewish version of the old debate between "nature" and "nurture," or between determinism and freedom. Today this discussion might take the form of a debate between human responsibility for our actions versus the constraints placed on us by genetics or gender or education or social opportunity. But to interpret this passage as biblical support for the notion of some sort of theory of the biological transmission of sin, with neither the knowledge nor consent of the sinner involved, is not warranted by the text.

Baptism in 1 Peter 3:21

The New Testament text that attaches the greatest significance to baptism is 1 Peter 3:21: "Baptism, which also [is] an antitype, now saves you, not the putting off of the dirt of the flesh, but an answer of a good conscience before God, through the resurrection of Jesus Christ."[28] The context is concerned with encouraging Christians who are undergoing persecution by pointing out that Christ has triumphed over all his enemies, and, therefore, so also will they. The explicit reference is to an intertestamental tradition that Enoch, when being translated to heaven, stopped off to preach judgment to the disobedient spirits, the *bene ha Elohim*, of the days of Noah.[29] The reference to Noah led to the statement that "eight souls were saved through water." The eight in the time of Noah were saved through the very water that threatened to destroy them. In the same way, so the writer seems to be saying, baptism, which symbolizes a death to one way of life and a birth to another, both destroys and saves. It is a picture that, as Jesus said, "one must lose one's life to save it." The imagery, therefore, is another variation on the theme, consistent in the New Testament, that baptism pictures a conversion of the most profound sort.

From this survey of the New Testament evidence regarding baptism, the following points may be adduced.

• Baptism in the New Testament was always by immersion.

• Baptism in the New Testament was an eschatological act both signaling the advent of the new age and serving as an act of initiation into it.

• While the specific Jewish antecedents of baptism are difficult to identify with precision, it appears certain that baptism functioned for Christians, even as it did for Jews, as an act of spiritual cleansing associated with the confluence of life and death in the person of the baptized.

• As such, baptism was associated with conversion, the inner transformation of the believer of the profoundest sort.

• Baptism in the New Testament was a confessional act, functioning as faith's response to the proclamation of the gospel.

• Baptism in the New Testament was a community act, initiating one into the community of the new age.

• Baptism in the New Testament was called neither symbol nor sacrament, and neither term is wholly adequate to express what the New Testament means by baptism. To call it a sacrament is to suggest something magical, that it works all by itself (*ex opera operato*), and the New Testament evidence will not support such a view. By the same token, calling baptism a symbol suggests that it is merely an arbitrary metaphor, completely inadequate to depict a spiritual transformation so catastrophic, so complete, so countercultural that it can only be properly described as "death" and "rebirth." The theological reflection on baptism in the Letters of Paul indicates that there is nothing "arbitrary" about this particular "symbol." It is a symbol with inherent power.[30]

Baptist Theology of Baptism

With the disclaimer that no Baptist can speak for another clearly in view, I shall summarize now what I regard as the "typical" Baptist theology of baptism.[31] Chief among Baptist principles governing the appropriate administration of baptism is the idea usually referred to as "believer's baptism."[32] In Baptist theology it is related to the concept of a "regenerate church membership," meaning that baptism must be administered after faith, not prior to it, and that it must be the conscious, free, and voluntary act of the believer. Baptism is a human response of faith, not a divine act of grace.[33] It is on this ground that Baptists reject infant baptism. H. Wheeler Robinson, a Baptist and former principal of Regent's Park College, Oxford, put it this way:

> The common element in all these interpretations of baptism is the necessary passivity of the infant baptized. Whether baptism be called dedication, or covenanting by parents, or sealing of a divine covenant, or an actual regeneration, it is throughout something done to, nothing done by, the baptized. So far as he is concerned, all of them are non-moral acts, though the act of the parents or sponsors is properly moral. The Baptist position is not simply a new phase of this succession of interpretations; it stands outside of them all as the only baptism which is strictly and primarily an ethical act on the part of the baptized.[34]

To put it succinctly, Baptists disbelieve in surrogate faith. The encounter with God required for salvation and regeneration is necessarily an individual encounter.

Moreover, Baptists believe that immersion is the only appropriate mode for the administration of baptism.[35] The Baptist distrust of authoritative tradition drives them to the New Testament model for baptism as immersion only; and as we have already seen, immersion is an especially appropriate picture for the Pauline and Petrine imagery that death and life meet in baptismal waters. The earliest evidence of a mode other than immersion being employed for Christian baptism comes from the *Didache*, or *The Teaching of the Twelve Apostles*, which dates to the early second-century AD. The key passage translates as follows:

Now concerning baptism, baptize in this way. Having before spoken all these things, baptize in the name of the Father and of the Son and of the Holy Spirit in living water. And if you should not have living water, baptize in other water [i.e. water of the same kind]. And if you are not able [to baptize] in cold [water], [then baptize] in hot. And if neither you should have, pour water three times on the head in the name of the Father and of the Son and of the Holy Spirit.[36]

The text is early and permits modes of baptism other than immersion. However, the tenor of the argument in which alternative modes are permitted is clearly concessionary and accommodationist: You should baptize in living water; but if living water is unavailable, it's permissible to baptize in cold water; but if cold water is unavailable, it's permissible to baptize in hot water, etc. By extension of the principle, I presume you could say: "If you can't immerse in running water, use a pool; if you can't use a pool, pour; if you can't pour, sprinkle, and if you can't sprinkle, I guess you could spit!" Baptists uniformly employ the New Testament model of immersion, although we rarely any longer do so in "living water," and I notice that even though we immerse, we like to have our baptisteries heated, a clear violation of the spirit of the *Didache*!

The third thing most Baptists would agree on is that baptism is an ordinance, not a sacrament.[37] That is to say, the act does not by itself bestow grace. Among Baptists, George Beasley-Murray perhaps has espoused the view nearest to a sacramental one. And yet, even Beasley-Murray cautions that the Bible, from the time of the prophets on, is at one in criticizing the notion of a purely external, automatic, materialistic view of religious objects and actions.[38] Moreover, as I indicated at the outset of this chapter, the great Baptist New Testament scholar, A. T. Robertson, regarded this as the *sine qua non* of Baptist theology, separating us from, in his words, "the great mass of modern Christians."[39]

These three things, then, I would regard as the key components of Baptist thinking about baptism: believer's baptism, by immersion, as a symbol (rather than a sacrament) of grace. As such, baptism's centrality in Baptist life is indicated by the fact that the immersion pool (baptistery) typically occupies the highest, central, most visible place in a Baptist church.

A Baptist's Theology of Baptism

The earliest Christian confession was, *Iesous Kyrios*, "Jesus is Lord."[40] Indeed, the distinguishing mark of a Christian in the early church was one's willingness publicly to confess faith in the words: "Jesus [Christ] is Lord."[41]

I witnessed that firsthand some years ago in the Caribbean. I had taken some seminarians to the Islands to work with a missionary for a few weeks. While we were there, several of the islanders made professions of their faith in Jesus. On the final Sunday before we departed, the missionary and I conducted a baptismal service in the ocean at beach side. The nationals had been reluctant to attend the services we had conducted. Many feared that there would be reprisals against them from the local authorities who objected to our presence there. But when we waded out into the water to baptize Peter, a young believer who was a local woodworker in the village, scores of townsfolk gathered on the beach to watch. I commented to the missionary: "Isn't it wonderful that so many of Peter's neighbors would come out to support him like this!" And the missionary laughed and said: "They're not here to support Peter. They're here taking names!" That was as close as I've come to New Testament baptism.

It's a powerful rite in which life and death, God and humanity, sin and grace meet in a cold, wet, cleansing bath. Despite our attempts to tame it—from roses to heated pools to gold-plated fonts—it still whispers of a wild-eyed prophet screaming in the desert about another world a-comin'. It's inelegant, undignified, humiliating—not a bad symbol, if you think about it, for a transformation so radical that it can rightly be called "death to an old way of life, and birth to a new."

When I baptize, I often speak from the water about the character of what we do. I say:

> When you join the Lion's Club or the Rotary Club, they shake your hand, pat you on the back, give you a pin and send you on your way pretty much as you were before. But when you join the church, we strip you naked as the day you were born, throw you in the water, half drown you, and then when you come up sputtering and spewing, we embrace you and call you "brother" and "sister." When you think about it, that's not bad preparation for

life in the Kingdom of God, a way of living in the world that will
make you odd, set you against culture, make you act "funny" and
feel "funny" and live "funny." We call it "baptism."

As a Baptist, I am often embarrassed at how anemic our Baptist
theology of baptism has become. Baptists, of all people, should seek
to understand and communicate the power of this powerful
symbol. But too often baptism is a forethought in our services, per-
functorily performed as a prelude to the "real" worship, or an
afterthought tacked on like a useless appendage to the end. Baptists
who rail against the mechanism and magic of the sacramentalists,
insisting that a symbol without significance is meaningless at best,
magic at worst, too often themselves reduce the rite to mere
formalism and pedantry.

Theologically, we seem oblivious to the logical inconsistency of
claiming, as Baptists often do, that baptism is a "mere symbol," and
then at the same time arguing that it doesn't "take" if enough water
isn't used. We excoriate the paedobaptists for baptizing unbelieving
infants, insisting that baptism doesn't "take" unless the baptized
"understands what s/he is doing." And yet, we baptize children,
some as young as three or four, who have about as much understanding of conversion as most adults have of quantum mechanics.
Besides, who among us who were baptized as adults really "understood" what we did when we submitted to the water? Twenty-nine
years ago I stood before my good friend George Balentine and,
when he asked whether or not I take this woman to be my wedded
wife, I said: "I do." I thought I understood what I was doing. But
now, twenty-nine years later, I'm still trying to "understand" what I
said when I said "I do." And so it is with my baptism. If one has to
"understand" before one can appropriately submit to baptism, then
would somebody please identify for me that absolute, nonnegotiable "something" that must be understood? And even if we
could establish such a thing, who among us will decide when it is
properly "understood?"

No. There is much muddled thinking among us Baptists about
baptism. And while I claim no special insight in this regard, I would
venture a description of baptism that, at this point in my thinking,
satisfies me. It is one Baptist's theology of baptism.

I would describe baptism as a sign signifying to all the beginning of a lifelong process of conversion to that Kingdom God revealed in Jesus Christ and one's adoption into the community of the kingdom people he is creating. I will comment briefly on each element of this description.

"A sign"

I prefer "sign" to "symbol" because whereas a symbol can be arbitrary, a sign participates in the reality of that which it signifies (The number "3" is a symbol of the idea of "threeness." The Roman numeral III is a sign.). Baptism is more than a mere symbol. The act of being buried beneath the water and being raised from underneath the water is a sign of the very kind of death and life that conversion demands. Some symbols say things. Some symbols do things. Baptism doesn't just say something; it does something. It is the spiritual heir of the Old Testament "prophetic act" in which the prophet "acted out" the word of God predicated on the idea that God's word can be stated and performed.[42] It sets in motion the action it represents. Therefore, it is a mistake to refer to baptism as a "mere symbol." There is nothing "mere" about baptism. My teacher and mentor, Frank Stagg, says it well with an analogy to a wedding:

> Water baptism is to the union with Christ what a wedding is to a marriage. Each presupposes a previous commitment, and each is a commitment. A wedding ring is a symbol, but a wedding is more than a symbol. In a wedding the mutual commitments already made in private are brought to outward expression in community. A wedding alone is not a marriage. Even so, water baptism without a previous personal commitment to Jesus Christ is but an empty gesture. . . . Since some cultures do not have what we know as a wedding, a marriage may be a marriage without a wedding. But a wedding adds immeasurably to the beauty and sacredness of a marriage. Even so, union with Christ can be real apart from water baptism, but baptism adds to the beauty and sacredness of that union.[43]

"Signifying a lifelong process of conversion"

The Christian life is not some slow, perfectly natural, inexorable, orderly process of faith development toward some esoteric goal of psychic wellness. It is, as Will Willimon says, "detoxification."[44] As

Will quips: "None of us takes naturally to water."[45] It is "hydro-therapeutic repentance."[46] And repentance, as C. S. Lewis reminds us, is no fun at all!

> It means killing a part of yourself, undergoing a kind of death. . . . Remember, this repentance, this willing submission to humiliation and a kind of death, is not something God demands of you before He will take you back and which He could let you off if He chose: it is simply a description of what going back to Him is like. If you ask God to take you back without it, you are really asking Him to let you go back without going back. It cannot happen.[47]

But neither is conversion some fleeting, momentary, ephemeral experience like Camelot that, once lost, can never again be regained. The salvation of which the New Testament speaks, this coming back to God, is more journey than event, though it is event. Thomas Oden talks about "the five days" of the believer's life: the day one is born, the day one is baptized, the day one is confirmed, the day one enters into a lifelong covenant of fidelity in marriage, the day one dies.[48] Baptism, as a rite of conversion or commencement, is well suited to signify the onset of this process, but is not very well suited to signify the continuation of it. Because we Baptists have jettisoned virtually all the rituals of the church, fearing formalism, we have tended to "front load" baptism with too much theology while ignoring the rest of the life of discipleship. It is for that reason that in most Baptist churches "rededication of one's life" has become the Baptist counterpart to confirmation, a rite of continuation and identification in sacramental traditions.[49]

Personally, I like the Roman Catholic idea of the sacrament as *viaticum* (from the Latin *via*, meaning "way"), the administration of the Eucharist to the dying as provision for the final leg of the "way" through life, literally "one for the road."[50] It seems to me that this ritual of affirming the presence of God on the journey, including its final leg, may have some application to a healthy biblical and ecclesiastical soteriology. Indeed, the concept of *viaticum*, God with us all along the way from womb to tomb, is much closer to the New Testament concept of salvation than the popular Baptist notion of salvation conceived of as an isolated event, largely emotional, that is accessed in the present only as memory. In the New Testament salvation is a vital, dynamic, synergistic experience with God through

Christ into which one grows throughout one's entire life.[51] In short, it is *viaticum*, God with us all along the way, changing us, redeeming us, saving us, making us his own.

It occurs to me: if this concept of *viaticum* as a primary soteriological metaphor could be extended to include the entirety of the Christian life and not just the last leg of it, with appropriate rituals along the way, baptism being but one of them, I think it could help significantly to assuage our Baptist propensity to reduce salvation to a single event that one was forced to try to relive or recapture over and over again as life moves in and out of its various vicissitudes. Both our understandings of ourselves and of God change as we move through life. Salvation cannot mean for me in my adolescence what it means in my adulthood. To freeze faith in its nascency is a denial of the New Testament teaching on salvation, the grace of God, and our character as persons.

Moreover, human beings are both cognitive and affective, thinking and feeling, knowing and doing creatures. There are times when just *saying* faith isn't enough; we need to *do* faith. That is particularly true if faith is more journey than event. We all need *viaticum*, those rituals of faith, those "rites of passage" that tap us on the shoulder at various watershed moments of our lives (the birth of a child, our emergence into adulthood, our marriage, at illness and death), and whisper: "Pssst. Don't forget, God is here too!"

It is at this point that, it seems to me, even Baptists need some "rite of Christian commencement"—baptism at birth, baby dedication, or something similar—to signify the beginning of this process, some "ritual of adoption" into the people of God that signals the advent of the journey and the presence of God at its outset. Such a ritual becomes an initiation of the *viaticum*, in which both parents and people own for the child what someday, if all do their job well, the child will own for him/herself. Farther along "on the way," then, believer's baptism can become as it were the Baptist counterpart to confirmation, the event in which one owns for oneself what was owned for him/her when one was a child. Without some ritual of *viaticum* ("setting a child out on his/her way to God"), Baptists are forced to admit that we really have no theology for children and either treat them as adults and baptize them as "infants" (as early as two and three years old), or put them off until they "understand what they're doing"—whatever that means, whenever that is.

"Signifying . . . one's adoption into the community"

Our Baptist proclivity toward individualism has caused us to undervalue the communal aspect of salvation. From the first, baptism was not a purely private affair, but rather signified one's incorporation into the eschatological people of God. Origen once said: "There is no salvation outside the church," and in the sense in which he meant it, I take him to be correct. Baptism does not mean whatever we as individuals want it to mean. It means what the church says it means. Indeed, baptism "means" church. Baptism is not initiation into some private, inner life of narcissistic self-reflection. It is, by its very nature, an act of community. You don't know what your baptism means until the church teaches you. You don't know what you did when you were baptized until the church tells you. You don't know who you are until the church tells you. Indeed, the major work of the church lies just here: disabusing you of the false and bankrupt notions of who you really are with which the world has seduced and confused and corrupted you. Richard John Neuhaus, when asked about his conversion to Roman Catholicism, replied:

> It is not quite accurate to say I "converted" to Roman Catholicism. I was converted at three weeks of age when I was baptized. Every day is a day of baptismal conversion, of dying and rising again with Christ, of taking new steps toward becoming more fully what, by the grace of God, we most truly are.[52]

Baptism is the place where this "dying and rising" is best signified. It's a powerful rite in which life and death, God and humanity, sin and grace meet in a cold, wet, cleansing bath. It's a messy, inelegant, humiliating, holy business. It's stripping down, letting go, giving up, so that we, in the life God gives us, might rise again.

"But it's so . . . so . . . inelegant," she said. Precisely. Significantly. Horribly. I remind you: none of us takes naturally to water. John Donne, I think, caught a glimpse of it when he wrote in Holy Sonnet 14:

> Batter my heart, three-personed God; for You
> As yet knock, breathe, shine, and seek to mend;
> That I may rise and stand, o'erthrow me, and bend
> Your force to break, blow, burn, and make me new.[53]

Notes

[1]A. T. Robertson, "The Spiritual Interpretation of the Ordinances," in *The Life of Baptists in the Life of the World: 80 Years of the Baptist World Alliance,* Walter B. Shurden, ed. (Nashville: Broadman Press, 1985) 50.

[2]Shurden, preface.

[3]Cf. *bathos,* "deep," etc.

[4]There is no evidence in the New Testament that baptism was ever administered through any mode other than immersion. Even Karl Barth, himself a Lutheran whose tradition practiced infant baptism by sprinkling, was forced to admit that the New Testament evidence is clear in this regard. See Karl Barth, *The Teaching of the Church Regarding Baptism* (London: SCM Press, 1963) 40ff. So also Jürgen Moltmann, *The Church in the Power of the Spirit* (Philadelphia: Fortress Press, 1993) 226ff; 240ff.

[5]One of the tractates in the *Mishnah,* "*Mikvaoth,*" deals exclusively with purification rituals associated with immersion pools.

[6]Though the Fourth Gospel attempts to minimize the impact of John's ministry on Jesus, the Synoptics agree that Jesus' ministry commences with the arrest of John, and that in some sense Jesus regarded his own ministry as a continuation of that of the Baptist's.

[7]Cf. John 4:1-2. See also Acts 18:25.

[8]Frank Stagg, *New Testament Theology* (Nashville: Broadman Press, 1962) 208-209.

[9]George R. Beasley-Murray, *Baptism in the New Testament* (London: Paternoster Press, 1962) 41.

[10]Ibid. See also Otto Betz, "Was John the Baptist an Essene?" *Bible Review* (December 1990).

[11]Cf. Mark 10:38.

[12]A comparison of Matthew's account of Jesus' baptism with Mark's account makes it clear that Matthew found problematic Mark's straightforward statement that in the days when John was preaching a baptism of repentance for the forgiveness of sins, among the "sinners" who came out to the Jordan to be baptized by John was Jesus. Incidentally, comparisons such as this argue persuasively for Markan priority.

[13]In 12:18ff. Matthew cites the entire First Servant Song (Isa 42:1-4), the longest scriptural quotation in the Gospel of Matthew.

[14]The linking of baptism as the sign of obedient servanthood with the making of disciples in the church is made explicit in the so-called Great Commission (Matt 28:18-20). The authenticity of the passage has long been contested *and* defended. For a discussion of the arguments, see Beasley-Murray, 77-92.

[15]Luke 12:50, author's translation. See also Mark 10:38ff.

[16]"The cup of which I drink you will drink, and the baptism with which I am baptized you will be baptized" (Mark 10:39, author's translation).

[17]Acts 2:16ff. Cf. Joel 2:1-5.

[18]Acts 2:38.

[19]That baptism in Acts was immersion is not threatened by the fact that Acts records that some entire "households" were converted and baptized. In the Roman

world, the religion of the *pater familias* became the religion of the entire household, so that when a pagan converted to Christianity, so also did his family, slaves, and servants. The fact that such a household would have included infants and small children does not automatically imply that they, too, were immersed, though it does not preclude it either. However, the fact that Acts records that ecstatic gifts typically accompanied the conversion of a household would suggest that infants were not included.

[20]See, for example, James D. G. Dunn, *Unity and Diversity in the New Testament*, 2nd ed. (Valley Forge PA: Trinity Press, 1993) 21ff; George E. Ladd, *A Theology of the New Testament*, rev. ed. (Grand Rapids: Eerdmans, 1994) 397ff; Robin Scroggs, *Paul for a New Day* (Philadelphia: Fortress Press, 1977), passim.

[21]Cf. Rom 6:3; 8:18-30; Gal 3:27.

[22]Rom 6:3-4, author's translation.

[23]Cf. Eph 4:22ff; 6:11ff.

[24]Cf. Col 2:11-12, author's translation.

[25]"Born with a fallen human nature and tainted by original sin, children also have need of the new birth in Baptism to be freed from the power of darkness and brought into the realm of the freedom of the children of God, to which all men are called." *Catechism of the Catholic Church* (Washington: United States Catholic Conference, 1994) 319. Origen (d. AD 251) is the earliest source of the tradition that the Apostles enjoined the baptism of children, "The Church has received a tradition from the Apostles to give baptism even to little children." The credibility of this tradition, however, is a matter of much dispute. See Beasley-Murray, 306.

[26]For a full discussion of the debate related to the correct translation of Rom 5:12, see C. E. B. Cranfield, "On Some Problems in the Interpretation of Rom 5:12." *Scottish Journal of Theology*, 22 (1969): 324-41.

[27]See 2 Cor 5:4 and Phil 3:12 where Paul uses the same phrase clearly meaning "because." Cf. C. E. B. Cranfield, *Romans 1-8*, Word Biblical Commentary, vol. 38A (Dallas: Word Books, 1988) 273.

[28]Author's translation.

[29]See Bo Reicke, *The Disobedient Spirits and Christian Baptism* (Copenhagen: Ejnar Munksgaard Forlay, 1946), for the definitive treatment of this text.

[30]Cf. Beasley-Murray, 262ff.

[31]I choose the term "typical" because, on the one hand, there really is no "orthodox" Baptist position on baptism, and on the other hand, to recognize the fact that what I am about to describe would not be representative of the baptismal practices of all Baptists. The three principles articulated here, however, I believe would find broad agreement among most Baptists.

[32]Cf. Robert G. Torbet, *A History of the Baptists*, 3rd ed. (Valley Forge PA: Judson Press, 1973) 516.

[33]It is at this point that notions of "prevenient grace" enter the conversation. Theologians of both the Roman traditions and the paedobaptist Protestant traditions stress the biblical idea of divine initiative prior to the human response of faith, symbolized by the fact that the child is unable to have faith by him/herself and requires his/her parents to "faith" for him/her as a picture of God's prevenient

grace in our behalf; cf. "In this is love, not that we loved God but that he loved us and sent his Son . . . for us" (1 John 4:10).

[34]H. Wheeler Robinson, *The Life and Faith of the Baptists* (London: Kingsgate Press, 1946) 73.

[35]I find it telling that the Baptist scholar George Beasley-Murray in his definitive work on baptism in the New Testament barely even addresses other modes of baptism. He dispatches the notion that New Testament baptism could have been administered by a mode other than immersion in one page! See Beasley-Murray, 133.

[36]Allen Wikgren, *Hellenistic Greek Texts* (Chicago: University of Chicago Press, 1949)104. Author's translation.

[37]The word "ordinance" comes from the Latin ordo meaning "to order something." It has to do with a "directive or command" of an authoritative nature. Hence, it has come to be applied to established religious rites such as baptism and communion in that these acts can be seen as responses to specific "commands" or "ordinances" of Jesus (See Matt 28:19; 1 Cor 11:24). A "sacrament," on the other hand, bestows grace on the participant in the ritual.

[38]Beasley-Murray, 300.

[39]Cited in Shurden, 50

[40]1 Cor 12:3.

[41]Cf. I. Howard Marshall, *The Origins of New Testament Christology* (Downers Grove IL: InterVarsity Press, 1976) 97.

[42]Cf. Beasley-Murray, 43.

[43]Stagg, 234.

[44]William H. Willimon, *Peculiar Speech: Preaching to the Baptized* (Grand Rapids: Eerdmans, 1992) 63.

[45]Ibid., 54.

[46]Ibid., 55.

[47]C. S. Lewis, *Mere Christianity*, rev. ed. (New York: Macmillan, 1981) 49.

[48]Thomas Oden, *Pastoral Theology* (New York: Harper & Row, 1982) 85.

[49]Incidentally, it is not coincidental that rededication tends to occur most frequently at about the same age as confirmation in the sacramental traditions, namely, the onset of puberty. When young people enter adolescence, their emerging sense of selfhood precipitates a crisis of faith as well as of personal identity.

[50]*Catechism of the Catholic Church*, 381.

[51]The language of salvation in the New Testament is rich, incorporating images and metaphors that speak of God's saving work as accomplished fact (1 Cor 6:11), present reality (1 Cor 1:18), and future goal (1 Pet 1:9). That Baptists have recognized this dynamic character of the New Testament teaching on salvation is evinced by *The Baptist Faith and Message Statement's* article on "salvation." The *Statement* defines salvation in terms of three aspects or qualities (corresponding to the past, present, and future qualities of the New Testament teaching on salvation): regeneration, sanctification, and glorification.

[52]Quoted in Willimon, 63.

[53]*The Norton Anthology of English Literature*, Vol. I, rev. ed., M. H. Adrams, gen. ed. (New York: W.W. Norton Co., Inc., 1968) 909.

Communion

G. Thomas Halbrooks

I still remember how we children hated to see it. Yet four times a year, the first Sunday of every quarter, there it would be—the table down front with a large white tablecloth covering all the plates and trays for the Lord's Supper. We usually wouldn't remember it until we came in the back of the church and saw it, and then we would say to each other, "Oh no; not today!"

It meant that after we went through the entire service, as we did every Sunday, then we had to go through the Lord's Supper part. We would be twenty to thirty minutes later getting out, and would we ever be hungry by that time! Even after we were old enough to join the church and take the elements, the little bit of bread and juice we got didn't help at all with the hunger.

Children at some of the other churches were able to go to the table after the service and eat the bread and drink the juice that was left, but the adults at our church would never think of allowing us to do such a thing. They didn't have the Lord's Supper very often; but when they did, they were much too serious about it to let any such foolishness happen.

Our church leaders also were serious about calling it the Lord's Supper. It was Jesus who had the first supper with his disciples and then told them to continue to do it in remembrance of him. It was the Lord's Supper. Since he began it and told us to do it, we did it to remember him. So the Lord's Supper was serious business, and our church leaders were confident that we didn't need any other fancy names for it that might imply it was something else.

In those years growing up in a Baptist church, I experienced some of the variety of views that Baptists have held regarding the Lord's Supper. Later, as I studied Baptist history and theology, I discovered that there were many more Baptist views than I had experienced in my earlier years. And those views had developed within a much larger context of views within the Christian community. While Baptists had followed some of those views, they had reacted against others.

But my assignment is not to present the Baptist theology of the Lord's Supper. It is to present my Baptist theology of the Lord's Supper or Communion. Yet, it was through studying the development of varying views that my own theology of Communion developed; therefore, I will present it in that way.

As Baptists follow the Protestant principle of *sola scriptura*, I will begin with a look at Communion in the New Testament. Then I will trace its development from the early church through the Reformation. The Reformation provided the context for the development of Baptist views, which I will then consider. In presenting all of this development, I will obviously be critiquing views from my own theological perspective. Finally, after looking at the development of Baptist views, I will present my own Baptist theology of Communion and in the process explain why I prefer the term "Communion" over the more widely used term among Baptists, "the Lord's Supper."

Communion in the New Testament

Although the early Christians continued their Jewish worship in the temple and the synagogues for a time, they also began to develop two of their own worship forms. The first was a service of the Word modeled on the Jewish synagogue service. It included prayer, scripture reading, preaching, an offering, and possibly singing. The focus varied from education to edification to evangelism. The word was proclaimed; people responded and were drawn together in Christian fellowship.

Christian fellowship was an important element of the second type of service the early Christians developed. It consisted of an *agape*, or fellowship meal, followed by a celebration of Communion, or the Eucharist, meaning "thanksgiving." In this service they sought to follow the pattern set by Christ in his last supper with the disciples.

The New Testament gives several descriptions of the last supper. All three synoptic Gospels give an account of the event, although the accounts vary slightly. John's gospel does not give an account, although some think that the discussion in John 6 refers to Communion. But clearly the earliest and most widely used account of the event was given by the apostle Paul in 1 Corinthians 11.

Paul explains to the Corinthians how Communion ought to be celebrated based on the earliest Christian tradition regarding the last supper. They are to follow the example of Jesus. He took bread, gave thanks, and broke it, saying, "This is my body that is for you. Do this in remembrance of me." Then he took the cup, saying, "This cup is the new covenant in my blood. Do this, as often as you drink it, in remembrance of me." He concluded by saying, "For as often as you eat this bread and drink the cup, you proclaim the Lord's death until he comes" (1 Cor 11:24-26).

Following this account of Paul, the early Christians viewed Communion as looking to the past, the present, and the future. It looked to the past to God's mighty act in Christ. It was a call to remembrance of Christ's death on their behalf. Communion also looked in the present to the communion or fellowship of the believers with Christ and with each other. They believed Christ to be truly present in some sense as they celebrated Communion. After all, he had said, "This is my body." And Paul had said explicitly, "The cup of blessing that we bless, is it not a sharing in the blood of Christ? The bread that we break, is it not a sharing in the body of Christ? Because there is one bread, we who are many are one body, for we all partake of the one bread" (1 Cor 10:16-17). Finally, Communion looked to the future in anticipation of Christ's return. Paul had said, "For as often as you eat this bread and drink the cup, you proclaim the Lord's death until he comes" (1 Cor 11:26). In the celebration of Communion in the early church, the themes of remembrance and communion always included the theme of anticipation.

Development in the Early Church and Middle Ages

Some changes took place, however, by the second century. The writings of Justin make clear that by the middle of the century the *agape* meal was no longer used. Instead, Communion had been joined to the service of the word, and the liturgy followed a general pattern. The understanding was also shifting. Ignatius referred to it as the medicine of immortality. By the third century some were no longer only remembering Christ's sacrifice in the past. Cyprian referred to Communion as a sacrifice in which the priest presents Christ's sacrifice anew on the altar. It came to be referred to as the "Mass" from the Latin words of dismissal used in the service. Although some diversity remained, it is clear that the understanding of Communion had developed in a manner different from the understanding in the New Testament.

Such development continued into the Middle Ages. Liturgies became more elaborate, having greater focus of priestly action and less on congregational participation. Communion was viewed as a meritorious work performed by the priest and as a re-presentation of Christ's sacrifice on the altar. During the sacrifice, Christ in some manner became fully present in the elements of bread and wine. It was viewed as a sacrament, an action which provided God's grace when done properly.

Speculation had developed as to when and how the body and blood of Christ became present in the bread and wine. Regarding the "when," the church decided that the event occurred when the priest said the words, *Hoc est corpus meum,* "This is my body." The uneducated masses did not understand the theology or the Latin and viewed it as a magical incantation. It was from their distortion of these words that the term "hocus pocus" developed.

Although the church had decided when Christ became present, discussion continued regarding "how." How was Christ fully present in Communion? Some thought it best not to try to explain it fully. They said that there was no real and objective change in the elements; rather, what is received is not the actual body which was born, crucified, and risen, but the spirit of Christ, a mysterious spiritual body appropriate to a sacrament.[1] But when Berengar of Tours affirmed such a position, it was clear that the church had moved strongly toward the view of a physical change in the elements. In 1059 Berengar was forced to recant his views. He concluded,

> The bread and wine placed on the altar are after consecration not only a sacrament but also the true body and blood of our Lord Jesus Christ and that these are sensibly handled and broken by the hands of priests and crushed by the teeth of the faithful, not only sacramentally but in reality.[2]

It only remained for the Fourth Lateran Council, 1215, to proclaim the doctrine of transubstantiation and for Thomas Aquinas, using the philosophical categories of Aristotle, to explain in detail how such a change or transfer of substance took place.

The church went to great lengths to create the proper setting for this great event of worship. They constructed ever larger and more elaborate churches and cathedrals. They developed elaborate pageantry with choirs, vestments, candles, crosses, bells, and incense.

No doubt the settings produced awe and reverence. But there was a great gulf fixed between clergy and laity. Only the priest was necessary for the mass; and if music was included, only choirs were necessary to sing it. The service was in a strange tongue. If people were present, their primary role was to see what happened. If they took Communion, they received only the bread—only the priest could receive the wine. It was not necessary for the people to receive both elements since Christ's body was fully present in each one. Furthermore, if the wine were given to the people, they might spill some. Since it was considered to be Christ's body, such an accident would create numerous difficulties.

For the pious faithful, no longer was there the mystery of God's presence in their midst in worship. God was holy other. They met God only in the elements in the Mass. God's presence had been fully explained, contained, and controlled. God came in worship at the designated time and in the place where the priest spoke the proper words. In the minds of many, the church had replaced mystery with magic.

Changes by the Protestant Reformers

It is not surprising that the Protestant Reformers wished to effect changes in worship. They all sought to base worship on scripture and put it in the vernacular. They all rejected medieval Communion theology. Yet they differed in their views on what changes should be made.

Luther believed that the word of God should always be read and proclaimed in worship, but he also believed that worship should conclude with Communion. Communion, however, was neither a meritorious work nor a sacrifice. Luther did believe that Communion was a sacrament, but he provided a new Protestant definition for the term. According to Luther, a sacrament was an action instituted by Christ which was a visible and physical sign of an invisible and spiritual reality. It did not confer God's grace automatically. Only those who had faith experienced the grace of God. Furthermore, although Luther did affirm the bodily presence of Christ beneath the elements, he rejected the concept of any change of the bread and wine into the body and blood of Christ, and he gave both bread and wine to the people.

The developers of the Reformed tradition followed many of Luther's ideas. They agreed that Communion was neither a meritorious work nor a sacrifice, and they agreed that Communion was a sacrament, following Luther's new definition for the term. But Ulrich Zwingli rejected Luther's view that Christ was bodily present beneath the elements. Instead, Zwingli said that as the congregation celebrated Communion, Christ became present in the hearts and minds of the believers. Calvin also rejected Luther's view of Christ's bodily presence, but he did affirm that Christ was spiritually present in the bread and wine in a mysterious way. He said that when believers participated in Communion, they were led to contemplate "those lofty mysteries which lie hidden in the sacraments."[3] In their views on Communion Zwingli and Calvin were moving closer to the understanding of the early Christians.

A third Reformation tradition on the European continent was that of the Anabaptists. Although they agreed with the others in following scripture and using the vernacular, their primary principle was to eliminate all "popish" practices. With their narrow scriptural literalism, they gave little recognition of the mystery of God's transcendence. Perhaps they avoided mystery because of their determination to eliminate all vestiges of medieval superstition. But in Communion it meant that they viewed it as a bare memorial. It was simply remembering what Christ did long ago, no more and no less. Whereas the medieval church had dissolved the mystery in Communion by explaining Christ's presence physically in it, the Anabaptists dissolved the mystery in Communion by explaining Christ's presence totally out of it.

The Anglican reform in worship followed more closely the principles of Luther and the Reformed tradition. The *Book of Common Prayer* was a beautiful literary expression of a Protestant reform of historic English liturgies. In Communion they followed the thought of Calvin and affirmed Christ's spiritual presence without attempting to explain it. But in their struggle for wholeness in worship they had two shortcomings. First, they were often weak in proclamation. Many ministers depended almost solely on the Prayer Book and put little if any time into preaching the word. The more serious shortcoming, however, was the demand for a fixed, uniform liturgy. The people were not free to respond to the movement of the spirit and worship God in the manner in which they felt led. For many, the

Prayer Book was a meaningful expression of worship. The rest were forced to defy the law if they wished to explore alternatives.

Those who rejected the Prayer Book were known as Puritans because they advocated purifying the church from the vestiges of "popery." They were Calvinists in theology, and some followed his worship pattern and views of Communion. Others, however, used a less structured form of worship and gave a greater place to extemporaneous prayer and proclamation. Although some followed Calvin, many tended to follow Zwingli or the Anabaptists in their views of Communion. It was out of this Puritan movement that Baptists arose.

Development of Baptist Views on Communion

As Baptists developed out of the Puritan movement in seventeenth-century England, they exhibited some of the Puritan concerns for purifying worship. They sought to eliminate the human forms of the established church and to base worship purely on the simple patterns provided by scripture. But they also sought to involve the congregation in worship and to provide openness for the movement of God's Spirit. True worship had to be scriptural and involve no books which would inhibit the movement of the Spirit. Not only did these earliest Baptists reject the Book of Common Prayer, John Smyth, the first Baptist pastor, believed that even the Bible had to be laid aside for worship after the text had been read prior to the service. Furthermore, participation was not limited to the preacher; lay people could speak as they were led by the spirit. Anyone designated by the congregation could preach and administer baptism or celebrate Communion.

Events during the mid-seventeenth century, however, caused Baptists to change their emphases. During this time more radical Protestant groups arose, some of which placed great stress on the Spirit and little on scripture. In the eyes of Baptists their worship was often chaotic with little order or form. Not wishing to be associated with these groups, but rather to align themselves more closely with the more respectable Congregationalist and Presbyterian dissenters, Baptists began to place less emphasis on the movement of the Spirit in worship and more on following scripture. They also stressed that only those officially set apart by the church as ordained ministers could preach or celebrate Communion.

As Baptists developed in England in the seventeenth century, they worshiped in a variety of ways, but by the end of the century a prevalent pattern had formed. Illustrating that pattern, the "Churchbook" of the congregation at Paul's Alley, Barbicon, provides the general basis for the following pattern.

Although worship varied during the seventeenth century, it tended to follow this fairly common pattern. A layman selected by the congregation began the service by reading a psalm. In some congregations he read it; in others he "read" it by "lining it out" for the congregation to sing after him to a known psalm tune. A time of prayer followed. The layman prayed, and others might follow him in a general time of prayer. After the prayers he read a portion of scripture. The minister then entered the elevated pulpit in the plain meeting house, and after reading his text, he preached, the sermon lasting as long as an hour. The minister concluded with prayer directed toward the application of the sermon. Then a psalm was read or sung as at the beginning, although in some churches a hymn was sung. The minister pronounced a benediction to conclude the service. The afternoon service followed the same pattern except once a month when Communion was observed before singing the closing psalm.

These Baptists celebrated Communion in a manner that was to become common practice. After the sermon and prayer the minister went to the table in front of the pulpit upon which had been placed bread and wine. He spoke of the deep meaning of the Supper and encouraged the members to receive it properly. Then taking the bread in his hands, he gave thanks and broke it, repeating the words of Christ, "This is my body, which is broken for you." After partaking of the loaf, he gave it to the deacons to partake and to distribute to the seated congregation, whom he urged to partake as an expression of their feeding on Christ the true bread. In the same manner he took the wine, gave thanks, poured it in the cup, repeated the words of Christ, partook, gave to the deacons to distribute, and invited the people to partake. Finally, after a brief meditation on the great blessing we have in Christ, the service concluded with the singing of a psalm. This pattern remained virtually unchanged during the first three centuries of Baptist life.

Although the early Baptists celebrated Communion monthly, in many congregations the frequency decreased to once each quarter during the late eighteenth and nineteenth centuries. The decrease in frequency may have been partially due to the change in views.

Some of the early calvinistic Baptists followed Calvin's views on Communion and believed Christ was spiritually present in Communion, but such views did not last long in the enlightenment milieu of the eighteenth century. The intellectual and moral emphases prevailed. Many Baptists followed Zwingli's views of Christ being present in the hearts and minds of believers or the Anabaptist view that Communion was a bare memorial, and the movement tended to be in the direction of the Anabaptist view. Some of that movement may have been a result of reaction against the views developed in the Middle Ages.

Such reaction also may have contributed to the preference for the term "ordinance" over the term "sacrament." Although some of the early Baptists used the term "sacrament" with the Protestant understanding, the tendency was toward using "ordinance" because Christ ordained that we do it.

The majority of Baptists who came to America from England brought these patterns and views of Communion with them and modified them slightly out of their own experience. These Baptists who followed this somewhat more structured pattern came to be called Regular Baptists.

Although the Regular Baptists began Baptist work in America, during the eighteenth century another Baptist group evolved out of the revivals of the Great Awakening. Known as Separate Baptists because of their origins out of Separate Congregationalism during and following the revivals, these Baptists clearly showed the marks of their revivalist roots. Whereas the Regulars were more prominent in the cities and towns of the East and relatively more formal and structured in worship, the Separates were more prevalent in frontier regions, especially as the frontier moved West and South, and were informal and openly evangelistic in tone.

With their entire concept of worship focused toward conversion of sinners, Communion did not hold an important place for the Separates, but they observed it because Christ commanded it. When they had the Supper, they placed it at the end of the service after everything else was finished; but they had it infrequently, most commonly once each quarter. They followed the same pattern used by the other Baptists.

In the meantime, however, other factors affected Baptist views of Communion and forced them further away from their roots. Scottish Common Sense Realism permeated much religious thought, including that of Baptists. Things were simply as they seemed. There was no mystery. There could be no mystical reality beyond the bare physical elements in Communion. There could be no reality beyond the symbols of bread and wine. Worship was intended to explain and convince and bring one to a decision of the will.

The Landmark movement in Southern Baptist life gave further reinforcement to such views. With a biblical literalism and legalism, Landmarkers taught that the important thing about the ordinances was to do them correctly, just as Christ had ordained that we do them. It seemed to matter little what they meant. Landmarkers expressed no concern for any mystery beyond the action.

Such views made it easier to move from the strong communal emphasis of early Baptists to a much more individualistic stress. This move from communal to individualistic was portrayed in Communion by the change in the form of the elements used. Because of the temperance movement, Thomas Bramwell Welch developed his unfermented Communion wine (later renamed Welch's grape juice), and by the end of the nineteenth century most Baptists were using it. But without the antiseptic qualities of wine and with the new knowledge of germs, they became concerned about using the common cup. The answer was individual Communion cups. By 1900 most churches had begun using them and soon began moving to individual pieces of bread. Concern for proper sanitation was addressed, but the strong sense of community that the common cup and loaf had contributed was lost.

By the end of the ninteenth century the purposes of Baptist worship appeared to be primarily to convert, to teach, or to call for right personal living. With such emphases Communion no longer had an important place. It continued to be done because Christ ordained it.

As the twentieth century dawned, Communion continued to have little importance in many Baptist churches. However, one of their most prominent biblical scholars indicated to Baptists that Communion should have an important place. In an address to the Baptist World Alliance in 1911, A. T. Robertson said that the Lord's

Supper had "much significance." He pointed out that through it "we symbolize our participation (communion) in the body and blood of Christ." Clearly it proclaims Christ's death and his return and our participation in his blessings. "But there is one thing more. 'We, who are many, are one bread, one body for we all partake of one bread.' In a mystic sense we are one loaf in Christ. This ordinance accents our fellowship with Christ and with one another."[4]

Robertson clearly indicated that in spite of all the eighteenth- and nineteenth-century developments among Baptists that tended to lessen the importance of Communion, in the early twentieth century there were still those in Baptist life who viewed it as having "much significance." Baptists would not overemphasize it, but neither would they treat it with indifference. As Baptists moved through the century, more of them recognized its significance. In spite of the influence of a trend toward entertainment in Baptist worship that further lessened the importance of Communion in some congregations, others sought to recover a deeper understanding. The liturgical renewal, which affected some Baptists and many other groups, gave impetus in that direction.

It has been through a consideration of this development through twenty centuries that I have developed my own views regarding Communion. Certainly I have been influenced by my understanding of scripture and by Baptist views and practices. But as a Christian I have also been influenced by the views and practices of others. As a Baptist, I am free to draw from all these views as I develop my own perspective in dialogue with other Baptists. Therefore, having considered developments through the twentieth century, I will present my own theology of Communion as we look toward the beginning of the twenty-first century.

A Baptist's Theology of Communion

In expressing a Baptist theology, I begin with scripture. All Baptist thought begins with a consideration of scripture; this is no less true for Communion. However, rather than follow the few scripture passages on Communion with a wooden literalism, I will seek to follow basic principles found there and to avoid views that would be contrary to scripture.

My Baptist theology of Communion must also include congregational involvement. Following the concept of the gathered church and a Baptist emphasis on the priesthood of all believers, I would hold that there is no division between clergy and laity. Thus, in Communion what the congregation does is as important as what the minister does.

Communion must also take place within the context of free church worship. Although worship, including Communion, should be done "decently and in order" and liturgical elements may be freely used or not used, there can be no fixed or required liturgy. This also means that the Communion service should not be excessively elaborate. There should be no complexity that stands between the laity and God, no liturgical obscurity that makes it difficult for the laity to experience God's presence in their midst.

Like all Christian worship, Communion is encounter with God. It is dialogue—revelation and response. God engages in self-disclosure to human beings, and we respond to that revelation. This encounter is christocentric. Christ is the focus of worship because Christ is the central expression of God's creative and redemptive action. In Communion the good news of that redemptive action in Jesus Christ is dramatically expressed.

Consequently, in developing my theology of Communion, I try to make it scriptural, congregational, free church, and expressive of a christocentric encounter with God. The focus of such a theology will not be on the nature of Christ's presence in the elements or the necessary qualifications of the administrator. But neither will it be a theology that asserts Communion is a mere symbol of what Christ did. Rather, the focus of my theology begins with a genuine remembrance of God's action in Christ with all of its implications.

The emphasis on remembrance follows Christ's injunction to "do this in remembrance of me" (1 Cor 11:24). Those who emphasize doing it to follow Christ's command tend to use the terms "Lord's Supper" and "ordinance," emphasizing that Christ ordained it and it is his supper.

But the emphasis on remembrance is more than simply following Christ's injunction. Communion is a remembrance of God's action in Christ on behalf of humankind. It is a remembrance of Christ's sacrifice or self-giving. The Greek word for remembrance is *anamnesis*. Jesus said, "This do for my *anamnesis*." The word means more than our word "remembrance." Dix and others have pointed out that *anamnesis* means not just remember, but to recall or

represent the past event in such a way as to make it currently opera-
tive,[5] to make its power available in the here and now. The early
Christians were not talking about performing another sacrifice;
rather, they were talking about making the power of Christ's offering of himself available in the present moment.

There is no way to explain fully how this happens, but an illustration may help to gain some understanding of what is meant by
this concept of remembrance. This April my wife and I celebrated
our thirty-fifth anniversary. Through the years we have celebrated
in various ways, but one thing we have always done is repeat our
vows to each other. Each year on April 4 I say to her, "I, Tom, take
thee, Jean, to be my lawful wedded wife, and do promise to love and
to cherish thee in sickness and in health, in poverty or in wealth, in
the good days and the bad days, as long as we both shall live."
Through this means of "remembrance," what happened long ago is
brought anew into the present moment with power.

Communion is more than a bare memorial that calls to remembrance something which happened long ago. It is a remembrance
that draws the fullness of God's past action in Christ into the present moment with power, so that believers experience anew God's
reconciling love.

This view of remembrance also gives room for a stress on
Christ's presence among the gathered body of believers. In Communion as we remember Christ's self-giving on our behalf and partake
of the signs of his body and blood, we experience his presence in
our midst. The bread and wine are far more than mere symbols.
They are signs that point to Christ's presence. Paul was very clear
about this: "The cup of blessing that we bless, is it not a sharing in
the blood of Christ? The bread that we break, is it not a sharing in
the body of Christ? Because there is one bread, we who are many are
one body, for we all partake of the one bread" (1 Cor 10:16-17).

Many profound discussions have taken place through the years
regarding the nature of this presence in communion—and some
not so profound. Several years ago such a discussion took place at
one of the weekly ministers' meetings in a small town. Most ministers in attendance had celebrated Communion the day before, and
two of the "higher church" ministers got into a discussion as to the
best way to dispose of the leftover elements. For them, it was an
important question since Christ was truly present in the elements of

bread and wine. During the extended discussion they noticed that the minister of the small Baptist church in town had remained quiet. They asked him, "What do you do when you have bread left over?" He replied, "I take it home and make peanut butter and jelly sandwiches."

I would take the elements with more seriousness than that Baptist minister did, but I would not have the same concern about disposing of the elements that the other ministers did. Christ's presence is not limited to any elements; it is with the body of believers. The bread and wine are signs that point to that presence. As we take the bread and cup, in our hearts we experience communion with Christ and with each other. It is a fellowship meal in the fullest sense. Through this Communion we are truly the body of Christ, for as Christ makes himself present to us all, he makes us all one in himself.

It is because of this understanding of Christ's presence that I prefer to use the term "Communion." It emphasizes the fellowship we experience with Christ and with each other. I am also comfortable with the term "sacrament" when understood in its Protestant sense. Although "ordinance" is an appropriate term in that Christ ordained that we do it, the term "sacrament" indicates that we do it not only because Christ ordained it, but also because it is something more. Communion is a sacrament in that it is an external and visible sign of an internal and spiritual reality.

Communion also points to the future, for through it we "proclaim the Lord's death until he comes"(1 Cor 11:26). The remembering of God's action in Jesus Christ and the experiencing of Christ's presence is also a reminder of his promise that he will come again.

Communion, therefore, is multifaceted, pointing to the past, present, and future. For all of God's action past, present, and future, we give thanks. Thus, in addition to Communion and Lord's Supper, another appropriate term to use is the term "Eucharist," or "thanksgiving." All three terms are appropriate, and they stress different aspects of the celebration. I prefer the term "Communion" because it emphasizes our communion with Christ and with each other as we celebrate it, and it points to a deeper and richer understanding of remembrance.

What about the other issues that are often raised in discussions of Communion? Who can celebrate it? Who can partake? How often should a congregation have it? How should it be done? To me, these issues are of secondary importance. If we have a clear understanding of what Communion is and what it means, the answers to these questions flow from these understandings and from our Baptist theology.

Anyone who is designated by a body of believers can celebrate Communion. It is the prerogative of a body of believers to call forth one whom they believe to be appropriate to lead them in the celebration. Likewise, the congregation can celebrate Communion as often as they like. I prefer to have it often enough so that it remains a meaningful experience but not so often that it becomes a routine. I like having it approximately once a month and on special occasions. But that is simply a personal preference.

Finally, the congregation can celebrate it in any way they choose. Most choose to have the deacons serve the members in the pews, which is certainly an historic and appropriate way. Some have the members come to the table on special occasions, such as Maundy Thursday or Christmas Eve. I prefer varying it. But I also prefer using the common loaf and cup in some way to emphasize our oneness in Christ. They can be used symbolically by the minister at the table when the congregation is served in the pews. They can be used by all when members come to the table. By using the method of intinction (taking a piece of the bread, dipping it in the cup, and then eating the bread), the symbolism can be maintained while at the same time addressing health concerns.

It is probably clear by this point that my theology of Communion, even in the term I use for it, varies from that of many other Baptists. But that is the Baptist way. We are free to develop our own theological understanding in dialogue with other Baptists. My theology of Communion has developed in just this way. I have studied scripture and the history of the church, I have talked with other Baptists through the years, and I have come to my own conclusions.

Out of this study and dialogue has come my Baptist theology. Communion proclaims God's action in Christ in the past and makes its power available to us now. It proclaims the future hope of Christ's return. It proclaims Christ's presence in the midst of the community of faith and draws us together in one body in the present. It is a visible and physical sign of an invisible and spiritual reality. As it addresses the past, present, and future in the Christian life, it is a tangible expression of Christian faith, hope, and love.

Notes

[1]Philip Schaff, *History of the Christian Church*, vol. 4 (Grand Rapids: Eerdmans, 1953) 550.

[2]Henry Bettenson, ed. *Documents of the Christian Church*, 2d ed. (New York: Oxford University Press, 1963) 147.

[3]*Institutes of the Christian Religion*, IV.14.5, Library of Christian Classics, vol. 21, edited by John T. McNeill (Philadelphia: Westminster Press, 1977) 1280.

[4]"The Spiritual Interpretation of the Ordinances," *The Life of Baptists in the Life of the World: Eighty Years of the Baptist World Alliance*, edited by Walter B. Shurden (Nashville: Broadman Press, 1985) 54.

[5]Dom Gregory Dix, *The Shape of the Liturgy* (New York: Seabury Press, 1982) 245.

Eschatology
Bill J. Leonard

> Then I saw an angel coming down from heaven, holding in his hand the key to the bottomless pit and a great chain. He seized the dragon, that ancient serpent, who is the Devil and Satan, and bound him for a thousand years, and threw him into the pit, and locked and sealed it over him, so that he would deceive the nations no more, until the thousand years were ended. . . . I also I saw the souls of those who had been beheaded for their testimony to Jesus and for the word of God. They had not worshiped the beast or its image and had not received its mark on their foreheads or their hands. They came to life and reigned with Christ a thousand years. (Rev 20:1-5)

These words from the book of Revelation have intrigued Christians for two millennia, influencing the development of innumerable systems and theories regarding the *eschaton,* the end of the age. Indeed, as the church approaches the third millennium, there seems no end to speculation regarding the apocalypse, the end of time, and the return of Jesus Christ. Even a brief survey of movements and ideas related to eschatology illustrates but a few of the many conjectures that have been set forth to describe and explain the meaning of Christian eschatology.

The *New York Times* reports that, on the way to the year 2000, concern for the second coming of Jesus is sweeping large segments of the American, indeed, the world, population. Popular renderings of eschatological speculation relate to the "rapture" of Christians out of this world, the development of a "one-world religion," and a one-world currency. Some even speculate that the year 2000 computer problem could be linked to the return of Christ.[1]

Concern for last things, millennialist speculations, and the return of Christ has existed from the beginning of the church. Somehow the Christian ideal of eschatology encompasses these theories and more. A discussion of eschatology begins with a definition of particular terms and ideas that relate to the study of the end times.

Definitions

The word "eschatology" is itself a general term for understanding the end of things, the end of time, the fullness of the Kingdom of God, the return of Christ, and the celebration of a new heaven and a new earth. Eschatology includes millennial speculations, social predictions, and hope for a new era of peace and justice. Today popular religion tends to link eschatological theology almost exclusively with predictions regarding the imminent return of Jesus Christ, but that is only one facet of a much broader category. Terms include the following:

- *Eschatology* is the study of "last things." It comes from the Greek word *eskhatos*, which means "last" or "final." The phrase *to eschaton* is not found in the New Testament. In 1 Corinthians 15:45 Jesus is referred to as *ho eschatos Adam*, or "the last Adam."[2]

- *Apocalypse* means "an uncovering" or "unveiling." *The Revelation of St. John* can also be known as the *Apocalypse of St. John*. The word has long been associated with last things.

- *Chiliasm* comes from the Greek *chilioi*, meaning "a thousand." It is another name for the millennium, or the thousand-year reign of Christ.

- *Millennialism* refers to a long period of unprecedented peace and righteousness, closely associated with the second coming of Christ.[3]

- *Millennialist* is the belief that history, through divine guidance, will bring in the triumph of Christian principles. It is a form of progressivism, which sees the church as leavening society until the Kingdom comes.[4]

- *Millenarians* are "minority groups" that anticipate the physical return of Christ as the world grows worse, believing that the world will be brought into divine subjection through radical supernatural intervention.[5]

• *Postmillennialists* believe that Christ will return after the church has helped to bring in the millennium through its faithful preaching of the gospel.[6]

• *Amillennialists*, or "no-millennialists," interpret biblical references to the millennium as a spiritual state in the hearts of Jesus' followers rather than as a separate historical period. They believe that the prophecies concerning the struggles with the anti-Christ and the reign of Christ are being partially fulfilled already in the present church age and that God will bring about an end to time as God chooses.[7]

• *Premillennialists* believe that Christ will return before the millennium to establish the Kingdom by his might. They are divided into numerous subgroups centering in the particulars of Christ's return.

• *Historicist premillennialists* believe that the prophetic scriptures, specifically in Daniel and Revelation, provide the entire history of the church in symbolic form. They examine the church's history to discover prophetic fulfillment and discover where the contemporary church is on "God's prophetic timetable."[8]

• *Futurist premillennialists* believe that no prophecies regarding the "last days" have been fulfilled in the church's history, but that they will be fulfilled in a short time just prior to Christ's return. Society will grow worse as the end nears, the anti-Christ will gain control, and the world will experience tribulation leveled primarily against those who do not recognize the anti-Christ's divine claims. The tribulation will end with the battle of Armageddon and the destruction of the anti-Christ and the return of Christ. Christ will bind Satan and establish his millennial kingdom, which will endure 1,000 years. At the end of that period Satan will be completely destroyed, the dead will be judged, and a new heaven and a new earth will be established.[9]

Futurist premillennialists differ as to the time of the "rapture," or the time when the true Christians, living and dead, are lifted away to meet Christ (1 Thess 4:15-17). *Pretribulationists* believe the church will be raptured before the beginning of the tribulation and the work of the anti-Christ. *Midtribulationists* believe the church will be raptured during the tribulation and after the rise of the anti-Christ. *Posttribulationists* believe the church will endure the tribulation period and be rescued by the rapture at the time of Christ's return.[10]

One of the more elaborate premillennialist theories comes from *Dispensational Premillennialism*, a movement that began in England with John Nelson Darby (1800–1882) and a group known as the Plymouth Brethren. In the United States those ideas were circulated through the work of Cyrus Scofield (1843–1921) and the publication of his notes in the *Scofield Reference Bible* in 1909. Scofield divided history into seven periods or dispensations leading to the return of Christ. As he saw it, the final dispensation, presaged by Christ's return, was imminent.[11]

Eschatology in Church History

These theories or others like them have characterized eschatological speculation since the beginnings of the church. The church at Thessalonica seems to have had a particular fascination with Christ's return. So concerned were some believers that they stopped work in anticipation of Christ's impending return. Saint Paul found their behavior problematic enough to write his famous admonition: "Anyone unwilling to work should not eat" (2 Thess 3:10). To read the New Testament is to be caught up in the immediacy of the Kingdom of God and the anticipation of the imminent end of the age. By the time the reader reaches the book of Revelation the stage is set for a vision of the last days filled with frightening images of dragons, beasts, nations, and martyrs. The description of the third enemy, the whore of Babylon, captures the dramatic imagery of the book: On her forehead is written "Babylon the great, mother of whores and of earth's abominations" (Rev 17:5). Who is this woman? John hints as to her identity including the statement that "the seven heads [of the beast] are seven mountains on which the woman is seated." This is a certain reference to the seven hills of the city of Rome.[12] Likewise, the writer of the book of Revelation links the anti-Christ to Rome and its emperors. From that point on, speculation regarding the anti-Christ flourished.

Apocalyptic movements punctuate the history of the church. As early as 175 CE,[13] a man named Montanus joined with two female prophets named Prisca and Maxmilla to announce that the end of the world was at hand. They believed they had received direct revelation from God and that Montanus himself was the promised "Paraclete" described by Jesus in the Gospel of John. The fall of Rome to "barbarian" invaders in 410 naturally created millennial fervor, prompting St. Augustine to write the *Civitas Dei,* the *City of God,* setting forth a Christian theory of history, reminding the church that empires come and go, while God and church endure.

Upheavals created by the Protestant Reformation also brought millennial intensity. One of the most infamous such events occurred in 1534 in the German city of Munster where Jan Mathys, Jan of Leyden, and other "prophets" claimed to have established the Kingdom of God. Troops laid siege to the city, ultimately conquering it and executing its leaders. The incident became a symbol of apocalyptic fanaticism well into the twentieth century. In England the Civil War and the execution of King Charles I in 1649 unleashed millennial speculation. The Fifth Monarchy Movement, widespread throughout the army and drawing heavily from the Baptists, anticipated the end of the age. Many of its members even took up the sword to help bring in the Kingdom, or the "fifth monarchy" of Christ's millennial reign.

America figured significantly in millennial speculation. Indeed, eschatology was a prominent factor in early colonial immigration. America became a seedbed for sects, many of which believed they had established the Kingdom of God on earth. Some colonial religionists surmised that the Native Americans were somehow descendants of the lost tribes of Israel. They were also discernible "heathen" who had never heard the Christian gospel. Thus the evangelization of these native peoples would result in the conversion of the Jews and the heathen. The gospel would be preached to the ends of the earth, thus hastening the return of Christ. Richard Mather (1596–1669), patriarch of the famous Mather family (father of Increase Mather, grandfather of Cotton Mather) arrived in America in 1635 and wrote extensively on the millennium, insisting that the end was near. By 1650 he saw the Christian message bearing fruit among the Indians. If they could be converted, then why not the Jews?[14]

Increase Mather (1639–1723) confessed his belief in a literal second coming, but without the immediacy evident in his father's writings. When the great London fire of 1666 led many to believe that the millennium was at hand, Increase Mather demurred. The time was not right. However, he did not hesitate to link America with the spiritual calling not unlike Israel. In a 1674 sermon, "The Day of Trouble Is Near," he declared: "Without doubt the Lord Jesus hath a peculiar respect unto this place, and for this people. This is Immanuel's land. Christ by his wonderful Providence hath . . . caused as it were New Jerusalem to come down from heaven; he dwells in this place."[15]

Roger Williams (1603–1683), Puritan dissenter and founder of the First Baptist Church in America and the colony of Rhode Island, also anticipated the immediacy of the millennium. Toward the end of his life he became convinced that all religious communions—Baptists included—were inadequate revelations. All churches were corrupt, and no proper authority existed for ministry or sacraments. Christ would return, restore the church to its "apostolic form," and reform the apostolic practices lost amid the confusion of sects. Williams thus refused to receive or administer any sacraments or to belong to any church. He became a "Seeker," awaiting the millennial restoration of true doctrine and practice.[16] These early colonial speculations tend toward a type of premillennialism, but without clear-cut systems.

Later colonials were more comfortable with postmillennial eschatological positions that they found verified in the religious awakenings that swept the region in the mid-1700s. Jonathan Edwards (1709–1758) was one of the most prominent preachers of the period whose postmillennialism is evident throughout his voluminous writings, particularly his *History of the Work of Redemption*. Edwards believed that the present age was moving toward the defeat of the anti-Christ and the beginnings of the kingdom of God. The revivals he observed in his church at Northampton, Massachusetts, were clear evidence that the kingdom was at hand. The millennium would be brought in, not with suffering, but with triumph. The church would experience a golden age prior to Christ's return. Edwards was the first postmillennialist American preacher.[17]

When the awakenings began to decline and a period of "coldness" returned to the churches, Edwards was concerned but not despondent. He called for continual "prayer concerts" that would implore God to send revivals. Prayer would not necessarily "hasten the day"—that was left to the will of a sovereign God—but it would prepare the hearts of God's people. He wrote:

> It is not unlikely that this work of God's spirit, so extraordinary and wonderful, is the dawning, or at least the prelude of that glorious work of God, so often foretold in scripture, which, in the progress and issue of it, shall renew the world of mankind . . . We cannot reasonably think otherwise than that the beginnings of this great work of God must be near. And there are many things that make it probable that this work will begin in America.[18]

Postmillennialism continued to occupy a prominent place among American evangelicals, evident in the early nineteenth century in the work of the well-known revivalist Charles Grandison Finney (1792–1875). Like Edwards, Finney saw the many conversions and religious enthusiasms in his revival meetings as a sign of the golden age of the church that would precede the millennium. His concerns also extended to social issues and the improvement of society. Finney and many of his followers were opponents of slavery, seeking to purge society of that dreaded practice. Finney himself became professor of theology and ultimately president of Oberlin College, a school founded by abolitionist professors and students. Oberlin became a center of anti-slavery efforts, Christian perfectionism, and evangelical feminism. Many of these evangelicals believed that success in such matters would be evidence that the Kingdom was near.

Millennial theories were also prominent in the development of numerous communal/utopian groups that have appeared throughout American history. These run across a spectrum from the celibacy of the Shakers to the sexual openness of the Oneida Community, from the apocalypticism of the Church of Jesus Christ of the Latter Day Saints to the New Age millennium of the Heaven's Gate Community.

The United Society of Believers in Christ's Second Appearing, better known as the Shakers, were a millennial and communitarian sect that began in England and came to America around 1774 under the leadership of a woman named Ann Lee (1736–1784). Through a series of dreams and visions Lee became convinced that sexual intercourse was the cause of the fall of Adam and Eve. She believed that God was both male and female, revealed in human form in the man Jesus. She and a small group of followers bought land near Watervliet, New York, and founded the first of numerous communities. Membership involved confession of sin, accepting the community of goods, and taking up the "cross" of celibacy. Soon Joseph Meacham (1741–1796) and a group of Baptists who brought new energy and organization to the fledgling body joined them. Evangelistic efforts help spread the movement from Maine to Kentucky. Shakers came to believe that "Mother Ann" was the female appearing of the Christ-spirit. (Shakers did not accept the deity of Jesus or Ann Lee.) Thus, Shaker communities mirrored the Kingdom of God where there was neither marrying nor giving in marriage (Matt 22:29). In a sense, Shakers believed they were the *avant garde* of the New Jerusalem. Shaker worship was given to ecstatic speech, spirit songs, and dances. The Shakers believed that the spirit world was very near and could be discovered by those with spiritual openness.[19]

Likewise, the Oneida Community founded by John Humphrey Noyes (1811–1886) in 1847 believed that they were the models of life as it would be in the "end times." Converted in the Finneyite revivals, Noyes came to the conclusion that Jesus had returned in 70 CE when the temple in Jerusalem was destroyed. Such knowledge had been lost to the church until Noyes rediscovered it.

Noyes' millennialism was particularly strong during the 1830s. He observed that "the Millennium was supposed to be very near. I fully entered into the enthusiasm of the time. . . . My heart was fixed on the Millennium, and I resolved to live or die for it."[20] Since the Kingdom had come, it was possible to live a sinless life of Christian perfection. While many evangelicals—John Wesley, Charles G. Finney, and others—promoted the idea of sanctification, Noyes' perfectionist views were unique. Noyes took the verse, "they neither marry nor are given in marriage," to mean that in the kingdom, marriage was not possible, but sex was. Persons who lived a kingdom life could have multiple sexual partners in the community of the converted. He and a few followers formed such a community in Putney, Vermont. Controversy over their practices forced them to move to Oneida, New York, in 1848 where the Oneida community was born.

Members strove for Christian perfection through mutual criticism among the believers. They shared various sexual encounters through a program known as "Complex Marriage," in which members were forbidden to have "exclusive love," for only one person. "Male continence" was a form of male birth control developed by Noyes. "Stirpiculture" was the name for community eugenics whereby certain members of the community were selected to have children together. Those with gifts for childrearing were charged with the responsibility of raising the children.

The community, which never had more than 200-300 members, supported itself by manufacturing animal traps and later Oneida stainless utensils. By 1880 the community had disbanded, and Oneida Company, Ltd., a business company, was established. Both the Shaker and the Oneida communities reflect the way in which eschatological speculations were worked out in two diverse communitarian groups. Each suggested that it was a sign of the kingdom that was to come.

Millennial speculation was not limited to strange communitarianists, however. During the 1830s millennialism gripped the eastern United States. A Baptist preacher named William Miller (1782–1849) calculated what he believed to be airtight "evidence from Scripture and history" that Jesus Christ would return sometime between March 1843 and 1844. He began declaring this word, first in churches in western New York and then in cities—Boston, New York—throughout the northeast. Protestants from a variety of traditions flocked to his meetings, and the Adventist movement was born. Miller's rhetoric was clear and profound.

> Hark! Hear those dreadful bellowings of the angry nations! It is the presage of a horrid and terrific war. Look! Look again! See lords and nobles, captains and mighty men aiming for the bloody fight! See the carnivorous fowls fly screaming through the air! See! See these signs. Behold the heavens grow black with clouds. The hail descends the seven thunders utter loud their voices. At the dread moment, look, the clouds have burst asunder the heavens appear! The great white throne is in sight. Amazement fills the universe with awe. He comes—Behold the mighty Savior comes. Lift up your heads, ye saints. He Comes! He Comes![21]

When the dates that Miller had set came and went, the Millerite movement experienced what came to be known as "the first Great Disappointment." One of his followers, through dreams and calculations, set a firm date of October 22, 1844. Miller was hesitant, but came to accept the date, later known as "the second Great Disappointment." Miller died a few years later, disillusioned and discredited. Not all his followers gave up the cause, however. Hiram Edson and Ellen Harmon White redefined Christ's coming as spiritual and preparatory, continuing to anticipate the *eschaton*. They suggested that Christ's coming had taken place in heaven, where he was "cleansing the tabernacle" in preparation for his complete return. White's prophecies expanded these ideas. The publication of her prophecies made Ellen White a major prophetic leader in what became the Seventh Day Adventist movement.

The Millerite movement brought premillennialism to prominence as an eschatological theory among American evangelicals. While Miller's calculations came to naught, premillennial speculation did not end with the days of Disappointment. Indeed, famed evangelist Dwight Lyman Moody (1837–1899) became a proponent of premillennial views. As Moody saw it, the wars, earthquakes, and immoralities evident throughout the world were proof positive that Christ's return was near. Like Miller, Moody saw the impending apocalypse as demanding unceasing efforts to evangelize the multitudes. His revival campaigns were aimed at converting as many people as possible before the end time fell upon the world. He declared that God had given him a lifeboat and ordered him to save as many as he could before it was too late.

Other well-known evangelists such as Billy Sunday and Billy Graham passed on Moody's premillennialism to the twentieth century. It also became an important part of the early fundamentalist movement, developing in the latter nineteenth and early twentieth centuries. A series of Bible conferences held at Niagara, New York, promoted premillennial eschatology along with other fundamentalist dogmas such as biblical inerrancy, the virgin birth, and substitutionary atonement of Christ, among others. While not all fundamentalists accepted premillennialism, it was a prominent doctrine among others.

Regarding millennial speculations, Baptists have promoted a variety of views. Walter Rauschenbusch (1861–1918), Baptist professor and father of the social gospel, was certainly a proponent of the postmillennial ideal, believing that the work of the church was to "Christianize the Social Order." He saw efforts to redeem persons from poverty and exploitation as a means by which the reign and rule of God would be brought into the world. Rauschenbusch wrote about "millennialism," responding to the premillennial view with some appreciation for its emphasis on the vitality of the faith and the activity of God in human history. He was also critical of the movement, writing:

> We should have no quarrel with Millenarianism if it held that the world, *minus* the redemptive forces of Christianity, sags downward instead of rising upward, that society naturally decays, that the increase in material wealth only hastens the rotting, and that the spread of intelligence but makes evil more malignant. But when Millenarianism asserts the same things concerning humanity, plus the redemptive forces of Christ, we feel in our hearts an impassioned protest, and that protest issues, not from unsanctified optimism, but from sanctified faith in Jesus Christ.[22]

During much of the twentieth century many Baptist leaders favored an amillennial approach, denying that millennialist references in the Bible were to be taken literally. Herschel Hobbs, renowned Southern Baptist pastor and leader, was a lifelong proponent of amillennialism.

Fundamentalism helped to bring premillennialism into Baptist life, with many popular preachers accepting such doctrines. Southern Baptists and Independent Baptists were particularly drawn to the premillennial position. J. Frank Norris (1877–1952), prominent Baptist fundamentalist and a founder of the independent Baptist movement, illustrates the evolution of premillennial views among the Baptists. As a student at Baylor University and the Southern Baptist Theological Seminary, Norris was a postmillennialist. Later he turned to premillennialism as part of his growing fundamentalist orientation. He insisted that "our motive is not to redeem America, China, or Russia; it is to get ready the body of Christ, the Bride, . . . for the coming of the Bridegroom." He thus noted that the premillennial approach "is the only missionary motive . . . not to clean out the stables, but to redeem the individual man and woman."[23] W. A. Criswell, for more than fifty years pastor of First

Baptist Church, Dallas, Texas, is one of the best known Southern
Baptist premillennialists. Under his leadership the Dallas church
added a section on the premillennial return of Christ to its version
of the Baptist Faith and Message, the Southern Baptist Convention's
confession of faith.

This survey of the various theories regarding the millennium
illustrates the way in which many segments of Christianity have
viewed eschatology. Among other things they illustrate that:

• Millennial speculations are irresistible for many persons and
  groups in Christ's church. Such theories are important to many
  people, and speculation as to the prophetic implications of Holy
  Scripture abounds in every age. In some sense, the Bible dares us
  to examine current events in light of their eternal potential. For
  many people, the biblical "codes" pointing to the end time offer a
  challenge of interpretation, expectation, and possibility. Historically speaking, Christians cannot seem to resist the temptation to
  develop calculations, timetables, and methods for analyzing the
  "signs of the times." In spite of innumerable "Great Disappointments" the millennial speculations will surely continue "till time
  shall be no more."

• If history is any illustration, millennial theories always seem to create "Great Disappointments" when theories fail and, in the words
  of the old preachers, "Jesus tarries." Anti-Christs come and go, the
  anticipated *eschaton* does not materialize, and calculations
  continue.

• Beyond all the calculations, mathematical systems, and indisputable "signs" is that most basic biblical concern: Hope. Hope is
  the essence of the church's eschatological quest.

The Eschatology of Hope

Hope is not mere wishful thinking or visionary fantasy. Rather, it is
a sense of assurance that God will have the final word in the world,
and that word will be good. Hope carries the church beyond theories and speculations to a basic trust in God. The church, the body
of Christ, is the community of hope. It is an imperfect, broken,

fallible, and sometimes sinful community, but it remains a community of hope, not because of its own sufficiency, but because it
ultimately belongs to God. At its core the church is a vehicle of hope
in the world.

In the sacraments, or ordinances, the church of Jesus Christ
declares its hope in the present and for the future. Baptism marks
the beginning of the journey; it signifies the door of the church, the
beginning of faith. While baptism occurs in the present moment, it
is also an eschatological promise. It symbolically unites the individual with all who have gone before and all who will come after. It
signifies that individuals have moved from one kind of life to
another, a pledge that God will keep the "new creation" for eternity.
Martin Luther, baptized as an infant, looked back to his baptism as
the moment not when he chose Christ, but when Christ chose him.
In spite of the difficulties of life, the doubts and fears, Christ kept
him in this world and the next. Baptism was a sign of hope that God
would not fail.

If baptism marks the beginning of hope, the Lord's Supper
offers hope for the journey. It is the continuing sign of God's presence by which "you proclaim the Lord's death until he comes" (1
Cor 11:26). At Christ's table Christians are assured that they belong
to the body of Christ, a family with eternal implications. The
Supper also reminds Christians that hope is found in community; it
is not simply an individual matter. To belong to the body of Christ
is to be part of a community of faith, the church.

Christian eschatology offers hope for justice. Whatever else the
"end time" may mean, it surely involves the promise of justice in
which wrongs are set right. Mary, the mother of Jesus, sang about
that promise of hope when she heard the news that she was to bear
a son. Her words are both a shout of praise and a hope for justice
for the oppressed.

> My soul magnifies the Lord, and my spirit rejoices in God my
> Savior, for he has looked with favor on the lowliness of his ser-
> vant. Surely, from now on all generations will call me blessed; for
> the Mighty One has done great things for me, and holy is his
> name. His mercy is for those who fear him from generation to
> generation. He has shown strength with his arm; he has scattered
> the proud in the thoughts of their hearts. He has brought down
> the powerful from their thrones, and lifted up the lowly; he has

filled the hungry with good things, and sent the rich away empty.
He has helped his servant Israel, in remembrance of his mercy,
according to the promise he made to our ancestors, to Abraham
and to his descendants forever. (Luke 1:47-55)

Human history is filled with injustice visited against the weak,
the poor, the exploited, and the innocent. Millions of people have
died because of evils beyond their control. The Holocaust against
the Jews is the great twentieth-century example of the injustices and
evils of the Nazi regime. Where shall those and all who have been
crushed by evil find justice? Surely if God is good, then there will be
a time of reconciliation when the evils of history will be set right.
This is not only a time of judgment for the sinful, but also at a time
when the "lowly" shall "be raised high."

African American slaves looked for such a time of retribution
and justice as they waited for deliverance from the yoke of slavery.
Their experience of "the troubles of the world" led them to hope for
a time when the judgment of God, the justice of God, would prevail. Nowhere is this hope more evident than in the "spirituals" sung
in pathos, memory, and promise. Lerone Bennett wrote, "Ex-slaves
say they slipped away to the fields and in 'hush-harbors' told God all
their troubles. Out of these proscribed meetings and the wakes and
other mournful events of the slave quarters came the spirituals that
were created, James Weldon Johnson said, by 'black and unknown
bards.'"

> Oh, Mary, don't you weep, don't you moan;
> Pharaoh's Army got drownded,
> Oh, Mary, don't you weep.[24]

There were also laments that looked for a time when they would be
understood:

> I'm gonna tell God all my troubles,
> When I get home. . . .
> I'm gonna tell him the road was rocky,
> When I get home.[25]

Through it all, there was the promise of deliverance: "Didn't my
Lord deliver Daniel, And why not every man."[26] Slavery and segrega-
tion pressed African Americans to work and hope for freedom and

justice, if not in this world, then in that great "gettin' up morning." Some have dismissed this idea as a form of escapism, but it is anything but that. It was a reading of scripture not by the oppressors, but by the oppressed. It was an understanding that justice was an eternal issue that would ultimately prevail.

Closely related to the hope for justice is the hope for wholeness. Eschatological hope points to a day when humanity and all creation shall know wholeness and completeness in the fullness of the Kingdom of God. Such wholeness, the dawning of a new day, is evident throughout the Bible. Justice and wholeness are linked in Isaiah's words:

> Your God comes to save you with his vengeance and his retribution. Then the eyes of the blind will be opened, and the ears of the deaf unstopped. Then the lame will leap like deer, and the speechless shout aloud; for water will spring up in the wilderness and torrents flow in the desert . . . The Lord's people, set free, will come back and enter Zion with shouts of triumph, crowned with everlasting joy. Gladness and joy will come upon them, while suffering and weariness flee away. (35:5-10 REB)

This eschatological wholeness also has implication for reconciliation among classic enemies. Wholeness applies also to relationships. Again, Isaiah writes:

> The cow and the bear will be friends, and their young will lie down together; and the lion will eat straw like cattle. The infant will play over the cobra's hole, and the young child dance over the viper's nest. There will be neither hurt nor harm in all my holy mountain; for the land will be filled with the knowledge of the Lord, as the waters cover the sea. (11:7-9 REB)

In the synagogue at Nazareth, Jesus reaches back to Isaiah in declaring his own work and reaffirming the wholeness that is to come.

> The spirit of the Lord is upon me because he has anointed me; he has sent me to announce good news to the poor, to proclaim release for prisoners and recovery of sight for the blind; to let the broken victims go free, to proclaim the year of the Lord's favour. (Luke 4:18-19 REB)

In fact, Jesus' entire ministry centered in the proclamation of the coming kingdom in which the broken were made whole and the old enemies reconciled. His healing work toward the blind, the lame, and the speechless were not simply beneficial acts of compassion toward specific individuals; they were signs of the Kingdom. In the Kingdom, wholeness comes to all. Hope, therefore, is the promise of wholeness that is to come and the grace to live with brokenness along the way.

Hope has an edge to it. It is filled with surprises, especially regarding those who find, or are found by, the Kingdom. As Jesus told it, in the "last days" the citizens of the Kingdom are a surprising lot, as described in the Sermon on the Mount: the poor in spirit, the pure in heart, the peacemakers, the persecuted, the unexpected ones. Jesus' own parables speak of the profound surprise at the last day, not only because it arrives unpredictably ("Keep awake therefore, for you do not know on what day your Lord is coming" (Matt 24:42), but also because of the people who get in. In parable after parable the surprising people—the in-valid ones, the Samaritans, the public sinners, the prostitutes, and the tax collectors—find their way to the head of the line. Even the people who show up at quitting time get the same wages as those who started out at the beginning of the day. God's sense of justice and wholeness is quite different than that of most human beings.

Such eschatological wholeness is not limited to humanity, however. It has implications for all creation. So Saint Paul linked hope and wholeness to the entire creation when he wrote:

> For the creation waits with eager longing for the revealing of the children of God; for the creation was subjected to futility, not of its own will but by the will of the one who subjected it, in hope bondage to decay and will obtain the freedom of the glory of the children of God. We know that the whole creation has been groaning in labor pains until now; and not only the creation, but we ourselves, who have the first fruits of the Spirit, groan inwardly while we wait for adoption, the redemption of our bodies. For in hope we were saved. Now hope that is seen is not hope. For who hopes for what is seen? (Rom 8:19-24)

Thus the *eschaton* brings completeness to all the created order so that it is truly a new earth, as well as a new heaven. Such wholeness is a promise to which the people of God cling in the present age. The *eschaton* is a paradox; it is at once present and future. We grasp hints of its presence in salvation, in sacraments, and the continuing work of God in the world. But it is always partial until the full "day of the Lord" arrives. German theologian Jürgen Moltmann made this insightful comment:

> Through his mission and his resurrection Jesus has brought the kingdom of God into history. As the eschatological future the kingdom has become the power that determines the present. This future has become the power that determines the present. This future has already begun. We can already live in the light of the "new era" in the circumstances of the "old" one. Since the eschatological becomes historical in this way, the historical also becomes eschatological. Hope becomes realistic and reality hopeful.[27]

On the way into the third millennium speculations concerning the "signs of the times" will surely continue. All will probably miss the mark and come to naught. Faith, however, calls us to hope. Beyond theories, systems, and calculations there is God who will have the last word. Faith calls for patience and the unceasing prayer of hope-filled people: "Even so come, Lord Jesus."

Notes

[1]Laurie Goodstein, "Thrillers Are Providing Spiritual Rapture Between the Pages," *New York Times*, 8 November 1998.

[2]John A. T. Robinson, *In the End God* (New York: Harper and Row, 1949) 68.

[3]Timothy Weber, *Living in the Shadow of the Second Coming* (Chicago: University of Chicago Press) 9.

[4]Ernest Tuveson, *Redeemer Nation* (Chicago: University of Chicago Press, 1968) 34.

[5]Ibid.

[6]Weber.

[7]George Marsden, *Fundamentalism and American Culture* (New York: Oxford University Press, 1980) 240, n20.

[8]Ibid., 10.

[9]Ibid.

[10]Ibid.

[11]Ernest R. Sandeen, *The Roots of Fundamentalism* (Grand Rapids, MI: Baker Book House, 1970) 59-80.

[12]James West Davidson, *The Logic of Millennial Thought* (New Haven CT: Yale University Press, 1977) 7.

[13]CE means "common era" and is equivalent to AD, Latin for *ano domini,* "the year of [our] Lord."

[14]Robert Middlekauff, *The Mathers* (New York: Oxford University Press, 1971) 31-32.

[15]Sacvan Bercovitch, *The Puritan Origins of the American Self* (New Haven CT: Yale University Press, 1975) 55.

[16]W. Clark Gilpin, *The Millenarian Piety of Roger Williams* (Chicago: University of Chicago Press, 1979) 56-62.

[17]C. C. Goen, "Jonathan Edwards: A New Departure in Eschatology," *Church History,* 28 (1959) 25-40.

[18]Jonathan Edwards, *The Great Awakening,* edited by C. C. Goen (New Haven CT: Yale University, 1972) 353.

[19]Stephen J. Stein, *The Shaker Experience in America* (New Haven CT: Yale University Press, 1992).

[20]Sandeen, 49.

[21]William Miller to Truman Hendryx, March 26, 1832; see also Ruth Alden Doan, "Millerism and Evangelical Culture," *The Disappointed: Millerism and Millenarianism in the Nineteenth Century,* Ronald L. Numbers and Jonathan M. Butler, eds. (Bloomington IN: Indiana University Press, 1987) 119-38.

[22]Walter Rauschenbusch, *Walter Rauschenbusch: Selected Writings,* edited by Winthrop S. Hudson (New York: Paulist Press, 1984) 91.

[23]C. Allyn Russell, *Voices of American Fundamentalism* (Philadelphia: Westminster Press, 1976).

[24]Lerone Bennett, Jr., *Before the Mayflower* (Baltimore MD: Penguin Books, 1962) 81.

[25]Ibid., 80-81.

[26]Ibid., 80.

[27]Jürgen Moltmann, *The Church in the Power of the Spirit* (New York: Harper & Row, 1975) 192.

Contributors

Michael G. Cogdill is Dean and Tyner Professor of Christian Ministry and Family Studies at Campbell University Divinity School, Buies Creek, North Carolina. Previously he was chair of the department of religion and philosophy at Campbell. Dr. Cogdill holds degrees from Mars Hill College, Mars Hill, North Carolina; Southeastern Baptist Theological Seminary, Wake Forest, North Carolina; and North Carolina State University, Raleigh. He has served as pastor of two churches in North Carolina, and remains active in Baptist congregational life as an interim pastor, worship leader, and Bible study teacher.

J. Bradley Creed is Dean and Professor of Church History at the George W. Truett Theological Seminary of Baylor University. Previously he was pastor of First Baptist Church of Natchitoches, Louisiana. He holds degrees from Baylor University and Southwestern Baptist Theological Seminary. Dr. Creed is a frequent speaker for churches, conferences, workshops, and groups.

R. Alan Culpepper is Dean of the McAfee School of Theology at Mercer University, Atlanta, Georgia. He previously served as professor of religion at Baylor University in Waco, Texas, and as associate dean of the school of theology and professor of New Testament at the Southern Baptist Theological Seminary in Louisville, Kentucky. He holds degrees from Baylor University, the Southern Baptist Theological Seminary, and Duke University in Durham, North Carolina. Dr. Culpepper is the author of numerous articles and of seven books, including *Anatomy of the Fourth Gospel, Interpreting the Gospel and Letters of John*, the commentary on Luke in the *New Interpreter's Bible*, and *John, the Son of Zebedee: The Life of a Legend*.

M. Vernon Davis is Dean and Professor of Theology of the Logsdon School of Theology at Hardin-Simmons University, Abilene, Texas. Previously he served as Vice President for Academic Affairs and Dean of the Faculty at Midwestern Baptist Seminary in Kansas City, Missouri, and as pastor of First Baptist Church of Alexandria, Virginia. Dr. Davis is the author of numerous church curriculum materials and journal articles and has published several award-winning sermons. A musician and composer, he is also the writer and composer of the hymn "Lord, Who Across the Ages."

G. Thomas Halbrooks is Dean of the Faculty and Professor of Church History at the Baptist Theological Seminary at Richmond, Virginia. Earlier he served as professor of church history at Southeastern Baptist Theological Seminary, Wake Forest, North Carolina. He has also taught at Mercer University in Atlanta, the Southern Baptist Theological Seminary in Louisville, Kentucky, and adjunctively at the Divinity School of Duke University, Durham, North Carolina. Dr. Halbrooks is a well-known writer and speaker in the area of Baptist life and thought, and has served as pastor and staff minister in Alabama, Indiana, and Virginia.

William L. Hendricks is retired as Director of Baptist Studies and Lecturer in Theology at Brite Divinity School, Texas Christian University, Fort Worth, Texas. His prior teaching career included faculty appointments at Southwestern Baptist Theological Seminary, the Southern Baptist Theological Seminary, Golden Gate Baptist Theological Seminary, Taiwan Baptist Seminary, Yugoslavian Baptist Seminary, Hungarian Baptist Seminary, and Ruschlikon Baptist Seminary. Dr. Hendricks holds degrees from Oklahoma Baptist University, Shawnee, Oklahoma; Southwestern Baptist Theological Seminary, Fort Worth, Texas; and the University of Chicago. A prolific writer and speaker, he is the author of eight books and numerous articles, and is a regular speaker and preacher at churches and denominational gatherings throughout the world.

T. Furman Hewitt is Director of the Baptist House of Studies at the Divinity School, Duke University, Durham, North Carolina. Previously a professor of Christian ethics at Southeastern Baptist Theological Seminary in Wake Forest, North Carolina, he also taught at Gardner-Webb University in Boiling Springs, North Carolina, and served as visiting professor at the Hong Kong Baptist Theological Seminary and as a pastor in Kentucky. He holds degrees from Furman University, Greenville, South Carolina; the Southern Baptist Theological Seminary, Louisville, Kentucky; and Duke

University, Durham, North Carolina. Dr. Hewitt has written numerous articles and is the author/editor of two books: *Life and Death* and *A Biblical Perspective on the Use and Abuse of Alcohol.*

Bill J. Leonard is Dean of the Wake Forest University Divinity School in Winston-Salem, North Carolina, after having served as chair of the department of religion and philosophy at Samford University in Birmingham, Alabama, and as professor of church history at the Southern Baptist Theological Seminary in Louisville, Kentucky. A graduate of Texas Wesleyan University and Boston University, Dr. Leonard is a popular speaker, author, and lecturer. He is the author/editor of twelve books, including *The Nature of the Church*; *Becoming Christian: Dimensions of Spiritual Formation*; *God's Last and Only Hope: the Fragmentation of the Southern Baptist Convention*; and a *Dictionary of Baptists in America.* He is currently writing a new history of Baptists for Judson Press.

Molly T. Marshall is Professor of Theology and Spiritual Formation at Central Baptist Theological Seminary in Kansas City, Kansas. A former professor of theology at the Southern Baptist Theological Seminary, Louisville, Kentucky, Dr. Marshall holds degrees from Oklahoma Baptist University, Shawnee, Oklahoma, and the Southern Baptist Theological Seminary. She has also studied at Cambridge University, the Tantur Ecumenical Institute in Jerusalem, Israel, and at Princeton Theological Seminary, Princeton, New Jersey. The author of three books and numerous articles, she serves often as lecturer at distinguished lecture series and as a preacher and speaker in churches and denominational meetings throughout the United States.

Gary Parker is Coordinator for Baptist Principles for the Cooperative Baptist Fellowship, Atlanta, Georgia. He was educated at Furman University, Greenville, South Carolina; Southeastern Baptist Theological Seminary, Wake Forest, North Carolina; and Baylor University, Waco, Texas. Dr. Parker has served churches in Missouri, South Carolina, North Carolina, and Texas, and has taught adjunctively at Eden Theological Seminary, Baylor University, and Southeastern Seminary. An accomplished writer, Dr. Parker is the author of nine books, both fiction and non-fiction, and has published numerous articles in magazines, journals, and denominational publications. He serves often as a supply preacher, interim pastor, and conference leader.

R. Wayne Stacy is Dean and Professor of New Testament and Preaching at the M. Christopher White School of Divinity, Gardner-Webb University, Boiling Springs, North Carolina. He has been a pastor and has held professorships at Gardner-Webb University; Midwestern Baptist Theological Seminary, Kansas City, Missouri; and Palm Beach Atlantic College, West Palm Beach, Florida. A graduate of Palm Beach Atlantic College and the Southern Baptist Theological Seminary in Louisville, Kentucky, Dr. Stacy is the author of numerous articles related to biblical studies and preaching.